Digital Triage Forensics

Digital Triage Forensics
Processing the Digital Crime Scene

Stephen Pearson

Richard Watson

Michael Harrington, Technical Editor

ELSEVIER

AMSTERDAM • BOSTON • HEIDELBERG • LONDON
NEW YORK • OXFORD • PARIS • SAN DIEGO
SAN FRANCISCO • SINGAPORE • SYDNEY • TOKYO
Syngress is an imprint of Elsevier

SYNGRESS.

Acquiring Editor: Angelina Ward
Development Editor: Greg Chalson
Project Manager: Paul Gottehrer
Designer: Alisa Andreola

Syngress is an imprint of Elsevier
30 Corporate Drive, Suite 400, Burlington, MA 01803, USA

Notices
Knowledge and best practice in this field are constantly changing. As new research and experience broaden our understanding, changes in research methods or professional practices, may become necessary. Practitioners and researchers must always rely on their own experience and knowledge in evaluating and using any information or methods described herein. In using such information or methods they should be mindful of their own safety and the safety of others, including parties for whom they have a professional responsibility.

To the fullest extent of the law, neither the Publisher nor the authors, contributors, or editors, assume any liability for any injury and/or damage to persons or property as a matter of products liability, negligence or otherwise, or from any use or operation of any methods, products, instructions, or ideas contained in the material herein.

Library of Congress Cataloging-in-Publication Data
Application submitted

British Library Cataloguing-in-Publication Data
A catalogue record for this book is available from the British Library.

ISBN: 978-1-59749-596-7

Printed in the United States of America
10 11 12 13 14 10 9 8 7 6 5 4 3 2 1

Working together to grow
libraries in developing countries

www.elsevier.com | www.bookaid.org | www.sabre.org

ELSEVIER   BOOK AID
International   Sabre Foundation

For information on all Syngress publications visit our website at www.syngress.com

Contents

Preface

This book is dedicated to the men and women who serve in our armed services and especially to those who risk their lives daily performing the Weapons Intelligence Team (WIT) mission. For every class that comes through the Weapons Intelligence Course (WIC) school house, a bond is developed between instructors and students, as many of us have served in Iraq or Afghanistan and know the personal sacrifices that will be made by each WIT member. Some of those members will make the ultimate sacrifice while serving our great nation. We want to thank our wives, Amanda Pearson and Linda Watson, and Corey Pearson (Stephen's son), for putting up with the long hours that we have spent working on this book. This book has been a labor of love for us, as we are committed to making sure that the service member in the field has the best training possible. Thanks go to Thomas Eskridge for his time and patience in the review of the material and to Kevin Lothridge and Lee Metcalf for the opportunities to participate in training programs that have caused us to research the cutting-edge techniques of our country's enemies. We thank the U.S. Army Staff Sergeant Lisa Dzienkowsi, NCOIC, WIC, FT Huachuca, AZ, for her service on the first WIT mission in Iraq in 2004–2005 and the selfless sacrifices that she makes daily to ensure the success of the WIC schoolhouse. We recognize all the instructors who spend endless personal hours making the WIC program such a success. We hope that with this book, many new battlefield investigators will be inspired to perform the mission so desperately needed.

Stephen Pearson and Richard Watson
March 2010

Introduction: Using the digital triage forensics model to collect and process cell phones and SIM cards

Digital media have made their way into just about every aspect of our lives. We carry iPods with training podcasts, music, and movies with storage capacities that rival our desktop or laptop systems. The cell phones we use today provide access to our e-mail and documents. Ten years ago, investigators would find the gold nuggets of evidence on systems owned by corporate entities because that was where the bandwidth and storage were located. In today's environment, with the advent of thumb drives, Compact Flash (CF) cards, and reliable online storage, the nuggets have moved to those closely held containers that are easily connected, used, and destroyed.

This new world of personal storage provides unique opportunities to anyone seeking intelligence or evidence on a suspect. Most recently, we have seen the use of these personal digital media devices being used to solve crimes spanning the spectrum of criminal offenses—from students being bullied online to plots being arranged to destroy schools or other national assets. Terrorists use computers and portable storage containers to pass strategic documents and plans. These devices can pass by unnoticed by anyone. During the attacks in Mumbai, India, in 2008, cell phones were seen as tools to orchestrate and collaborate during tactical actions. Insurgents in Iraq use cell phones to record their criminal activities so that they can be paid for their work. Cell phones make a convenient medium to detonate improvised explosive devises.

We know that the evidence and/or data are out there and it is in real time. Investigators and intelligence gatherers need to be able to collect and exploit this real-time data, providing the command with actionable intelligence as well as evidence that will later be used to convict suspects of their crimes.

In June 2008, the cellular networks in Iraq were upgraded to the digital standard of 1900 MHz. This new bandwidth allows the user to take advantage of the full digital capability that a cell phone has to offer. New threats to the evidence or intelligence gathering process have been identified with the use of this new topology. New safety concerns for the on-scene investigator have also now been raised as the insurgents target the investigators in the battle space.

With current practices and procedures, field commanders are potentially denied real-time actionable intelligence that is available from the digital media being seized because of the long time it takes to identify and exploit the media.

Under the current models, teams analyzing the data have little time for a complete and/or thorough examination of the media collected from the battlefield. This time barrier has come to be because there is no time to do it properly. This perception comes from several factors.

- First, the imaging process can be lengthy;
- Second, investigators may not have access to the available media to image the data;
- Third, it involves providing the investigator the programs, knowledge, and training in the collection of data, allowing the media to be exploited for the field commanders.

To address the aforementioned concerns, specialized teams such as the Weapons Intelligence Teams (WITs) are being employed to conduct a unique task on today's battlefield crime scene. The WIT is being tasked to gather and identify digital media and triage the media to find out whether the media contain any actionable intelligence. The task of processing the battlefield crime scene in itself is complicated, but will be further complicated with safety and tactical considerations as well as the time limit for scene processing of 5–60 min on average.

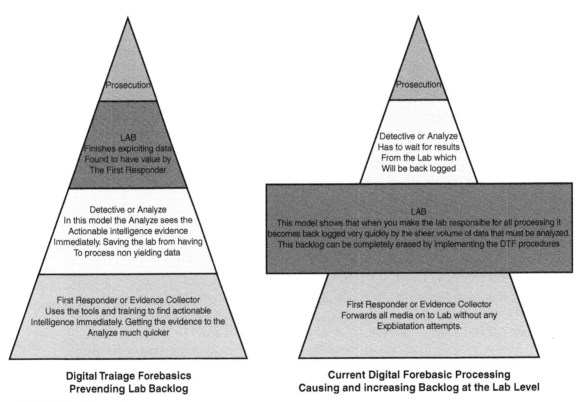

■ FIGURE 1 Processing pyramid.

Compare that with today's modern law enforcement world; there is typically no time limit for the processing of a crime scene. Compare that with stateside Law Enforcement personnel who have no tactical implications or time challenges associated with their crime scenes.

At the traditional digital crime scene, great care must be taken to preserve the evidence in its most pristine form, allowing for itemized evidence collection, labeling, and chain of custody documents to be created. The combat crime scene does not allow for this diligence in evidence collection due to its safety and tactical element. When collected from the combat crime scene, evidence is routinely lumped together and maintained in a single evidence container. The itemized evidence is not identified until it is returned to the Forward Operating Base (FOB) for further processing. This modified collection process is a reality of the battle field crime scene and the operations tempo (OPTEMPO) that our specialized teams, such as WIT, exist in.

The problem of providing actionable intelligence is further challenged by the process of analysis after the media have been gathered. Currently, the exploitation or analysis of the captured media is done only at the lab level (see Figure 1).

The teams on the ground such as WIT are not allowed to exploit media. This makes little sense, as teams such as WIT have the equipment and training to be able to conduct exploitation at the FOB. In some cases, the WIT equipment is better than in the labs in the battle space.

In this book, we strive to define and present the digital triage forensics (DTF) process from the investigator/operator level. The chapters are designed to be a template to teach small-team DTF collection and processing. This is by no means the end-all text. As we are writing this book, things are already changing. The investigator/operator has to be aware of the changes and be prepared to change Tactical Training Plans (TTPs) quickly to recognize and defeat the next potential threat.

About the Authors

Stephen Pearson combines more than 29 years of law-enforcement experience with in-depth expertise in today's most pervasive Internet and computer technologies. During his tenure in both federal and civilian law-enforcement agencies, Stephen has had the opportunity to see all facets of computer crime investigations. Stephen began developing tools and training for the investigation of computer crime investigation in 1994 when assigned to the United States Army Military Police School at Ft. McClellan, Alabama. Stephen retired from the Military Police Corps as the Non Commissioned Officer in Charge of the Advanced Technology Criminal Investigation Courses in 2003. Stephen pursued his career in the computer crime investigations world by becoming an investigator with the Pulaski County Sheriff's Office. During his tenure at the sheriff's office, Stephen used his technological skills for numerous cases, one of which led to the safe recovery of an abducted child during a joint FBI and sheriff's department investigation. In 2003 Stephen took the position of CEO of the High Tech Crime Institute (HTCI). Over the past 8 years HTCI has grown into a multi million dollar organization specializing in the training of complex tasks to the end user. Most recently, Stephen has been directly involved in the development and implementation of computer crime and forensics training for the U.S. armed forces in Iraq and Afghanistan.

Stephen is recognized by the federal government as an expert witness in DOS file structures and has been consulted on numerous high-profile investigations. Stephen developed the ground-breaking Cyber Squire Internet child safety program for the United States Army at Ft. Leonard Wood. It became a standard program for the local school system for child Internet safety.

Stephen has been awarded numerous decorations, including the Meritorious Service Medal, Army Commendation Medal, and Army Achievement Medal. In September 2002, Stephen was awarded the Military Police Corps Order of the Marechaussee (Bronze), the highest peacetime Military Police award, for his superior performance and dedication to training excellence. Stephen holds a Bachelor of Science degree in Computer Information Science (*Summa Cum Laude*) and Associate's degrees in Administration of Justice and Computer Information Science. Stephen is currently working on his MBA at Webster University. He holds the Microsoft Certified System Engineer certificate (+ Internet) and is also an Army Master Instructor.

Richard Watson is the Vice President of Actionable Intelligence Operations Training with the High Tech Crime Institute, Inc. (HTCI) and manages offices in Colorado, Arizona, and Missouri supporting the war fighter at Ft. Carson, Ft. Huachuca, and Ft. Leonard Wood United States Army installations. Richard conducts business development throughout the United States, focusing on actionable intelligence solutions through digital media exploitation and digital forensics triage. Prior to working for HTCI and after completing 8 years of active military duty, Richard worked for the U.S. Department of Energy Protective Forces and was a

Colorado Law Enforcement Officer. Richard is also a United States Air Force reservist with more than 27 years of service, active duty and reserve, where he is a Special Agent with the Air Force Office of Special Investigations. He has conducted military criminal investigations and counterintelligence operations throughout the world. He also served in Iraq from 2006 to 2007 as a member of a Weapons Intelligence Team prosecuting over 130 pre-/post-blast Improvised Explosive Device investigations.

Richard holds a bachelor's degree from the University of Nebraska/Omaha and associate's degrees from Central Texas College and the Community College of the Air Force. He has earned the Bronze Star Medal, Air Force Combat Action Medal, and Army Combat Action Badge while serving in Iraq. Richard resides in Colorado with his wife, Linda.

Michael Harrington, Technical Editor (CFCE ENCE) is an Independent Digital Forensic Trainer and Consultant and owner of Harrington and Associates LLC. Michael was a Sergeant with the Michigan State Police in the Digital Evidence Unit, joining the Department in 1995. He has also worked for Micro Systemation AB as its Director of North American Training and was owner of Innovative Digital Forensic Solutions LLC, which produced the popular Pandora's Box mobile phone forensic software.

He writes a blog on Mobile Forensics at http://mobileforensics.wordpress.com.

New age of warfare: How digital forensics is reshaping today's military

Not since the use of improvised explosive devices (IEDs) by the Irish Republican Army in the United Kingdom have we seen extensive use of IEDs as we have during combat operations against American and coalition forces in Iraq and Afghanistan as a primary force multiplier and sometimes tactical advantage. These IEDs have been taken to a level of use in modern warfare that has shown to be effective for an enemy with inferior technology or organized modern army. From homemade explosives to modified military ordnance, IEDs have become the preferred weapon of choice for insurgents operating in Iraq and Afghanistan. Weapons technical intelligence (WTI) is being developed daily on today's IED components so that tactics, techniques, and procedures (TTPs) can be developed to thwart activities directed at U.S. ground forces as they move about the battlefield. Weapons intelligence teams (WITs) are being fielded to further WTI collection as well as the exploitation of IED materials and electronic digital media. With so much emphasis on all realms of forensics, Baghdad has become the hub for battlefield evidence collection and relevant in prosecuting the war. Military intelligence and evidence have merged as a vehicle to capture and prosecute enemy combatants taking full advantage of modern technology to root out actionable intelligence through digital forensics, thus creating battlefield cops out of everyday modern soldiers.

YESTERDAY'S "BOOBY TRAP" IS TODAY'S IED

Today's battlefield in Iraq and Afghanistan has generated many changes in how U.S. military services conduct warfare in the twenty-first century. One evident change is how U.S. enemies are using anything they can to blow up U.S. ground forces and cause massive casualties instead of face-to-face combat as in past wars. Enemy forces that do not have superior numbers and firepower are creating IEDs as a force multiplier causing chaos and fear wherever they are detonated. Unfortunately, these devices are being used against civilian populations as well when enemy forces

Digital Triage Forensics. Doi: 10.1016/B978-1-59749-596-7.00001-2

target local government officials, such as host nation police and security forces. This tactic has proven to stall cooperation between our military forces and the host nation government. Judges and community leaders have been the target of IED attacks in an attempt to sap the will of the local population and further the enemy's political agenda.

In past armed conflicts, small explosive devices have been used or altered to create "booby traps," thus wounding, maiming, and killing a very small number of soldiers. These traps were not used as a major tactic to employ against our military forces, but as a way to slow us down and create casualties to tie up two to four personnel to take care of any dead or wounded created from the trap. Don't get me wrong, IEDs are not a new phenomenon; they just have not been as prevalent on the battle field as they are in this century.

There have been enormous amounts of military ordnance that have been created that are explosive in nature and are designed for specific missions, such as land and water mines. These devices are usually hidden from unsuspecting enemy forces and are detonated when struck, run over, or stepped on. The claymore mine is an antipersonnel explosive device that can be preset and detonated manually by the emplacer or set as a "booby trap" and set off by the unsuspecting victim. You may be wondering how this differs from IEDs. The difference is that military ordnance is manufactured to specific guidelines and in many cases for specific weapon systems that they can be fired from, such as mortars and artillery shells. IEDs are generally military ordnance that has been "improvised" in some way to be detonated by means other than the originally intended one (see Figure 1.1).

Other IEDs that have been developed by local insurgents have been created by manufacturing containers, filling them with military grade explosives or homemade explosives (HME) and rigging them with some sort of initiation device (see Figure 1.2). More will be discussed about different types of IEDs in Chapter 3.

The insurgents in Iraq have been quite successful in using IEDs against U.S. troops and other military forces since U.S. forces landed on their soil in 2003. In 2009, IED activity began ramping up in Afghanistan as focus turned to the U.S. military forces with the United States' attempts to defeat the Taliban. With all of the United States' high-tech ways of conducting warfare, IEDs have proven that low-tech still has its place in modern warfare. The amount of sophistication that goes into an IED depends on training and background of the actual IED maker and the amount of money available in the region to purchase bomb making materials, to

■ **FIGURE 1.1** Artillery Shell IED emplaced in a road. *Photograph taken by the author, Rich Watson.*

■ **FIGURE 1.2** Homemade IED container with victim-operated pressure switch. *Photograph taken by the author, Rich Watson.*

name just a few. During my time in Iraq, I was located in AR Ramadi, a large city in the Al Anbar province of western Iraq. Most of the IEDs I saw were not as sophisticated as devices seen in Baghdad. I referred to some of the common IEDs I saw as "Red Neck IEDs" as they were made from any materials they could find. Some worked and some did not.

Weapons technical intelligence

So where have all these developments taken us today in modern warfare? The use of IEDs is considered asymmetric warfare and is quite effective for the enemy to use. Because of the use of IEDs, WTI was added to traditional Technical Intelligence (TECHINT) of weapons as a response to the threat. TECHINT is basically the gathering of information about weapons systems of U.S. enemies. WTI is just a category of intelligence gathered from technical and forensic collection of IEDs. Intelligence and forensic evidence gathered help soldiers, sailors, marines, and airmen in their battle spaces to learn the TTPs of the enemies they face.

Every time IED materials are collected from pre- or postlast investigations, the components, wiring, and overall build of the device is examined to determine if new techniques are being implemented to develop IEDs that could defeat the United States' current TTPs. One device that we're focused on in this book is the use of cell phone technology and its use as an IED component.

As you will read in Chapter 5, cell phones are used extensively to detonate IEDs and to store and transmit photographs and data related to insurgent cells, IED sites, and future IED attacks. Cell phone technology has advanced rapidly in the last 15 years and they are now small computers that are capable of being used not only as phones but also powerful electronic processing devices. For a long time, desktop computers and laptops have been the most powerful sources of computing ability available for everyday use. Now cell phones are replacing even laptops as a primary means to conduct business and everyday life with the ability to access the Internet from almost anywhere. As you will see in Chapter 4, computers still have a major role in storing large amounts of data by insurgent cells that can effectively be exploited even when data is supposedly deleted from the system's hard drive. Because of cell phone and computer usage in relation to IED manufacturing, you'll no doubt see these items listed as part of WTI lexicon documentation in the future.

THE INVENTION OF WIT

During the early stages of the Iraq war, it was evident that IEDs were making a huge impact on U.S. ground forces. Something needed to be done to combat these devices and prevent them from producing casualties and causing fear among the U.S. ranks every time they left their forward operating bases (FOB); hence, the creation of WITs.

I interviewed United States Army Staff Sergeant (SSG) Lisa Dzienkowski about her initial experience as a WIT member, as she was selected to be one of the first to pioneer this new needed enduring capability. SSG Dzienkowski told me that in 2004 it was decided by the presidential staff that IEDs were becoming a problem for U.S. ground forces, which weren't really prepared or trained or equipped to cope with defeating the IED threat. The Counter-IED Targeting Program (CITP) was then established; however, CITP was not necessarily intended to conduct the "on the ground" exploitation and collection of IED devices, so WITs were established to take on this role. A task order was sent from the National Ground Intelligence Center (NGIC) to the United States Army Intelligence and Security Command (INSCOM), and INSCOM tasked the 732nd Military Intelligence (MI) Battalion from Schofield Barracks, Hawaii, and another unnamed unit from Fort Meade, MD. Between 15 and 18 volunteers were taken from each unit, and that group became the first Weapons Intelligence Detachment in Iraq. SSG Dzienkowski went through about a month of training, but actually only 2 weeks or so were focused on Weapons Intelligence. She really didn't know what would happen once they got to their mission. Their biggest challenge was interfacing with the explosive ordnance disposal (EOD) teams they were assigned to and selling the WIT mission to the unit they supported. Some EOD teams were resistant, along with some units who didn't even want to send the teams outside the wire. The teams fought through the hurdles and challenges, and did everything they could to prove that the WIT mission was important and needed. There were six teams; three were originally located in the Baghdad area, with one team bouncing around quite a bit and eventually ending up near the western border of Iraq. SSG Dzienkoski's team was in Baqubah, one team was in Samarra, and another team was in Mosul. Each team basically wrote its own standard operating procedures (SOPs) and reports with little guidance. All of the teams communicated with each other and would adjust if another team found something that worked better, but it really was a proof concept all around. Most teams were successful at convincing units and EOD teams that the WIT mission was important and much needed, even though it took practically her entire deployment to get that point driven home. SSG Dzienkowski is currently assigned to the WIT school house as the Non-Commissioned Officer in Charge (NCOIC) (Figures 1.3 and 1.4).

In 2004, when SSG Dzienkowski was assigned to a WIT element, they took with them five pelican hard cases of equipment to their mission, not knowing what kind of equipment was really needed. As each iteration of WITs has completed tours of duty in Iraq, the U.S. military has gotten a

■ **FIGURE 1.3** SSG Dzienkowski receiving an incident briefing from Iraqi security forces. *Photograph courtesy of SSG Dzienkowski.*

■ **FIGURE 1.4** SSG Dzienkowski standing in a blast hole while investigating a postblast scene. *Photograph courtesy of SSG Dzienkowski.*

better understanding of the evolution of the WIT mission and the equipment required to exploit IED evidence. Now in 2010, the WIT kits consist of one large pelican case with some of the most technologically advanced exploitation tools available. The primary focus of a WIT element is to collect evidence found at pre-post blast scenarios and weapons caches using the tools provided in the WIT kits. This includes basic biometrics, explosive residue detection, and digital media exploitation. Chapter 3 will discuss in more detail the actual mission sets required of WITs and how they process the scenes that they respond to during their tours of duty.

WIT training found a home with the 203rd MI Battalion at the Aberdeen Prooving Ground, MD from 2004 to 2008 and then was moved to its current school house located at FT Huachuca, AZ. Currently, students are "volunteered" to be participants in this critical mission. Typical career fields selected are members of MI, Military Police, and EOD technicians taken out of their traditional roles. In past operations, personnel from the U.S. Air Force and U.S. Navy have been selected and put together to create a joint mission. Career fields from those services have included Special Agents of the Air Force Office of Special Investigations (AFOSI), Intelligence, and Master of Arms (Figure 1.5).

Today, WIT members go through 7 weeks of training to prepare for their mission, in addition to Combat Skills refresher training and Combat Life Saving skills training. Some of the subjects taught at the WIT school house include, but are not limited to, the following:

- Report Writing
- FOB Operations
- IED Threats
- Foreign Weapons
- Media Exploitation
- Tracking
- Biometrics

■ **FIGURE 1.5** WIT 5, AR Ramadi, Iraq. Pictured from left to right; author Rich Watson (AFOSI), MSgt Kyle Waller (EOD), SSgt Nick Bradley (Intel), TSgt Travis Goes (Intel), and SPC Landon Lang (25th ID Airborne). *Photograph courtesy of author Rich Watson.*

At the end of their WIT training, all students take an extensive written test and are placed in a field training environment for 3 days where they operate as WIT members and go to scenarios, day and night, designed to test all of the skills they learned throughout the course. WITs are now training Iraqi Army personnel to conduct WIT operations as part of assisting the Iraqi government's transformation to take charge of their country. WIT has a very important and dangerous role in today's modern warfare scenarios and can be utilized anywhere in the world and against any enemy that our nation may face.

"CSI" BAGHDAD: TODAY'S INTELLIGENCE IS TOMORROWS EVIDENCE

Intelligence gathering plays a major role in today's warfare as intelligence provides us with knowledge about what the enemy may be doing or is going to do in the future. Intelligence can be about enemy weapons, troop strengths, troop movement activity, and future operational plans, to name just a few. Intelligence gathering techniques are widely varied from human informants on the ground to satellites orbiting the earth and taking photographs of targeted locations. No matter how it is gathered, intelligence information is used in determining courses of action to be taken in offensive and defensive combat actions in the affected battle space, but when does that intelligence information start to fade into the gray area of evidence? www.dictionary.com defines intelligence as "information of strategic or military value." It also defines evidence as it is applied to law as "data presented to a court or jury in proof of the facts in issue and which may include the testimony of witnesses, records, documents, or objects."

IED materials today are considered to have intelligence value and evidentiary value as well, but how can we use these materials in both categories to make cases against IED makers and employers? The answer is sound, and ethical collection processes as well as documented collection actions requiring a chain of custody to be established on all materials collected. A lot of intelligence that is gathered cannot be used in a court of law as the many varied collection techniques would not meet the standards of our justice system as information (evidence) that was "lawfully" collected. Yet, if our intelligence collectors knew ahead of time that the information they gather could be used as evidence in the future, they could be trained to properly collect and document that information whether the intelligence gathered is in the form of documents, IED components, or digital media.

Now that you understand the difference between military intelligence and evidence, you will be able to better understand the role and mission of WIT. WIT members are not only gathering evidence at pre-post blast scenes they investigate, but are gathering intelligence on enemy TTPs and activity within their area of responsibility (AOR) as well. The information and evidence collected by WIT will be used to successfully prosecute enemy insurgents in courts of law.

ACTIONABLE INTELLIGENCE AND ITS EFFECT ON THE BATTLEFIELD

Actionable Intelligence can be defined in several ways such as "having the necessary information immediately available in order to deal with the situation at hand," but for the purposes of this book, we will define it as "intelligence that can be acted upon within a 12 to 72 hour period of time." No matter which definition is used, the meaning is the same, useful information that can be quickly acted upon.

WIT members exploit cell phones, computer hard drives, thumb drives, SD cards, SIM cards, and other digital media, looking for actionable intelligence that could be used immediately to thwart planned attacks against U.S. and coalition forces. Actionable intelligence gathered could be, but is not limited to, pictures taken by the enemy showing convoys, pictures of key buildings on FOBs, pictures of insurgents placing IEDs, and written plans for future operations against U.S. and coalition forces. Such actionable intelligence could change the course of battles and save many lives. Actionable intelligence is the "golden nugget" that WIT members are in constant search of.

SOLDIERS TO "BATTLEFIELD COPS"

As discussed earlier, WIT members are culled from many career fields within our military services. For most of them, conducting battlefield investigations is a new and foreign concept. Throughout WIT training, they are given crash courses in basic investigative techniques that most police officers spend months learning and spend years perfecting. WIT members become "first responders" of the IED world with their EOD counterparts. Some teams become very successful and glean great results during their tours of duty, but because WIT is not a voluntary assignment, there can be problems associated that can have major effects on our military's success in defeating the IED threat and could ultimately cost soldiers their lives.

Unfortunately, there have been WIT members who do not want to be part of the WIT mission and while they are in school, fail to rise to the occasion, and prove they are capable of being flexible to the mission requirements placed upon them. Those WIT members then deploy and do the minimum amount of work required, do nothing to be successful, and help place negative stigmas upon WIT members and the WIT mission. Like any career field, people who want to be in that career will strive to be successful and bring credit upon themselves and the organization they work for. These negative attitudes some military members bring to the mission not only discredit the Counter-IED initiative, but also discredit their service. The U.S. Army has identified the WIT mission as a sustainable mission and is taking measures to create an additional skill identifier (ASI) for those U.S. Army soldiers who attend the WIT training. The end goal is to create a military occupational specialty (MOS). Once an MOS is created, we will see soldiers who want to be part of the WIT mission enter the career field and bring unprecedented successes to the IED defeat mission. It is not known at this time what the other services may do to identify those who will be trained in the WIT mission.

Rule of Law challenges

The U.S. Army Field Manual 3-07, Stability Operations, defines the Rule of Law as "a principle of governance in which all persons, institutions, and entities, public and private, including the state itself, are accountable to laws that are publicly promulgated, equally enforced, and independently adjudicated, and which are consistent with international human rights norms and standards."[1]

On January 1, 2009 a Security Agreement was established between the U.S. Government and the Government of Iraq. Since then, we have been performing operations with Iraqi Security Forces and have developed prosecutable cases based on Iraqi criminal practice and procedures. Now U.S. and coalition forces are not only mandated to follow developed Rules of Engagement (ROE), but also Rules for Escalation of Force. These rules help our military members make use of force decisions and require constant updating as enemy TTPs evolve and change.

So how does Rule of Law affect WIT members in Iraq? We are seeing a shift from U.S. forces conducting the WIT mission to training Iraqi police and security forces in forensics, biometrics, and digital forensics so that they can perform the mission. WIT may now arrive on a pre-post blast IED scene and conduct only a partial investigation of the scene as the Iraqis conduct most of the scene investigation. This is all part of partnering with the Iraqi Government so that they can take control of their country.

Afghanistan police and security forces are not quite that evolved, but the Rule of Law will come more into play as that country is stabilized. Until then, WIT members must realize that the role they were trained to play will eventually turn from evidence collectors to WIT trainers for the host nation. This is an evolution that will be a constant in any conflict U.S. forces become involved in.

SUMMARY

In this chapter, we have discussed how IEDs have evolved from basic booby traps to primary attack methods of insurgents in Iraq and Afghanistan to the point where traditional TECHINT created a subcategory called WTI that includes technical and forensic collection as part of IED makeup. We have also discussed the need that arose to counter IEDs and the development of the WITs to actually do the hands-on collection of IED evidence and components and pioneer a new sustainable need within the U.S. military forces. We have also looked at the evolution of military intelligence and evidence merging to create a sustainable vehicle for successfully prosecuting enemy combatants under the Rule of Law in Iraq as our soldiers, sailors, airman, and marines become "battlefield cops" outside of their normal military duties and responsibilities.

REFERENCES

1. Headquarters Department of the Army. U.S. Army Field Manual 3-07, Stability Operations. Washington, DC: Stability Operations; October 6, 2008.

Chapter 2

Digital triage forensics and battlefield forensics

INTRODUCTION

In this chapter, we will focus on digital triage forensics (DTF) and how this concept has been developed to what it is today using the computer forensics field triage process model (CFFTPM). We will also discuss the differences between DTF and CFFTPM and define their roles for producing actionable intelligence. You will learn that battlefield forensics is sometimes unorthodox to the everyday investigator who conducts investigations in controlled crime scenes and also the challenges the weapons intelligence team (WIT) members face when exploiting improvised explosive device (IED) scenes on the battlefield. While these teams risk their lives to collect IED evidence, you will read that there is a problem with standardizing the training given to the WITs and other military and civilian entities. How evidence gets to laboratories for processing, what and who make up these labs, and what levels of exploitation are used to finalize the contents of this chapter.

DTF AND BATTLEFIELD FORENSICS

DTF is not a new idea and certainly is not a new investigative thought process. Our growth as a society and the need for a more connected world grow every day. Global businesses and governments are pushing the boundaries of electronic transfer and storage daily. The thirst for quicker, faster communication has also challenged the investigator of today to be able to gather and process information much more rapidly. The investigator needs to stay close behind the criminal enterprises. Yes, behind. The world of investigation is a reactionary one, and typically, the investigator finds himself or herself in the catch-up mode. Very few

Digital Triage Forensics. Doi: 10.1016/B978-1-59749-596-7.00002-4

law enforcement agencies can afford to dedicate an investigator to staying on top of the latest technology. It is usually the investigators' own desire to learn that keeps them abreast of the new technologies. For example, in 1995, I was an instructor at the Military Police School at Ft McClellan, Alabama, supporting its instructors with a very forward-thinking chain of command. The school's initial training of computer crime investigation was more an overview of how to use the brand new Microsoft Office programs. Its initial classes were very low tech. However, it only took a year for the school to recognize that future crime investigation would be on the Internet, and the complexity of its training grew quickly. In 2003, the school was on the cutting edge of providing training for computer crime investigation. It was an exception to the rule. In the early days, the Internet did not exist to as far as the average person was concerned. Most people were buying their first home computer not as a necessity but as a luxury. In those days, criminals did not see computers as an enhancement for criminal activities. This is not true today. The criminals, terrorists, and states opposing the United States have recognized and understand the value of technology and Internet as a combat or criminal multiplier. Can you imagine a company or government of any significant size without e-mail or a Web page in today's world? Whether we like it or not, over the past 13 years, digital media has made its way into every aspect of our lives, and for Americans especially, it has quietly become our most visible Achilles' heel.

Let us do a little mental exercise. Close your eyes and imagine going a week without using any technology. No Facebook, Myspace, Twitter, Fantasy Football, Voice Over Internet Protocol, etc. Are you done laughing or did your cell phone ring and interrupt you?

In our connected world today, criminals seek the power of free services and tools that come with the Internet. The criminal element has embraced the use of the digital media much more quickly than the law enforcement agencies that have been tasked to enforce the laws, protecting the citizens. These free tools on the Internet open the door for many poorly funded criminal and terrorist enterprises to act and coordinate as a larger, more organized entity. The other enticing draw for the criminal element is that it is possible to attain a certain level of anonymity. An Article written by Rick Ross in 2003 called "Criminal environmental extremists may be recruiting children"[1] warned us of the recruiting efforts of organizations on the Internet that target the youth of the Internet. Gangs and terrorist organizations use the Internet routinely to recruit new talent and to spread their ideological causes.

HANDS ON

Online Skill

On your computer, bring up your favorite search engine. In the search dialogue box, type in "Gangs Online" and read through some of the pages that are presented to you. Now, type in "Terrorist Organizations Online" and read through the sites that are brought up. Now, go to www.youtube.com and type in "gangs recruiting" and watch a few of the videos that appear. You will see very quickly that the criminal and terrorist organizations have moved to the Internet and have embraced the use of digital media.

Investigators in the battle space do not have the luxury of time as we will discuss later on. Investigators today have a need for actionable intelligence: whether it be the patrol officer at a traffic stop or a battlefield investigator collecting evidence at a postblast investigation (PBI), the need for a quick turnaround of intelligence can be critical. As the criminal element has taken to technology, they, like many of us, do not follow the simple rules to hide or encrypt that data. This then provides the investigator with a unique opportunity. Exploitation of the digital evidence can provide a wealth of actionable intelligence, but the problem is getting to it.

Too often, investigators gather evidence that is not exploited for days or weeks, as it is sent to a central location where the experts can process the media. This removes any possibility of gathering actionable intelligence. The processing model that centralizes the data to one location is antiquated. In the early days of digital media, processing this model was fine. Unfortunately, the load of digital evidence began to overwhelm the labs that were designated to perform the analysis of the electronic media. The current model is shown in Figure 2.1.

The DTF model alleviates this backlog by implementing a triage forensic step as shown in Figure 2.2.

This backlog of electronic evidence was recognized in the mid-2000s and written about in the paper "Computer Forensics Field Triage Process Model" published in 2006. In this paper, the proposal was made to create a new methodology for processing digital evidence. The investigative process proposed was called the CFFTPM and is defined as those investigative processes that are conducted within the first few hours of an investigation, that provide information used during the suspect interview and search execution phase. Due to the need for information to be obtained in a relatively short time frame, the model usually involves an onsite/field analysis of the computer system(s) in question.

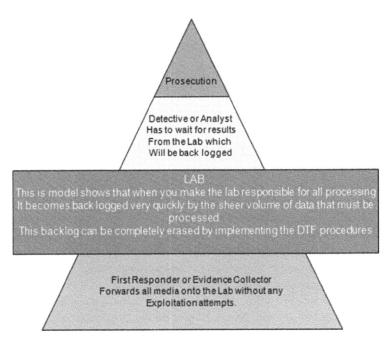

■ **FIGURE 2.1** The traditional forensic model.

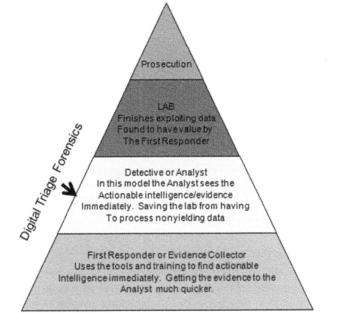

■ **FIGURE 2.2** The digital triage forensic model.

The focus of the model is on the following:

1. Find useable evidence immediately;
2. Identify victims at acute risk;
3. Guide the ongoing investigation;
4. Identify potential charges; and
5. Accurately assess the offender's danger to society.

At the same time, it involves protecting the integrity of the evidence and/ or potential evidence for further examination and analysis.

Being able to conduct an examination and analysis on scene in a short period and provide investigators with time-sensitive leads and information provide a powerful psychological advantage to the investigative team. Suspects are psychologically more vulnerable within the first few hours of their initial contact with police, especially when this contact occurs in their place of business or dwelling (Yeschke, 2003).[2] They tend to be more cooperative and open to answering questions even after being "Mirandized." This cooperation can be critical in certain cases such as abductions, sexual predatory offenses, etc. What is crucial to the investigator during this initial time period is the knowledge of the full extent of the crime and/or involvement of the suspect and "triggers" that further increase the suspect's willingness to talk and cooperate. These triggers may be found in the digital evidence located on the suspect's system(s) (e.g., e-mail correspondence, digital maps, pictures, chat logs, etc.).

The CFFTPM uses phases derived from the integrated digital investigation process (IDIP) model of Carrier and Spafford (2003)[3] and the digital crime scene analysis (DCSA) model developed by Rogers et al.[4] The phases include planning, triage, usage/user profiles, chronology/timeline, Internet activity, and case-specific evidence. These six phases constitute a high level of categorization and each phase has several subtasks and considerations, which the Conference on Digital Forensics, Security and Law, 2006, classifies according to the specifics of the case, file system, operating system under investigation, etc.

The use of higher order categories allows the process model to be generalized across various types of investigations that deal with digital evidence. The need for a general model has been identified in several studies as a core component of a practical/pragmatic approach for law enforcement investigations (ISTS, 2004;[5] Rogers and Seigfried, 2004;[6] Stambaugh et al., 2001[7]). Before discussing each of the model's phases, it is important that qualifications be placed around the use of the CFFTPM, as the model is not appropriate for all investigative situations.

Table 2.1 Comparison Table of All the Models

Traditional	CFFTPM	DTF
Planning	Planning	Planning
Identification	Triage	Identification
Collection	Identification	Collection
Preservation	Collection	Preservation
Examination	Preservation	Triage
Analysis	Examination	Examination
Report	Analysis	Analysis
	Report	Report

This CFFTPM model was the starting point that I used for the creation of the DTF model. The CFFTPM model does not take into consideration the challenges posed by the battlefield crime scene. Table 2.1 summarizes the differences.

All the models start out the same with the planning stage, which is critically important to successful operations. In the traditional and DTF models, the identification, collection, and preservation are done at the scene; in the CFFTPM model, the triage element is added, allowing the investigator to be able to perform some limited triage examinations at the scene. The CFFTPM model allows the investigator to be trained to gather and exploit data at the scene immediately. This triage process is a great improvement over the normal model, as the investigator is given the opportunity to gather immediate intelligence. The triage also allows the investigator to prioritize the evidence that he/she may send to the lab to aid it in not having to process junk data.

So, how is the DTF model different from the CFFTPM model? In the DTF model, the triage processing is not done at the scene; instead, it is done at the Forward Operating Base (FOB). Why was this necessary to move the triage step? The answer is simply safety and time. The triage processing was moved after watching the work-flow process of the investigator in a battlefield environment. To fully understand how the workflow of the battlefield investigator affects the placement of the triage process, we should fully define the DTF model.

DTF is defined as the process of identifying electronic evidence containers that can yield actionable intelligence for the battlefield commander while maintaining the integrity and pristine nature of evidence. Actionable intelligence is obviously the difference in the model. We defined actionable intelligence earlier as intelligence that can be acted upon within a 12–72 hour period. An example of using actionable intelligence with this model in a combat theater might be when a patrol moving down a supply route encounters a possible insurgent. The patrol, after detaining the individual, discovers a cell phone. The cell phone is sent back to the FOB and quickly analyzed by the team investigator. A review of the noninterpretable data from the cell phone reveals pictures of an intersection within close proximity to where the individual was detained. The pictures reveal photos showing wires protruding from the ground. The investigator immediately realizes that this individual has pictures of an IED. The investigator looks at the timestamp of the pictures and notes that the pictures were taken just 2 hour ago. No significant activity has occurred in that intersection in the last 5 hour. The patrol alerts an Explosive Ordinance Disposal (EOD) team that is dispatched to the scene. The EOD team successfully disarms the IED, preventing a serious event from occurring. In this instance, the actionable intelligence gathered from the cell phone was able to create a preblast event instead of a postblast event where soldiers may have been injured or killed.

In the preceding example, we can see why we move the triage to after the scene collection. The proper triage of the evidence must occur quickly in all situations. As was stated earlier, the two defining differences from the CFFTPM model and the DTF model are safety and time.

■ *Safety* for a combat investigator is the amount of exposure he/she must place himself/herself in to be able to gather evidence from the battlefield crime scene. While the investigator is exposed, he/she risks sniper attacks, indirect or direct fire, secondary IED, or mortar attacks.
■ *Time* is defined as the time that an investigator has to conduct the battlefield investigation. Typically, the investigator will have from 10 to 60 min to collect and process the battlefield crime scene. This includes the collection of the digital evidence. Imagine telling a stateside investigator that he/she has 60 min to process and investigate a car bomb in a mall parking lot!

Battlefield forensics versus controlled crime environments

The battlefield crime scenes in Iraq brought these two new conditions clearly into focus. By no means does this suggest that the investigator is doing a poor job; however, the investigator must work more diligently to prioritize the evidence and move more quickly and proficiently. To their credit, the WITs in Iraq have become very proficient at conducting these types of investigations. In this situation triaging the evidence at the scene is just not practical.

So, do these new models alleviate the need for traditional forensic models and the further processing of the evidence by the lab? No, they absolutely do not do so. The CFFTPM and DTF models are not designed to do a complete review of the data containers. In the DTF model, specifically only those data containers that may reveal noninterpretive evidence such as pictures and video are reviewed completely unless an interpreter is available: then, maybe textual data will be reviewed. The triage process does not typically look for unallocated data storage or encrypted data. The triage analysis is looking to identify those containers producing actionable intelligence and to prioritize the digital device when it goes to the lab to assist in making the full analysis more effecient. For the DTF process to work, the investigator must employ a collection method or procedure that is fast and effective in all situations.

Today's civilian investigators cannot even imagine what it would be like to collect evidence within the battlefield. Here, in the United States, investigators have as much time as needed to investigate their scenes as well as collect evidence in a controlled environment. Civilian investigators do not have to worry about secondary IEDs that may go off while on the scene. They do not have to worry about being attacked or shot at by snipers, and they do not have to wear body armor and carry a combat load of ammunition and weapons while trying to conduct their evidence-collection efforts.

WIT members have to learn to quickly assess their scene, prioritize in their mind what items of evidence are most crucial to collect, photograph the scene and surrounding area, and grab and bag the evidence, sometimes in as little as 5 min. To the civilian investigator, this would be mind boggling and he/she might ask how the WIT can be effective in its evidence-collection efforts. Through the WIT members' training, seasoned law enforcement professionals guide them in sound evidence-collection methods that are geared to collect the best possible pieces of evidence in the quickest manner that still maintains the integrity of the evidence so that it can be properly exploited and used in a criminal court. Are pieces of evidence missed or contaminated during these hurried collection efforts? Sure, but considering the exigency of the situations WIT members face in their environment, the "good" evidence they do collect is used in Iraqi courts to successfully convict those IED makers who have killed or tried to kill U.S. forces and Iraqi civilians.

Consolidated discipline training

One of the issues in making the DTF model work is consolidation of training. There are many contract companies teaching the force today, and standardization of training is an ongoing problem. This would appear to be common sense, but in reality it is not widely practiced. In our experience with other contractors, we often find that companies are afraid of losing their intellectual property, and this prevents a fluid exchange of ideas. At times, this is a well-founded fear but one that must be overcome.

The success of any training program relies on a uniform training doctrine. One very successful approach to the training model is in the cluster strategy employed by the National Forensic Science Technology Center (NFSTC) in Largo, Florida. This innovative approach to training was the brainchild of Kevin Lothridge, the chief executive officer (CEO) at NFSTC. By working closely together with several companies, such as the High Tech Crime Institute, Inc., Ron Smith and Associates, Forensic Technologies, and other organizations with completely different skill sets, training options are widely expanded. These organizations keep but one goal in mind—to provide the absolute best training to clients. To that end, they work under teaming agreements to provide a wide variety of training specialties in an efficient environment. By combining the efforts of multiple specialists into a uniform model, this approach creates a training selection that offers the full view of battlefield scene collection and processing.

Participating in a cluster of complementary organizations requires intercompany exchange of training materials to ensure that everyone is teaching with a single voice and that no one will be trained with a different procedure no matter what class they are in. This one simple requirement has had a tremendous effect on the curriculum being offered. Other policies and procedures ensure that the student gets the highest level of effective training possible.

The second part to the success of the innovation center is the extensive investment that has been made in the infrastructure of the center. The student literally has a hands-on experience from day 1. Scenario sites at the center provide a real-world look and feel to what the student may encounter when at a battlefield scene.

The innovations center is going to be a model that many other centers are going to try and emulate in the future. Visit NFSTC at http://www.nfstc. org/training/state-of-the-art-training-lab/

HOW DOES EVIDENCE GO FROM THE BATTLEFIELD TO THE LAB?

As WITs collect evidence from IED scenes and caches, they warehouse it at their FOB in the most secure fashion available to them, maintaining a chain of custody. Once they have collected, processed, and exploited their evidence to the best of their abilities, the evidence is packaged and shipped to the Combined Explosives Exploitation Cell (CEXC) at Camp Victory in Baghdad. In the early days of WITs, team members used to hand-carry all evidence to CEXC via helicopter or convoy. Nowadays, WITs can package the evidence, sign over the chain of custody to the helicopter commander or the convoy commander, and, once the evidence arrives at Camp Victory, a member of the CEXC can sign for it and take the evidence to their lab.

The CEXC supports the operational units by conducting further exploitation of evidence in a state-of-the-art lab and controlled environment. Members of the lab are experts in their fields from federal agencies such as the Federal Bureau of Investigations (FBI); the Alcohol, Tobacco, Firearms, and Explosives (ATFE); the EOD; and the Joint IED Defeat Organization (JIEDDO), to name a few, as well as lab technicians from all over the world.

The CEXC conducts investigations of significant events, updates electronic warfare frequencies, tests explosive residues, and identifies IED trends and bomb maker signatures. Methods used in their exploitation of evidence consist of triaging the evidence to determine the priority of processing the evidence, photography, technical exploitation, forensic exploitation, and biometric exploitation.

The Joint Expeditionary Forensic Facility (JEFF) is another lab where evidence can be sent for studying machinery and tool markings on IED evidence. This is especially important when explosively formed projectile (EFP) liners are discovered, as the lab technicians may be able to determine where the EFP was made and collect data as to how it was made. The JEFFs primarily exploit non-IED evidence such as firearms and they conduct tool mark analysis as well.

The Terrorist Explosive Device Analytical Center (TEDAC) is a lab ran by the FBI at Quantico, Virginia. The TEDAC's mission is to manage exploitation of IEDs of interest to the U.S. Government and is the warehouse for IED evidence. TEDAC also coordinates with other government agencies to further exploit and research IED materials and components.

FIVE LEVELS OF EXPLOITATION OF WTI MATERIALS

The above-mentioned labs all have their roles in exploiting IED evidence, but there are five levels of exploitation that you need to be aware of. Each level has its own unique mission and exploitation requirements that ultimately support the battlefield commanders. These commanders require feedback from exploitation efforts at all levels to remain offensive in their Area of Operations (AORs). The five levels of exploitation are the following:

Level 1: Tactical
Level 2: Operational

Level 3: Strategic
Level 4: National
Level 5: Special Activities

An explanation of the five levels of exploitation as they relate to IED evidence follows. Level 1 exploitation involves collection of evidence at IED pre/post blast scenes and caches by WIT members and maneuver units in the field. This is the most basic and important collection level, as, without the evidence, no analysis or actionable intelligence could be obtained. WIT members are trained in Level 1 exploitation so they can garner any actionable intelligence from their evidence and report it within a 72-hour time frame. This is especially crucial when digital media are present. WIT members can image hard disk drives with Parabens Forensic Replicator and use triage forensic tools such as Parabens P2 Commander to conduct analysis of the hard disk drives. Cell phones can be analyzed with Parabens Device Seizure tool. There are other triage forensic tools available for use in the marketplace; however, WITs are supplied with Parabens products at this time.

Level 2 exploitation is conducted by the forensic labs in theaters such as CEXC and JEFF. Both labs use many evidence exploitation methods that are very sophisticated and specialized. This level of exploitation is typically conducted in theater, so information gleaned from Level 2 exploitation can be used to immediately support the battlefield commanders.

Level 3 exploitation involves scientific examination and analysis of IED evidence and provides direct support to the attacking the enemy's network.

Level 4 exploitation is managed by the Defense Intelligence Agency (DIA). This level of exploitation combines collection, exploitation, and analysis with national policy and requests assistance from other national labs such as within the Department of Justice and the Department of Energy.

Level 5 Exploitation is collection, analysis, and research by government agencies and private research firms that focus on developing methods to enhance collection efforts in the field.

SUMMARY

The benefit of using the DTF model is clear in the battlefield or combat situation. Current processing models are designed to be used in traditional investigative environments and do not take into consideration safety and time that must be evaluated when in a hostile environment. The benefits of the DTF process are the following:

■ It returns actionable intelligence in a speedy reliable manner.

- It identifies devices that require further analysis by a true digital forensic lab.
- It permits timely coordinated processing that allows the investigator a minimal amount of time at the crime scene or objective.

It is important to remember that training without proper policy implementation will result in the failure of the DTF model. Training must also be uniform across the board, providing for a one-voice training effect. This can only be accomplished when contractors feel that they are a part of a team and that their intellectual property is going to be protected.

Controlled crime scenes cannot even compare to crime scenes on the battlefield, yet WIT members successfully conduct evidence collection that leads to prosecution of bomb makers and emplacers using sound battlefield evidence collection methods developed over the years.

Without the many layers and levels of exploitation and the laboratories that support the efforts of the evidence collectors, no progress would be made against our enemies as we take the fight back to them by analyzing and exploiting battlefield evidence to create new Tactical Training Plans (TTPs) for our battlefield commanders to use.

In the next few chapters, we are going to show the DTF model employed at the combat theater level. We will cover traditional storage containers such as laptops and thumb drives, etc., moving into the more complex processing of cellular devices. The programs and procedures that we will be using to illustrate the DTF process are currently being used in Iraq and Afghanistan to perform the DTF process.

REFERENCES

1 Ross R. Criminal environmental extremists may be recruiting children. Posted in Environmental Extremists, Animal Rights and Environmental Extremists at 6:03 p.m. by Rick Ross. www.cultnews.com/?p=1404; 2003.
2 Yeschke C. The art of investigative interviewing – second edition. Boston: Butterworth Heineman; 2003.
3 Carrier B, Spafford E. Getting Physical with the Digital Investigation Process. *International Journal of Digital Evidence* 2003;2(2):20.
4 Rogers M, Goldman J, Mislan R, Wedge T, Debrota S. Computer forensics field triage process model, Paper presented at the Conference on Digital Forensics, Security and Law. www.digitalforensics-conference.org/CFFTPM/CDFSL-proceedings2006-CFFTPM. pdf; 2006.
5 Institute for Security Technology Studies. *Law enforcement tools and technologies for investigating cyber attacks: A national research and development agenda.* Retrieved September 9, 2004 from http://www.ists.dartmouth.edu.
6 Rogers M, Seigfried K. *The future of computer forensics:* A needs analysis survey. Computers and Security(Spring 2004).
7 Stambaugh H, Beaupre D, Icove D, Baker R, Cassaday W, Williams W. Electronic crime needs assessment for state and local law enforcement. Retrieved September 1, 2005 from http://www.ojp.usdoj.gov/nij/pubs-sum/186276.htm; 2001.

Chapter 3

Conducting pre/postblast investigations

INTRODUCTION

In this chapter, we discuss the role of WIT in conducting pre- and postblast investigations of IED scenes as well as preparing for those missions. Scene safety will be discussed as the WIT operator conducts IED scene analysis to determine what types of IED events have taken place. We will discuss the common forms of IED attacks, scene investigation limitations as well as evidence collection and postmission reporting. Finally, we discuss detainee operations as they pertain to the WIT mission.

WITs ROLE WITHIN THE EOD TEAM

When WITs are deployed to their AOR, they are married up with an EOD team, who responds to 9-Line calls when IEDs, caches, and postblast scenes are detected by the maneuver units in the field. WIT members are being thrust upon EOD teams to conduct their missions, creating a dangerous environment for the WIT member as well as the EOD technician. The EOD community is a very tight-knit group who work and play hard together. EOD work is dangerous and there is no margin for error. EOD technicians live on the edge daily and accept the risk that they may blow themselves up, but they never want to be the one that causes the death or injury of an innocent. WIT members respond to IED incidents and can become a liability to the EOD team, a liability some EOD personnel do not want to take on. Prior to the official WIT mission, EOD had been conducting a quasi-WIT mission in the form of photographing the scenes, collecting some evidence if it was feasible, and writing a short report as to what happened at these scenes. As you will see later in this chapter, WIT now takes the mission to new levels by not only collecting and documenting the scenes, but also providing an in-depth analytical report used to study TTPs of the enemy, analyze trends in IED activity within an AOR, and exploit any evidence found to glean any and all actionable intelligence available to them.

When a WIT element arrives at an EOD unit, they should make every effort to explain their mission to them as well as the strengths and

Digital Triage Forensics. Doi: 10.1016/B978-1-59749-596-7.00003-6

weaknesses within the team. The EOD leadership may have past experiences with WIT, good or bad, that could affect the initial reception the WIT members receive. The EOD technician assigned to a WIT should conduct the initial liaison with the EOD team as they speak the same language and have a common core of experience and bond, even if they are from different military services. On rare occasions, the EOD technician assigned to the WIT can cause problems as he/she may feel slighted about being assigned to WIT and not to a deployed EOD team. This attitude creates dissension within the WIT element and makes the team ineffective. WIT members have in the past become mission liabilities or portrayed themselves as superior and not a team player. Such issues can cause an EOD team not to want them on missions and refuse to take them along or tell them to drive their own vehicle within the responding convoy. If the EOD team has had good experiences with WIT members, they will more than likely be given the benefit of doubt until they either prove they can be professional and a force multiplier or a hindrance.

WIT may respond to 9-Lines with EOD in their own vehicle or ride in the EOD vehicle as an actual member of the EOD team. Methods of responding to IED events will depend on how dangerous the roads are within the AOR, available vehicles to respond in, and how many EOD teams the WIT element will have to support. Some WIT travel in their own vehicle with at least three members (driver, team leader, and gunner) or they split into a one person WIT supporting multiple EOD teams and riding with that team to IED events. In either method, the WIT members need to integrate themselves with the EOD team and become a functional team member. A WIT member can accomplish this by volunteering to help get equipment out of the vehicle while on scene, provide security when not performing a WIT function, and be additional eyes and ears for the safety of the team. This may sound like common sense or not that much to ask, but those few simple tasks I mentioned will go a long way with the EOD team and show them you are not going to be a hindrance or liability. Over time, successful WITs will have cultivated excellent relationships with their EOD team and will have laid a positive foundation for the next WIT that the EOD team will encounter (Figure 3.1).

PREMISSION PREPARATIONS

Premission planning starts stateside, even before the WIT leaves the United States and continues after arriving in the AOR that they are assigned to. As a team is formed and each of the members train and learn

■ **FIGURE 3.1** 1st Platoon Marine EOD from Camp Pendleton, CA, 2006; AR Ramadi, Iraq. *Photo taken by author Rich Watson.*

together, each person's strengths and weaknesses will start to show. As the team becomes more proficient in learning their mission, each member's role within the team will become evident. One team member may be an excellent report writer, another a great photographer, and another member could be proficient in lifting fingerprints. A team should plan in advance how they will operate as a team at IED scenes based on those strengths and weaknesses. The only issue with this sound planning theory is that when they arrive in their AOR, teams can be split to support multiple EOD teams or other FOBs that require WIT support. In these instances, the WIT members must be prepared to accomplish all aspects of their WIT training.

Once WIT members arrive at their FOB, the first order of business is to ensure all of the WIT equipment needed has arrived and has been inventoried. If any equipment is damaged or missing, the WIT member will need to contact the WIT Headquarters element at Camp Victory. The second order of business is to begin the liaison efforts mentioned previously with the EOD team(s) that the WIT member will be working with. The third order of business will be to review previous WIT reports from the AOR. This will help the team quickly get up to speed on the types of IEDs found in the past, common locations of IED sites, and other information pertinent to the AOR. If the WIT member is relieving an existing WIT element, many of these preparations will be made easier by their presence and there usually will be 1-2 weeks overlap called "right seat/left seat." During this overlap phase, the new WIT member will ride with an outgoing WIT member (right seat) to learn the EOD team's operating nuances as well as the AOR while responding to 9-Line calls. After a week, the outgoing WIT member will become secondary and the new WIT member will take over as the primary WIT investigator (left seat). By the time this training overlap is completed, the new WIT member should be able to take the mission and run it.

When planning to go on missions, it is important to pay attention to your personal equipment and ensure it is set up in the best configuration for portability and functionality. Besides carrying your weapons and wearing all of your battle gear, you will be carrying your WIT tools for evidence collection. The WIT kits contain two photography bags that can be used not only to carry the supplied cameras, but also house fingerprinting materials, evidence bags, etc. that a WIT member will need on the scene. These "go-bags" are designed to be portable and not to hinder the WIT member while wearing all of his/her protective gear and weapons. As the WIT member conducts missions, he/she will learn better what evidence collection items to take and what items to leave back at the FOB as they may be rarely used or not used at all.

Another premission planning suggestion is to look at the vehicles you will be driving or riding in to ensure all aspects of those vehicles are operational. Also look where items are stored, where you will stow your gear, and where you will be riding. If you will be riding with EOD, ask ahead of time what your responsibilities will be while on missions. Ensure all communication devices are functioning, as well as the electronic counter measure devices installed for that particular vehicle (Figure 3.2).

SCENE SAFETY

When responding to an IED scene or cache, safety at the scene is of utmost importance. Once you leave the protection of your armored vehicle, many hazards await you. Upon arrival, the battalion that has the battle space where the IED scene is located will have a protective cordon set up that EOD and WIT will enter to process the scene. All team members that actually leave the vehicle to conduct their portion of the mission will first scan the area from their feet out to 25 m looking for booby traps and secondary IEDs that may be waiting for them. This process is called "5 & 25s" and is very important and each member must do this scan religiously each time they exit their vehicles. The enemy targets EOD teams as they are their nemesis who defeat their bomb making efforts.

■ **FIGURE 3.2** EOD Cougar commonly used to respond to IED scenes, 2006; AR Ramadi, Iraq. *Photo taken by author Rich Watson.*

Since WIT responds with EOD, they become a target as well. There have been many instances where teams have discovered secondary IEDs implaced and designed to detonate while the teams are investigating the scenes. The enemy watches our teams and their TTPs to see how they operate. It is imperative that EOD and WIT change their approaches to blast scenes when driving in and how they set up to conduct their mission. There will be instances where the enemy will place a "dummy" IED and watch how EOD and WIT respond to the scene. A few days later they will place a real IED in the same place. The IED itself could be booby trapped or a secondary IED could be placed where their truck was parked when they responded to the dummy IED. By not changing approaches or operating procedures, especially when returning to the same scene from a previous mission, could prove disastrous.

Besides secondary IEDs and booby traps, the second safety consideration is the possibility of snipers in the area. While on scene and outside your armored vehicle, you can feel very vulnerable and exposed. Do not stand in one place too long and scan your surroundings and rooftops constantly. This is a time where those team members that are outside of the vehicle provide security when not performing a mission function. Every time I left the vehicle, especially in urban areas, the hair on the back of my neck would stand up because I was wondering if a sniper was somewhere out there. In the early years of WIT, the enemy would see EOD arrive at IED scenes and conduct their mission. Then, they started seeing one or several other soldiers show up and start photographing scenes and picking up items off the ground and putting the items in bags. They did not know what these soldiers' roles were, but in 2006, a battalion in the northern area of AO Topeka outside AR Ramadi, Iraq stumbled on a sniper training area in the desert. They discovered rifles, ammunition, and training manuscripts. The training manuscripts described tactics and techniques for the sniper. Also in this manuscript there was a section describing targets to select. It mentioned that when EOD teams arrive on an IED scene, the soldier with the camera should be shot. They were not sure at that time what WIT was, but they thought whoever they were, they were important enough to be shot. So, who on your team is going to carry the camera?

One last hazard that a WIT team may face is indirect fire from small arms, rocket propelled grenades (RPGs), and mortar fire. There have been times when EOD and WIT have been attacked by small arms fire from enemy forces moving through the area while on IED scenes. While you are in Iraq or Afghanistan, you will become familiar with the times of day when prayer is conducted and you will hear the calls to prayer over loudspeakers throughout any city you may be in. The TTP that the enemy has used in the past is to wait for the EOD team and WIT to arrive at an IED scene and then make a call to prayer to let the enemy forces know the U.S. forces have arrived so that they can make their attack. If you hear the call to prayer when it is not the time for prayer, expect the enemy to show up.

RPGs and mortars are prevalent and readily available for enemy forces and are fired at EOD teams and WIT quite often. The scary part of this type of attack is that you can't hear them coming in on you until they either fly over your head or land and detonate. Sometimes that can be too late (Figure 3.3).

ON SCENE IED ANALYSIS

Upon arrival at an IED scene, typically the EOD team leader will meet with the cordon commander to determine the situation. This may be a pre- or postblast site and on occasions, a cache. Caches are fairly simple to assess. The WIT member needs to look at the location of where the cache is stored and answer the questions: Why did the enemy select this location for a cache? What was the purpose of the cache? With the contents in the cache, who or what were they possibly targeting? Caches can be a wealth of information for WIT when they discover IED materials as well as any digital media. WIT members will collect IED items such

■ **FIGURE 3.3** Mortar detonation outside of a WIT vehicle while on an IED scene, 2006; AR Ramadi, Iraq. *Photo taken by author Rich Watson.*

as detonators, timers, cell phones, telephone base stations, tools, circuitry components, computers, and other digital media that may be found such as flash drives, cameras, compact disks, and SIM cards. WIT will also, time permitting, collect fingerprints of any physical items that cannot be taken as evidence, samples of HME, and swab samples from any component that could have explosive residue left behind. The EOD team will document any and all munitions and explosive devises discovered and will destroy them in several ways. The EOD will sometimes blow up the munitions in place, destroying not only the munitions, but the structure they were stored in as well. Another option is to remove the munitions and take them to the FOB where they are stored until a sufficient amount has been collected. When the EOD feels they have to remove them from their storage area, all of the munitions are loaded into trucks and driven out into the desert where they are piled together and destroyed (Figures 3.4–3.6). This is a safe method to destroy the munitions so that they will not fall back into the hands of the enemy. It is also a great stress reliever as the explosion created is quite a "fireworks" display!

Upon arrival at a preblast IED scene, typically the EOD team leader will meet with the cordon commander to determine the situation. The WIT member should, at this time, take long-range photographs of where the IED is suspected to be and 360° photographs of the surrounding site. We will

■ **FIGURE 3.4** Loading munitions to be destroyed, 2006; AR Ramadi, Iraq. *Photo taken by author Rich Watson.*

■ **FIGURE 3.5** EOD personnel preparing to destroy captured munitions', 2006; AR Ramadi, Iraq. *Photo taken by author Rich Watson.*

■ **FIGURE 3.6** Cache of ordnance used to make IEDs, 2006; AR Ramadi, Iraq. *Photo taken by author Rich Watson.*

discuss photography in detail later in this chapter. Afterward, a Talon robot will usually be deployed to assess the IED type and how it can be rendered safe. From the protection of the armored vehicle, an EOD team member will drive the Talon robot remotely to the IED. The WIT member should sit next to the Talon robot driver and take notes as to the type of IED present, its explosive makeup, and look for any new technology or design incorporated into the IED (Figures 3.7–3.9). The WIT member should look at the location of the IED and answer the questions: Why did the enemy select this location for an IED attack? Where is an aiming point for this IED? Who or what were the enemy possibly targeting? What type of IED was this?

Upon arrival at a postblast scene, The WIT member will need to take as much time as allocated to analyze the scene. Once the EOD team determines the area to be safe and free of unexploded ordnance (UXO), WIT can photograph the scene extensively and start any evidence collection processes. The WIT member needs to look at the location of where the IED was placed and answer the questions: Why did the enemy select this location for an IED attack? Where is an aiming point for this IED? Who or what were the enemy possibly targeting? What type of IED was this? The WIT member should consult with the EOD team as to what their assessment of the IED event was and what possible explosives, munitions, and methods were used to detonate the IED (Figure 3.10).

■ **FIGURE 3.7** A Talon robot advancing toward a suspected IED, 2006; AR Ramadi, Iraq. *Photo taken by author Rich Watson.*

■ **FIGURE 3.8** A Talon robot, 2006; AR Ramadi, Iraq. *Photo taken by author Rich Watson.*

■ **FIGURE 3.9** View from an enemy firing point toward their aiming point, which is the top of the hill as a dirt road crests it; 2006, AR Ramadi, Iraq. *Photo taken by author Rich Watson.*

■ **FIGURE 3.10** An EOD technician investigating a postblast scene; 2006, AR Ramadi, Iraq. *Photo taken by author Rich Watson.*

In all three of the aforementioned IED scenes that a WIT member could respond to, factors that need to be examined are common. On scene, IED analysis is just the first step to the WIT reporting process as the WIT member is not only gathering the facts and evidence from each scene, but any and all intelligence associated with the scenes as well. These important facts will help the WIT members in writing their WIT report after each mission. We will discuss WIT reports later in this chapter under postmission reporting.

PHOTOGRAPH! PHOTOGRAPH! PHOTOGRAPH!

The most important step in the WIT process that a WIT member will conduct is taking digital photographs. Lots and lots of digital photographs! Digital photography in the WIT mission is so important because it will describe the scenes without a word being spoken. Anyone can look at a series of photographs and get the basic idea of an event that occurred. Since cameras were invented, soldiers and the media have been documenting wars and destruction. Photographs tell the stories of lives changed forever, death and destruction; they have been taken to collect intelligence as well. Digital photographs become the foundation for WIT intelligence reports and save the WIT member from having to write everything down on paper to keep a record of the event when he/she has such a limited time on the scene. With the advent of digital cameras, WIT members can snap hundreds of photographs using SD cards or other digital storage containers that are quick and easy to change whereas rolls of film are cumbersome, easily damaged, and limited in the amount of photographs that can be taken.

Each WIT kit that is deployed is equipped with four cameras. There are two Nikon Coolpix point and shoot cameras that can easily be carried in a pouch on the WIT members equipment or in a cargo pocket on their uniform. The kit also includes a JVC digital movie camera that can be used to record the scene as the WIT member narrates or used to take still photographs. The last camera supplied is a Ricoh 500 ruggedized camera with GPS technology, infra-red picture-taking capabilities, and pictures taken can be incorporated into Falcon View software technology. In previous WIT kits, there were Nikon D70 SLRS Cameras with three interchangeable lenses. Although the Nikon D70 cameras took fantastic pictures, the nature of a desert combat environment led to the Ricoh cameras being deployed with the WIT kits because the Nikon D70s were too fragile and could not hold up to the rigors of the battlefield they were deployed to. Often, the Nikon D70s would break when WIT members would have to dive for cover when they came under attack or the lenses would break when accidentally dropped. Having to carry multiple lenses for different types of photography situations became an issue as well. The Ricoh 500s have worked well to this point and are less bulky than the Nikons, but some complaints from WIT teams have said they use up batteries quickly, so they have to carry several extra batteries for resupply.

All WIT members receive photography training while attending the WIC. They are taught standard law enforcement methods and how to take crime scene photographs. The three main types of photographs a WIT member is taught to take are

- Overall scene photographs
- Medium-range scene photographs
- Closeup photographs

Overall scene photographs are taken when the WIT member first arrives at an IED scene. These pictures should be taken from all directions if possible when outdoors and from all corners of rooms or buildings when indoors. These pictures will give the viewer a good feel of the structure or terrain where the IED event took place. These pictures can be taken while the EOD team leader is assessing the situation as the WIT member cannot do anything until the EOD team ensures the area is safe. There will be times at preblast IED scenes, when these will be the only type of photographs one may get, so the WIT members should take as many photographs as they can. While taking overall photographs, the WIT member should be looking for IED aiming points and locations where the enemy could remotely detonate an IED from. These areas will help the WIT member assess the enemy's intentions as to whom or what they were targeting.

Medium-range scene photographs are mostly taken indoors when the WIT member has the opportunity to move about the room. Most outdoor medium-range photographs are taken at postblast scenes. The medium-range photographs help bring in more detail of the scene and focus to the immediate area where an IED event occurred. They also show where evidence may be located, dimensions and size comparisons of blast holes, the layout of IED components, and any dead bodies or body parts as a result of an IED blast. The medium-range photographs will also assist the WIT member to remember where items were on the immediate scene so they can recreate their scene sketch that must be included in their WIT report.

Closeup photographs are used to fully document items of evidentiary value and fully detail those items. The closeup photographs should be taken last on scene as once a piece of evidence is documented with a close up, it can be collected and removed from the scene. Back at the FOB, WIT members can take even more detailed photographs of evidence in a controlled and safe environment. Detailed pictures should be taken of evidence showing all of its sides, any serial numbers or engravings, wiring design, and any modifications to the wiring that may have been completed by the bomb maker, detailed fingerprints prior to attempt a lift, and any circuitry that may be exposed (Figures 3.11 and 3.12).

As mentioned earlier, photographs may be all that you take from an IED scene and become crucial to the WIT member's ability to write a report

■ **FIGURE 3.11** A Senao cordless telephone base station modified to remotely detonate an IED; 2006, AR Ramadi, Iraq. *Photo taken by author Rich Watson.*

■ **FIGURE 3.12** Close up picture of wiring to a 9 v battery used with a command wire detonator; 2006, AR Ramadi, Iraq. *Photo taken by author Rich Watson.*

about the incident. This could occur based on the dangerous nature of the scene. There have been many instances where WIT members could not leave the armored vehicle because bullets were bouncing off the vehicle from small arms fire. In this situation, usually on a postblast scenario, the EOD team leader may drive the vehicle up to the scene and make the best assessment from inside the vehicle. The WIT member can obtain photographs by taking them through the bullet proof windows. Another trick to get photographs when the scene is unapproachable or too dangerous is from the video monitor that the Talon robot driver uses to guide the robot. The Talon has a camera mounted with day and night capabilities. As the EOD member drives the robot, the WIT member can take still photographs from the screen. This way you will be able to get a picture of what the IED or IED scene looks like and can use those pictures in the WIT report. We have found the best camera to use with taking pictures of the robot display is the JVC video camera in still shot mode.

Night-time photography can be challenging, especially when the team is driving "blacked out" with no headlights and using night vision devices to see. You want to avoid using white light to photograph scenes as you light up yourself and your team members, thus making everyone potential sniper targets and you will cause aggravating bright white flashes to anyone wearing night vision devices. Be cognizant of your surroundings and keep safety in mind over getting any photographs (Figure 3.13).

■ **FIGURE 3.13** Night shot of a Vehicle Bourne IED; 2006, AR Ramadi, Iraq. *Photo taken by author Rich Watson.*

PREBLAST INVESTIGATIVE STEPS

Upon arriving at a preblast IED scene, typically the EOD team leader will meet with the cordon commander to determine the situation. All EOD and WIT members that exit the vehicle should conduct 5 & 25s around their vehicle looking for any secondary IEDs that may have been planted. The WIT member should at this time take long-range photographs of where the IED is suspected to be and 360° photographs of the surrounding site. Once the EOD team determines the type of IED they are dealing with, they will determine a course of action to either render the IED safe or blow it up in place (BIP). There are several types of IEDs that can be encountered that have general descriptions for the purpose of labeling. They are the following:

- Command wire IEDs (CWIED)
- Victim operated IEDs (VOIED)
- Remote controlled IEDs (RCIED)
- Vehicle bourne IEDs (VBIED)
- Human bourne IEDs, also known as "Suicide Bombers"
- Other

CWIEDs are IEDs that are created to be detonated with the use of a command wire that leads from the IED to an initiation device activated by an enemy combatant. Command wires have consistently been copper wire, but can be anything that can carry an electrical current. Copper wire is used extensively as it is thin and can be hidden well from unsuspecting soldiers. The initiation devices will have some sort of power source, usually 9 v batteries and there could be a battery booster at the end of the wire where it is attached to the IED. This type of IED can be dangerous to the enemy insurgent as it places him at risk of being discovered, captured, or killed before the IED can be set off. Mechanical failure can occur as well prior to detonation (Figures 3.14 and 3.15).

VOIED are IEDs that require an unsuspecting victim to initiate activation. Typically, these types of IEDs target foot soldiers and vehicles. VOIEDs have some type of initiation device when stepped on or driven over. The most prevalent initiation device is a pressure switch attached to the IED. These pressure switches are commonly made from hack saw blades, foam or wood, wire, and a 9 v battery pack (Figures 3.16 and 3.17).

VOIEDs can be left in place without any monitoring, but are indiscriminant about whom they will maim or kill. Many innocent Iraqi civilians have been severely injured or killed by VOIEDs that had been left in place. Unfortunately, many children have been the unsuspecting victims of such IEDs.

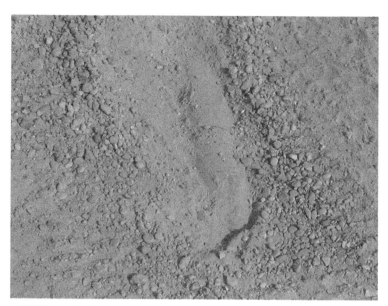

■ **FIGURE 3.14** IED showing copper command wire running across the center middle of the IED; 2006, AR Ramadi, Iraq. *Photo taken by author Rich Watson.*

■ **FIGURE 3.15** Typical initiating device with copper wire; 2006, AR Ramadi, Iraq. *Photo taken by author Rich Watson.*

RCIEDs are very popular with the enemy as they can be close enough to watch the detonation, yet far enough to remain safe from being shot or captured by U.S. and coalition forces. RCIEDs consist of a command wire going from the radio controlled device to the IED. The radio controlled device can be a cell phone, long-range cell phone (LRCT), or Senao

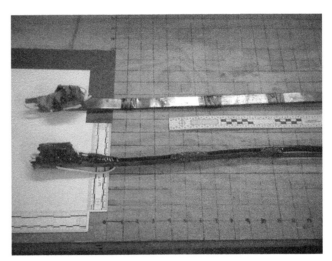

■ **FIGURE 3.16** Pressure switches made from thin metal strips, black tape, foam, wires, and 9 v batteries; 2006, AR Ramadi, Iraq. *Photo taken by author Rich Watson.*

■ **FIGURE 3.17** VOIED; 2006, AR Ramadi, Iraq. *Photo taken by author Rich Watson.*

telephone base stations. These devices can be very basic, with simple to elaborate modifications. The initiation devices for RCIEDs are usually another telephone, either one that belongs to the Senao base stations or cell phones. The cell phones used to detonate RCIEDs can be your every-day cell phone, uniquely modified to set off multiple RCIEDs at once.

Even though the enemy may feel safer using such an IED initiation device, there are limitations and some areas in Iraq are seeing an enemy TTP change of relying on more VOIEDs and CWIEDs. A reason for this change in tactics is our continued use and improvement of electronic countermeasure devices (Figures 3.18 and 3.19).

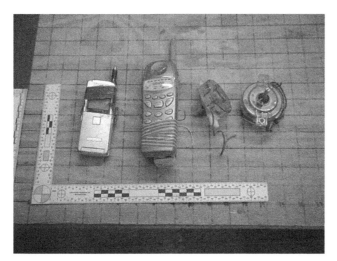

■ **FIGURE 3.18** Cell phones used for RCIEDs; 2006, AR Ramadi, Iraq. *Photo taken by author Rich Watson.*

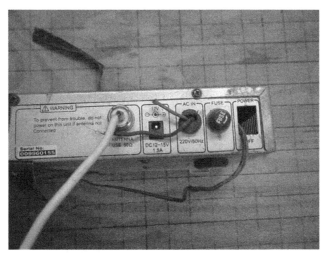

■ **FIGURE 3.19** A modified Senao base station rigged to detonate an RCIED; 2006, AR Ramadi, Iraq. *Photo taken by author Rich Watson.*

VBIEDs can be one of the most destructive IEDs that can be used against persons, other vehicles, or physical structures. The amount of explosives that can be packed into a vehicle is limited only by the size and space of the vehicle's compartments. During my tour in Iraq, I saw VBIEDs made from everyday sedans to Iraqi-style dump trucks. Besides munitions and other types of explosives packed into the vehicle, some bombers will add cans of gasoline to create more thermal effects upon detonation, adding to the destructiveness of this type of IED.

VBIED drivers are typically volunteers who are willing to kill themselves for their cause, but sometimes the drivers are not so willing after they start down the road and think about it. The VBIED maker will sometimes install a radio control device to detonate the VBIED if the driver "chickens out." Drivers dedicated to the cause have their hands and feet tied to the steering wheel and accelerator just in case they are shot or killed while driving the car toward their intended target. Tying them to the steering wheel and accelerator at times keep the vehicle on its intended path toward creating death and destruction (Figures 3.20–3.22).

Suicide bombers will attack crowds of people causing mass death and destruction. They will strike in bazaars, on public transportation, military

■ **FIGURE 3.20** The remains of a VBIED after the driver "chickened out" and detonated as he was turning around to leave. The intended victim was an Iraqi police officer; 2006, AR Ramadi, Iraq. *Photo taken by author Rich Watson.*

■ **FIGURE 3.21** The remains of a dump truck VBIED after an attack on an Iraqi police station; 2006, AR Ramadi, Iraq. *Photo taken by author Rich Watson.*

■ **FIGURE 3.22** The remains of a VBIED after the driver attacked a U.S. forces convoy. The convoy gunners shot the vehicle as it quickly approached them causing the VBIED to predetonate; 2006, AR Ramadi, Iraq. *Photo taken by author Rich Watson.*

checkpoints, and Iraqi police and training centers, to name a few. Suicide bomber vests are homemade and contain any type of shrapnel or projectiles that will cause mass maiming or death. Marbles and ball bearings are very common as they are hard and aerodynamic in flight. Suicide bomber devices can be rigged with many different types of explosives and initiation devices. There are other types of IED devices out there, but the ones listed are the most common that WIT and EOD will encounter while conducting their missions.

After EOD determines what type of IED they are dealing with, they initiate a plan to either disable the IED or blow it up. The WIT member should get as many photographs as possible, as that could be all they get from the scene. If the IED is rendered safe, EOD will remove it from the scene. WIT members should be able to take quality pictures of the device when safely back at the FOB and retrieve any other evidence of value from the components of the device.

If EOD makes the decision to blow the IED up in place, the WIT member may or may not collect any physical evidence from the device. Depending on the safety factors of the scene, the EOD team leader may move closer to the destroyed IED either on foot or by driving the vehicle up to the location. EOD would do this to collect any evidence that survived the blast after they blew it up or to ensure manually that the IED was rendered safe via the actions of the robot. Once EOD is positive the device is rendered safe, it is transported back to the FOB. Manually rendering an IED safe is very dangerous. There have been EOD technicians killed by IEDs that were booby trapped to detonate when the initial initiation device was disabled and the IED picked up (Figure 3.23).

There can be investigative limitations that will prevent the WIT member from processing a preblast IED scene. Some investigative limitations have been mentioned previously, but are worthy of mention again. Investigative limitations can be caused by the environment or safety factors of the scene. It may be unsafe to get out of the vehicle due to enemy activity. If the IED device is blown up by the EOD team and there are remote control problems with the Talon robot, the WIT members may not get any photographs of the device, let alone any physical evidence. The WIT members may get minimum information, relayed from the cordon commander to the EOD team leader and then to them. The WIT member may not have an opportunity to interview any soldiers who were involved in discovering the IED or any civilian witnesses who might have seen those who placed the IED.

■ **FIGURE 3.23** The rear of an EOD cougar that was destroyed when a VOIED was thought to be rendered safe and placed in the back of the vehicle. Unfortunately, one Marine EOD technician and one Navy Corpsman were killed in the detonation and one WIT member was severely injured; 2007, AR Ramadi, Iraq. *Photo Courtesy of Marine SSG Daniel Bogart.*

There are many types of IED evidence that can be collected from a pre-blast IED scene. The obvious are physical pieces belonging to the IED. Items to look for are command wires, push button detonators, LRCTs, cell phones, pressure switches, tape, batteries, wires, and base stations, to name a few. Once back at the FOB, the WIT member can examine the evidence he/she brought back further for fingerprints, explosive residue, etc. The WIT members have many tools in their WIT kit to use when exploiting evidence. If the WIT member does not feel confident in lifting fingerprints, the evidence item can be contained until it reaches the lab at CEXC, where it can be further exploited. The WIT members have buckle swabs available to swab components that may have trace DNA and they have a Field Forensics explosives residue detection kit available to them to swab parts and pieces from the IED to assist in determining the explosives used to make the IED. Once any and all exploitation of evidence is concluded, the evidence is packed and shipped to CEXC for Level 2 exploitation.

After the mission is completed, the WIT members must file a WIT report that describes the mission they went on, stating facts about where and how the IED was placed, whether there were any enemy combatants captured and details of how the IED was discovered and by whom. The WIT members will also list in the report, all evidence they collected and the results of any exploitation they conducted on the evidence. The last thing the WIT members will add to their report is their assessment of the IED scene. The assessment is where the WIT members can write what they personally think about the IED scene as to why the IED was placed where it was, who the enemy were targeting, why they chose the location for the IED and what other similar devices have been used in the past and what the IED trends are for the AOR. This assessment is very important and the WIT members should put as much thought into this section of the report as possible because the readers of the report rely on them to provide the best intelligence available for that AOR. The WIT members, along with the EOD teams in an AOR, are considered the experts in the field when it comes to IEDs and must be diligent in providing the best and most accurate picture of IED events as possible.

POSTBLAST INVESTIGATIVE STEPS

Upon arriving at a postblast IED scene, typically the EOD team leader will meet with the cordon commander to determine the situation. All EOD and WIT members who exit the vehicle should conduct 5 & 25s around their vehicle looking for any secondary IEDs that may have been planted. The WIT member should at this time take long-range photographs of where the IED detonated and 360° photographs of the surrounding site. Once the EOD team determines it is safe to enter the postblast scene area, they will drive the vehicle inside the cordon and get as close as safely possible to the blast scene. Another option is to make a manual approach to the blast scene, if the terrain prevents the EOD vehicle from getting to the blast scene.

Once at the blast scene, 5 & 25s should be completed again. If there is any chance for a secondary IED to be in play, it is at this time. On one postblast scene that I went to, we pushed up closer to the blast hole that was located in the middle of a "T" intersection. Insurgents led a M1A2 Bradley on a chase luring it to the "T" intersection. Fortunately, the M1A2 took the turn at the intersection wide and was not damaged by the IED blast. The insurgents were caught and our EOD team and WIT were called out. 5 & 25s were conducted by us as well as several soldiers that were part of the cordon. We discovered the IED device was a CWIED as we found a car battery in a trash pile that had copper wire going from it to the blast hole and from the battery into a nearby building. After a few moments on scene, one of the EOD technicians asked me to come with him away from the vehicle. After we stepped a safe distance away, he stated our vehicle was sitting on an IED as the EOD team leader noticed detonation cord sticking out of the ground behind the rear left tire. We later found out that one of the soldiers that helped conduct our 5 & 25s saw the red detonation cord and did not mention it to the EOD team leader. This mistake could have cost our entire team their lives. After moving the vehicle away from the suspected secondary IED, the EOD technicians blew up the ground around the detonation cord and discovered two projectiles rigged as an RCIED. After the projectiles were destroyed, we found the RCIED device several meters away in an old rice sack in a trash pile. That was a close one!

As listed earlier, there are several types of postblast IED scenes you can go to. CWIEDs, VOIEDs, and RCIEDs are the typical scenes a WIT member will respond to. VBIEDs and Suicide Bombers will create their own evidence collection nuances for the WIT member to deal with.

After the EOD technician determines the area safe for the WIT member to conduct his/her mission, start with photographing the scene. If your team is attacked, you may be leaving and not coming back to the scene. Pictures may be all you get. Take photographs of the blast area and the blast hole. Try not to include the EOD technicians in your photographs of the blast hole as they will get in the hole looking for shrapnel and any other evidence that can help them determine what components and amount of explosives were used. Time permitting, measure the width and depth of the blast hole or place something by the hole and photograph it. The item can be used to gauge the size of the hole.

Sometimes, very little or no evidence will be found at the blast scene as evidence could have disintegrated in the blast or been thrown farther than your security element will allow you to go. Other than a VBIED or Suicide Bomber, it may be difficult to determine what type of IED was placed and detonated. The EOD team will give you their best assessment as they are the experts in the explosives field. When in doubt, go with their assessment (Figures 3.24–3.26).

There can be investigative limitations that will prevent the WIT member from processing a postblast IED scene. Some investigative limitations have been mentioned previously, but are worthy of mention again. Investigative limitations can be caused by the environment or safety factors of the scene. It may be unsafe to get out of the vehicle due to enemy activity. The WIT member may get bare minimum information relayed from the cordon commander to the EOD team leader. The WIT member may not

■ **FIGURE 3.24** Fragmentation from munitions used in an IED attack; 2006, AR Ramadi, Iraq. *Photo taken by author Rich Watson.*

■ **FIGURE 3.25** A Marine EOD technician examining a blast hole at a postblast scene; 2006, AR Ramadi, Iraq. *Photo taken by author Rich Watson.*

■ **FIGURE 3.26** VBIED postblast scene; 2006, AR Ramadi, Iraq. *Photo taken by author Rich Watson.*

have an opportunity to interview any soldiers who were involved in the IED incident or any civilian witnesses that may have seen who placed the IED. Blown up vehicles and deceased insurgents or U.S./coalition force members may have been removed from the scene by the time EOD and WIT arrive. Postblast scenes differ from preblast scenes as after an IED has detonated, U.S. and coalition forces will be in the scene when the chaos erupts. Evidence will be destroyed and later, after a cordon is established and the on scene forces feel safe, they will walk through the blast scene and collect "souvenirs" to take back to their respective FOBs and units even before EOD arrives and declares the area safe. The WIT member's evidence literally grows legs and walks away.

Evidence collection at postblast scenes can be like looking for a needle in a haystack. Evidence from any postblast IED will most likely be small and hard to identify. The WIT members should conduct a grid style search for evidence starting at the blast hole and working outward. The WIT members should also ensure they collect dirt samples from the bottom of the blast hole as well as a control dirt sample away from the blast hole. These samples will be used to help determine what type of explosives may have been used in the making of the IED.

If a VBIED is present, attempt to identify the type of vehicle used, any serial numbers on parts of the vehicle, license plates, and any other identifying features. If the driver is still intact or a portion is still intact, you may be able to get finger prints from the driver's hands and biological evidence such as DNA and blood samples from body parts. The WIT member may also find passports and other identification on the body as well as family photographs. These items could be found on Suicide Bombers as well.

After the mission is completed, the WIT members must file a WIT report that describes the mission they went on, stating facts about where and how the IED was placed, whether there were any enemy combatants captured, details of the detonation and information on any U.S. or coalition forces wounded or dead. The WIT members will also list in the report, all evidence they collected and the results of any exploitation they conducted on the evidence. The last thing the WIT members add to their report is their assessment of the IED scene. The assessment is where the WIT members can write what they personally think about the IED scene as to why the IED was placed where it was, who the enemy were targeting, why they chose the location for the IED and what other similar devices have been used in the past and what the IED trends are for the AOR. This assessment is very important and the WIT members should put as much thought into this section of the report as possible because the readers of the report rely on them to provide the best intelligence available for that AOR. The WIT members, along with the EOD teams in an AOR, are considered the experts in the field when it comes to IEDs and must be diligent in providing the best and most accurate picture of IED events as possible.

During the discussions between pre- and postblast investigations, we covered many examples of these two scenes that are similar and yet distinct to each type of event. We discussed many ways to process the scene and many ways that EOD teams have operated in the past. The information provided has been tried and true during past WIT missions, but is by no means the only way to operate while conducting missions. WIT and EOD teams remain flexible to the scenes they respond to and constantly update their TTPs to keep the enemy off balance. TTPs of today may not work 6 months down the road and will need to be changed. In the end, WIT members rely heavily on the brave men and women of the EOD teams that they respond with to IED incidents. At the end of the day, a WIT member may not agree with the actions of his EOD team leader, or decisions made in the field, but the bottom line is the EOD team leader is responsible for the safety of the EOD team and WIT members and his/her decision is final. Remember, no evidence is worth risking your life or the lives of the team members for. A WIT and EOD team will never respond to all IED activity in their AOR as there are just not enough resources, so do not fret over one scene that may not have been processed or evidence that may not have been collected for the sake of collecting.

DETAINEE OPERATIONS AS IT PERTAINS TO WIT

At the end of the day, what WIT members do in the field will hopefully build IED evidence against an unknown person who may be caught later and linked to the evidence or provide the Iraqi courts with solid evidence against insurgents captured in relation to an IED event. This is an important end goal that culminates in the success of the WIT mission and best defines the sacrifices they make daily.

Sometimes, WITs forget or do not think about this final piece of their mission as it is not really explained to them very well when attending WIC. Some WIT members may not attempt to link IED evidence to past or present detainees as many of the WIT members do not have law enforcement backgrounds, and therefore do not think as cops do. It is imperative that this portion of the WIT mission be fostered and better understood not only by the WIT members, but by their leaders as well.

When the Special Agents from the Air Force Office of Special Investigations were assigned to WIT, evidence was getting linked with captured insurgents, which helped the prosecuting authorities make a case against them, thus allowing the courts to hold the defendants until a trial was set. Since the agents were pulled off the WIT mission to better serve the war effort in counterintelligence operations, there has been a decline in this thought process for the WITs. This mission is all about collecting evidence and actionable intelligence for the purpose of capturing IED makers and eliminating the IED threat. So why would WIT members risk their lives daily to collect evidence and intelligence and not follow through to the very end? One of the main issues is the WIT leadership does not embrace that aspect of the mission and rely on the labs to make the case against the insurgents.

WIT members must engage all aspects of detainee operations when arriving at their FOB. The first military unit they should contact would be the servicing Judge Advocate General (JAG) from the FOB. The JAG officers assigned know who all of the players are in the justice arena for detainee operations from Tactical Human Intelligence Teams (THT) to the nearest military detention facility, which may be on the same FOB. JAG will appreciate a WIT member's effort in trying to link IED evidence to detainees involved in IED events. JAG will also give the WIT member sound advice on how to present evidence found on IED scenes, prepare it to be further analyzed by labs like CEXC and assist them overall in making sound, legal, and ethical cases against insurgents involved in IED attacks and bomb making. If a WIT member is willing to learn and listen to JAG, they will become a huge proponent for their mission that could open doors to hurdles WIT may have not foreseen as well as praise them to the FOB leadership. The more military commanders hear positive praise about WIT, the more likely will they be to assist the teams. I mentioned earlier in this chapter about liaison with EOD teams. This philosophy has the same impact with the judicial system and its components that WITs must work around as they are not versed in military law enforcement and are not part of the military justice culture.

Once WIT members establish their presence on the FOB with JAG, they should seek out the THT members assigned to each battalion in their AOR. The THT members are the MI link to those battalions and are usually the first persons to speak to enemy insurgents that are captured. The THT will create a dossier on each insurgent and document all information about them, and any evidence that was taken from them. Usually, the THT can detain a prisoner for up to 24 hours and then either must set them free or forward them to a detention facility (Figures 3.27 and 3.28).

■ **FIGURE 3.27** Three insurgents who were captured when their vehicle was spotted surveilling U.S. forces; 2006, AR Ramadi, Iraq. *Photo taken by author Rich Watson.*

■ **FIGURE 3.28** RPGs found hidden in the insurgents vehicle from Figure 3.27; 2006, AR Ramadi, Iraq. *Photo taken by author Rich Watson.*

WIT members should explain to the THT how the WIT mission can assist in making a case against detainees that are brought in from IED incidents or who are captured with IED evidence. WIT should strive to obtain the detainees' capture record for their report and in return, provide the THT with WIT reports that they produce. By providing WIT reports to THT, they can brief and train their battalion soldiers on the latest IED trends in their particular battle space. This has proven to pay huge dividends in the past as soldiers new to IEDs and IED activity in their battle space have been saved from possible death from the valuable education they received because of the WIT and THT relationships and information sharing. This information sharing also assists soldiers in identifying IED components and how to properly report their findings to on scene WIT members so that the IED evidence stays as pristine as possible and lastly, prevents a soldier from handling IED evidence that could be booby trapped.

The final part of the detainee operations equation that a WIT member will have influence over are the detention facilities. The WIT member needs to introduce himself/herself to the detention facility leadership and sell the WIT program as a viable intelligence and evidence gathering mission that can assist them in making cases against their detainees. As with the THT, WIT members should provide detention leadership with their WIT reports to educate them and provide more documentation for a detainee's capture folder. The more evidence that can be linked to the detainee, the better chances of a conviction by the Iraqi courts. The WIT member needs to get the buy in from JAG, THT, and the detention facility to make everything work.

Detainee operations are a vital link in destroying the IED threat. Keeping bomb makers in jail and forcing them to trial with sound evidence collected by WIT members will send a clear message to the insurgents that their IED activities will lead them to incarceration or death and hopefully provide a strong deterrent to their activities.

SUMMARY

We have discussed the WIT roles and responsibilities within the EOD community and how productive liaison efforts with the EOD teams are important, not only for operational purposes, but for the success of the mission as well. Premission planning, as well as scene safety prior to and after arriving at IED scenes, has been discussed. Photography has been heavily recommended as the primary means of recording IED scenes and the only thing of value that might be taken away from a scene. During our discussion of pre- and postblast investigations, we have discussed the common types of IEDs a WIT member will be exposed to as well as how and what evidence to collect from them. There are many investigative limitations that can hinder WIT operations, but the mission can still be completed successfully. Reporting the incident and bringing detainees to justice with the actionable intelligence and evidence collected at the IED scenes round out the WIT process.

Chapter 4

Using the DTF model to process digital media

THE CHANGING LOCATION OF DIGITAL EVIDENCE CONTAINERS

The trend to move away from a hard-drive, fixed-system computer work-station, or laptop has been in the works for many years. In the early 1990s, people stored data on hard drives in the work environment, as this was the only place where you could store them. Hard drives were very large and very expensive. Most people could not afford large hard drives or expensive home equipment.

INTEVIDENCE

Intevidence is a word that has been created out of the firestorm that surrounds the world of intelligence and evidence collection. Each side sees the materials on the battlefield as belonging to its own discipline. If you ask a military intelligence type what battlefield material is, he/she will tell you that it is intelligence and therefore need not to be protected as a legal artifact. If you ask a law enforcement type the same question, he/she will say it is evidence and needs to be maintained as such. The problem is that it is both. So to try and bridge the gap between the two worlds, the word "intevidence" was born. I define intevidence as follows:

"Intevidence (noun): The collection of objective or battlefield materials with the procedural steps that will maintain the minimum judicial requirement of "chain of custody," ensuring that the materials can be used in any intelligence or judicial venue."

Eventually, this changed as the home computer became more affordable and more available. As the 1990s progressed, people began to store more and more data on the home computer. People began to work more from home, as they could afford equivalent or sometimes even better and faster equipment. The home systems quickly caught up and surpassed the office computers. The problem then became how to transfer data back and forth

Digital Triage Forensics. Doi: 10.1016/B978-1-59749-596-7.00004-8

between home and work. Floppy disks did not hold that much data and the Internet was way too slow to use reliably at this point. The computer industry recognized this and created a larger medium of storage, the compact disk (CD). The CD had its problems though; it was hard to learn how to store files on it, and the early CDs would routinely fail. The CD, which was to be the floppy killer, fizzled at the start line. The CD was not going to wipe out the floppy as thought. The computer industry went back to the drawing board and devised several new storage media such as the LS 120, Jazz drives, zip drives, and thumbdrives. As these media went through their paces, the thumbdrive began to shine. The thumbdrive was to become the next useful storage medium. The thumbdrive was then called the floppy killer, and it lived up to its nickname. In a few years, it would completely replace the floppy disk. In many ways, the thumbdrive surpassed the CD and burgeoning DVD medium as the personal portable storage of choice. You can now find thumbdrives and USB external media being used in every computer application. Where will we go next? The answer is clear. The next step for mass storage will be the mesh or cloud networks, allowing us to store data onto the virtual network. The insurgent and enemy forces already use these networks to plan and conduct operations around the world. The insurgents and our enemies learned very early on that America's Achilles heel is its technology. Because the enemies of America have learned our technology weaknesses, operators are going to be involved in technology investigations for the foreseeable future. We have to provide these operators and investigators the tools and techniques to be able to investigate and solve technology threats, while providing actionable intelligence to the battlefield commanders.

WHAT HARDWARE DO I NEED TO CONDUCT A CRADLE-TO-GRAVE BATTLEFIELD INVESTIGATION?

The operator on the battlefield is in need of hardware and tools that will allow the operator or investigator to be able to conduct a full capture and analysis of the digital media found in the battlefield arena. The High-Tech crime Institute, Inc. (HTCI) (www.gohtci.com) has been working with the battlefield operators to produce a battlefield collection kit since 2006. HTCI's Battlefield kit has been tried and tested through 14 generations, and is currently deployed in Iraq and Afghanistan. Each time, the battlefield kit was reduced in size and weight but it increased in flexibility and capability. The mantra that HTCI has followed is not to add more equipment but to optimize the equipment that the operator already carries onto the battlefield. HTCI has optimized each generation of its battlefield kit to reduce the overall size and cost of the kit by about 60% of its original cost.

Weapons intelligence team kit: Cradle-to-grave collection

The weapons intelligence team (WIT) kit is a unique design provided to operators and investigators in combat theaters fighting the war on terrorism. The WIT kit system has been thoroughly tested in the combat environment. This kit is designed to provide absolutely the best battlefield forensic equipment. The system is designed to be used in both full forensic collection situations and triage forensic situations (see Figure 4.1).

The kit is composed of four major components:

- Document, media, and cellular exploitation system
- Video evidence collection kit
- Photographic evidence collection kit
- Biometric evidence collection kit

As an integrated unit, the investigator/operator has the ability to employ as much or as little of the system as needed. The entire kit is enclosed inside a 1630 Pelican Case with a lid organizer, allowing convenient deployment of all the tools. Let's take a look at the kit and the subcomponents that make up each of the sub kits. I think that after looking at the kit you will see the reason why it is in such high demand among the small unit and tactical investigation units worldwide.

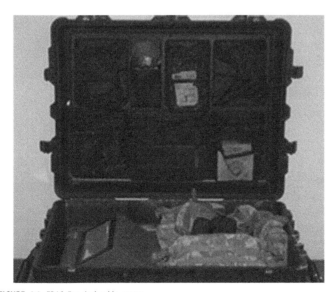

■ **FIGURE 4.1** EDAS Fox deployable system.

The first subcomponent is the document, media, and cellular exploitation system. This subcomponent provides the investigator/operator the tools to gather data from any digital medium system regardless of the type of container it may be in. The system will gather data from all USB connected devices, hard drives, floppy drives, CDs, and DVDs. The subcomponent comes with a full page scanner and software to allow document processing. In addition, the system provides a complete cellular collection and exploitation system.

The HTCI isolation chamber, which allows the complete isolation of the cellular media being captured, is also included with the cellular exploitation system. At the core of the subcomponent is the EDAS Fox Deployable laptop, preloaded with the Paraben P2 Commander digital forensic application and Paraben's Replicator application to capture and create the digital media in a forensic manner.

The EDAS Fox Deployable laptop has Paraben's Device Seizure application to process the cellular devices captured by the investigator/operator. The document, media, and cellular exploitation system subcomponent includes the following:

- Pelican Case lid organizer
- 26″ Telescoping nine-piece mirror inspection kit
- AAA/AA battery recharger
- 9 V battery recharger
- 9 V battery
- AA NIMH battery
- AAA NIMH battery
- Roll photographic tape 1 in.
- Black and white 6 in. ruler
- Reversible two-piece ruler, L and straight
- Crime scene evidence tape
- Mini tripod
- Laptop backup system hard drive (250 GB)
- 500 Gig HD SATA evidence capture drive
- Rugged backpack to allow portability of the subcomponent
- EDAS Fox deployable laptop
- P2 Commander
- Paraben replicator
- GPS photo-link software
- Foxview software
- Garmin world map
- ATTAC Postblast investigation software

- Microsoft Office 2007
- Computer tool kit (case)
- U.S. military Lensatic compass
- Forensic Elite explosive detector (softcase)
- Replacement kit for forensic Elite explosive detector
- Forensic Quest
- Forensic Quest battery pack
- Forensic Quest adapterkKit 2.54 Gig thumbdrive
- Handheld document scanner
- Digital media analysis capture bag
- 1 TB external USB HD
- One-touch HD enclosure
- Analysis station and cables
- Notebook tray for analysis station
- SATA tray for analysis station
- Indelible markers
- Voice recorder
- HTCI isolation chamber for cellular devices
- Nitrile barrier evidence gloves (100 pk)
- Evidence collection bags (100 pk)
- Paraben device seizure cellular toolkit camouflage bag with Cellex identifier
- SIM card reader
- HTCI SIM evidence collection cases
- Cable set for cell phones
- Plastic magnifying glass
- USB parallel blue and silver cable
- SIM card evidence holder
- 3 V battery
- AAA batteries
- AA batteries

The photography subcomponent was designed to allow the investigator/operator to be able to document and locate the battlefield crime scene using global positioning system (GPS). This includes cameras and rulers that are used with the photographic kit to produce a careful documentation of the scene. The subcomponent contains the following:

- Camouflage carrying bag with the photoidentifier
- Garmin GPS with cable
- 100 ft tape measure
- Ricoh 500 SE-M w/strap
- Battery and charger for Ricoh 500

- USB cable for Ricoh 500
- Car adaptor for Ricoh 500
- PVS-14 night vision adaptor for Ricoh 500
- Nikon Cool Pix camera
- Nikon USB cord
- Nikon video cord
- USB SD card carrier for SDHC with cord
- 2 GB San disk card
- Bushnell binoculars

The video subcomponent was designed to allow the investigator/operator to be able to provide a video documentary of the crime scene. The video camera provides high-quality still photographs that are usable to collect fingerprints. Included are a video camera and rulers that are used with the video kit to produce careful documentation of the scene. The subcomponent contains the following:

- Camouflage carrying bag with the video identifier
- JVC 30 Gig video recorder and still capture camera
- Garmin GPS with cable
- 100 ft tape measure
- Nikon Cool Pix camera
- Nikon USB cord
- Nikon video cord
- USB SD card carrier for SDHC with cord
- 2 GB San disk card
- 4 GB SDHC card

The biometric collection subcomponent was designed to allow the investigator/operator to be able to gather biometric evidence from any crime scene. The biometric collection kit allows the collection of DNA, fingerprints, chemicals, and other biometric data. The kit includes fingerprint cards, fingerprint collection spoons, and collection powders. There are also bags and tags to allow the proper documentation of the crime scene. The subcomponent contains the following:

- Biometric collection kit in a camouflage carrying case
- Postmortem cardholder
- Postmortem fingerprint cards 20r/20l
- Criminal fingerprint cards
- Hinged print lifters, white 2 in. × 4 in.
- Hinged print lifters, black 2 in. × 4 in.
- Backing card, white, 3 in. × 5 in.
- Backing card, black, 3 in.× 5 in.

- White fingerprint powder, 2 oz
- Silver/black fingerprint powder, 2 oz
- Semi-inkless fingerprint pad
- Bureau reference scale 1/6 in. and 1/6 in. × 3″ rev scales
- Adhesive backed photo scale pack, white/black, 50 per pk
- Sharpie marker, black-twin tip
- Transparent latent print lifting tape, 2 in. × 360 in.
- Evidence bags, plastic, 9 in. × 12 in.
- Glove, nitrile, large
- Fiberglass brush, 6 in. whisper

An operator will be able to collect and process evidence in any challenging environment such as the battlespace or in arenas requiring a rugged and durable forensic collection solution using the HTCI EDAS FOX deployable system. No matter what kit you choose to use, it is important to always test your equipment and follow a verification processes.

Hardware verification

Most investigators do not spend a lot of time talking about verification of computer hardware, but it is critically important to make sure we go through the process of certifying any computer that we are going to use to collect intelligence/evidence. There are many opinions on this but the basic fact is this: If you do not certify or calibrate your tools, you cannot testify that the tool is working correctly in a judicial venue.

It is imperative therefore that the investigator/operator verify the hardware prior to its use. Once you certify the hardware that you are going to use, you need to make sure that you recertify the hardware on a set schedule. Remember, any changes made to the hardware, whether it be installing or upgrading to new hardware or installing and updating new software, will require the recertification to be performed on the hardware to ensure it is still able to process evidence correctly. All it takes is one Dynamic Link Library (DLL) file to be loaded incorrectly or a conflicting memory allocation to cause failure of your forensic applications. This verification process is used routinely in scientific applications and other traditional investigative collection tools; ergo, it only makes sense to apply it to your digital forensic hardware.

The following are the recommendations for certifying a forensic computer system.

The machine should be a standalone one.

If you are using a Windows-based system, try to use Windows XP Professional, as this is a standard operating system used by law enforcement around the world to conduct digital forensics. This is one situation where being the leader is not always the best idea. It is always better to use a system that has been certified in judicial venues for use in digital forensics.

Audit the hardware of the machine and compare this audit with the manufacturer's system specifications sheet and the Microsoft hardware computability list (HCL). You may need to take the case apart to see all the components installed. Inspect the original documentation that came with your system; this should be what is in the system currently.

Audit the software installed on the computer. Make a record sheet that has the following minimum information:

- Name of the program
- Date bought or upgraded
- License type: key or dongle
- License number

Keep this book with the workstation. Repeat the audit on a scheduled basis quarterly or semi-annually.

Ensure to maintain compliance during the interim.

Recertify if any hardware or software is added to the computer forensic system (see Figure 4.2).

CHARACTERISTICS OF DIGITAL MEDIA

We have talked about the hardware and how to verify that hardware when conducting a digital forensic investigation. But what is it that we are investigating? We need to look at the characteristics of the actual media you are about to capture.

Digital evidence, like any other evidence, has its own characteristics. Digital media is much like DNA, as it has unique qualities that can identify a specific device to an event much like DNA can identify a specific person to an event. As the investigator looking for DNA would gather evidence from the crime scene, so does the digital investigator when looking through the digital media container.

Program Name	Purchased	License Type (Key or Dongle)	License or Dongle Number	License Expires
Program 1	13 January 2010	Dongle	123467890	12 January 2011

■ **FIGURE 4.2** Sample worksheet.

The residue of deleted or partially overwritten files still remains on the digital medium and is retrievable using software that allows the investigator to see the residual data in some type of logical form. Digital evidence is also fragile; it can be corrupted, lost, or destroyed by bad procedure or policies used by the investigator. This is why it is so important to ensure that the investigators are properly trained to be able to gather digital evidence containers from the scene correctly.

One unique characteristic of digital evidence is its ability to be cloned. This cloning ability allows the investigator to make an exact copy of the digital media container for review. This prevents the investigator/operator from having to use the original evidence in analysis or investigation. The investigator/operator can make numerous copies of the digital evidence and pass them out to other investigator/operators so that they can help perform a peer review of the evidence providing a second opinion to the investigator/operator. The investigator can also send the entire case off to another digital forensic lab to have them do the complete analysis while the investigator/operator maintains control of the original evidence. Obviously, this is different from traditional evidence, where it cannot be copied or cloned and is typically consumed in the analysis of the evidence at the lab. This, in some ways, makes digital evidence more valuable when it is produced in court.

The greatest danger to the digital evidence is usually the investigator/operator. As long as we train our investigator/operators and arm them with good policy and procedures and provide proper facilities to maintain the digital evidence, there should never be a time when digital evidence cannot be used or introduced into any legal venue.

STEPHEN'S QUICK AND DIRTY GUIDE TO UNDERSTANDING DIGITAL FORENSICS

Simply stated, the true definition of digital forensics is widely debated in the law-enforcement forensics community. A lot of ego is on the block when one talks about defining the process. There are those that want to be known as forensic scientists and those that simply want to be known as button pushers. In between, there is the majority of digital forensic examiners that see themselves without the cape and "S" on their shirts. So what is digital computer forensics?

We can answer this question by looking at the four pillars that make up digital media forensics. The four pillars (or principals) of digital forensics are the following:

Pillar 1: No action taken by law enforcement agencies or their agents should change data held in a computer or storage media, which may subsequently be relied upon in court.

Pillar 2: In exceptional circumstances where a person finds it necessary to access original data held in a computer or storage media, that person must be competent to do so and be able to give evidence explaining the relevance and the implications of his/her actions.

Pillar 3: An audit trail or other record of all processes applied to computer-based electronic evidence should be created and preserved. An independent third party should be able to examine those processes and achieve the same result.

Pillar 4: The person in charge of the investigation (the case officer) has the overall responsibility of ensuring that the law and these principles are adhered to.[1]

If you incorporate the pillars into your processing policies and procedures, you really cannot go wrong. The pillars provide a solid foundation for the investigator to follow and build from. I personally define digital forensics as the *proper collection of digital data as well as media for the purpose of analysis that provides inculpatory and exculpatory information that can be used in any venue that seeks a factual ruling.* I define digital triage forensics collection in much the same manner with two important caveats: *Proper collection of digital data as well as media for the purpose of analysis to yield actionable intelligence. The analysis will also provide inculpatory and exculpatory information that can be used in any venue that seeks a factual ruling. The proper procedural collection of the digital data and media from the initial scene will be dependent on the agent's safety and time required for the proper collection. The agent's safety will supersede any procedural requirements.*

The bottom line of digital forensics is simply using investigation skills with computer-based applications and tools to provide evidence that can be used in court. You will notice that I do not use the word *evidence* in the definition; instead I use the word *information*. There is a reason for this and that reason is that information is the processed data. When you collect data from the drive, it must be processed. The accepted term for the data after processing is information. This makes sense to me, as this information will then be analyzed looking for evidence.

---

[1]ACPO guidelines—http://www.acpo.police.uk/asp/policies/Data/ACPO%20Guidelines%20v18.pdf

Digital forensic ethics

Digital forensic ethics are very important. The reason they are so important is because they can show an individual's bias in an investigation. If a bias can be proven, then the testimony to the evidence collected by the investigator can be seen as tainted and possibly not usable in the judicial venue at all. There are some key points that you need to remember when talking about the digital forensic ethics.

Don't lie and report only factual findings. This may seem like common sense but it has been seen in court where the investigator has been caught not telling the truth about professional certifications or training that they may have received. Investigators, at times in their attempt to appear more credible, may stretch the truth on their professional education. If you get caught lying in a digital forensic investigation, you're done for. Once you have been found to be a liar on the stand, you will never be able to testify in a digital forensic investigation again. Why? The answer is very simple: this is one of those disciplines in which the evidence will never be seen by the judicial panel. The judicial panel will never see the 1s and 0s that make up the evidence on the media. What the judicial panel does get to see is the interpretation through software of the 1s and 0s that can produce something of evidentiary value. In this respect, it is the investigator's integrity that is critical when conducting the digital investigations. If that integrity can be questioned by the judicial panel, then the evidence produced by that investigator/operator will also be questioned. The bottom line is, don't ever lie because you will no longer be able to present interpreted evidence in court. Another issue that can show the investigator/operators bias is a relatively new issue in our world of social media. Social media provide the defense attorney the ability to be able to read or review personal Web sites or social networking sites looking for the factual bias that the investigator/operator may have.

As an example, let's say that we have a young soldier who is acting as an investigator/operator in a war zone and collects evidence that will be used in a judicial panel either in the United States or in the embattled country. The defense attorney has the responsibility to ensure the best defense for their client and therefore goes out into the social media sites and finds the personal page of that investigator/operator. On that personal page is found statements and pictures that show a strong bias to the population of the embattled nation that the investigator/operator is working in. The site does not differ between the host population and the insurgent or terrorist faction. The statements reflect a lack of understanding of the country that they are protecting. The defense attorney may find statements making fun of the population or generalizations of the population, etc. This can all be used to show that the investigator/operator has a bias against the population and therefore it is easy to say that the investigator would not be able to report factual findings in an unbiased manner. If the defense can show bias by the investigator/operator, then the evidence can become tainted. So, the bottom line is, in the world of social media, blogging, and personal Web sites, be very careful about what you post and what you let others post to your personal pages, as everything today can be used to show a personal bias. It would be a shame to lose a case in a judicial venue just because somebody posted a silly or inappropriate comment on your social media site.

Investigator/operator need to always provide factual findings. It is not for you to decide whether somebody is guilty or innocent; it is your job to provide factual evidence that can be adjudicated to determine the guilt or innocence of an individual. By adding or leaving out information from a case report, the judicial panel may see you as favoring one side or the other. To prevent this, always produce a complete report where possible and provide the judicial venue with factual findings. This may not always be possible, as there are instances where investigations are shortened by time or technology constraints. If you have to provide a limited examination for any reason, make sure to document the reasons or circumstances that surround the limited examination.

Integrity of the evidence is also a critical point. It is very easy to lose control of the collected evidence. The simplest form of control for an investigator/operator is the chain of custody. There is no expectation that an investigator/operator at a combat objective or crime scene has the luxury of time to properly place evidence tags and labels on every item that was collected. This is absolutely understandable and is called exigent circumstance. The investigator in the battlefield environment works under the exigent circumstances as a rule; instead, in the United States, the exigent circumstance is an exception to the rule. But even in this world of exigent circumstances, due diligence is still required and it is imperative that the investigator tries to do as much as possible to gather and collect the end evidence or intelligence in the most pristine manner. It is also important that at a minimum, the chain of custody is maintained by the investigator/operator, which is not an unreasonable request of the investigator/operator in the field.

As we've talked about earlier, professional ethics in the forensic world is extremely important. Always ensure that you enter into an investigation or case with your eyes wide open. Do not let others influence you into looking for specific things or a specific type of evidence just because that's what they need to prove this person guilty. It is your job as the professional forensic investigator/operator to bring out both inculpatory and exculpatory evidence. It is also your professional responsibility to ensure fairness, as you are the expert when it comes to the digital media that is being processed. This is something that cannot be taken lightly by anyone. So the bottom line is, always apply ethics and morals that have been taught through law-enforcement academies and/or military training. If you find yourself entering into an investigation with preconceived notions about the individual you're investigating, then take the higher road and have someone else process that evidence. This may save the evidence later on in court when they try to prove your bias or can prove your bias toward the individual being prosecuted.

Using the digital forensic process

The procedural framework to process digital media is defined in the "Electronic Crime Scene Investigation Guide: A Guide for First Responders."[2]

There are five basic steps in conducting a computer forensics examination:

- Preparation
- Collection
- Examination (this is the first step in the DTF process)
- Analysis (this is the second step in the DTF process)
- Reporting

We are now going to look at each of these steps very quickly so that you understand each of the steps.

Preparation

When we talk about preparation, we are talking about the investigator himself or herself. The preparation that is necessary for the investigator takes place many months or even years prior to the actual investigation. This is the training that the investigator receives during the on-the-job experience prior to conducting an investigation. In too many instances, in our digital forensic world, investigators are known as pushbutton investigators. In other words, they come in with a tool, they push a button, and they walk back out with what some call evidence. Some argue that this is all that the investigator needs to do. Clearly though, there is a need for some understanding of what it is you have done, because if you do not

---

[2]National Institute of Justice, 2001. http://www.ncjrs.gov/pdffiles1/nij/187736.pdf

know that, how can you testify that your procedural steps meet the legal requirements for the collection of the evidence? Remember that when you go to court, there will be someone on the other side listening, reviewing, and waiting to ask you questions about your competence as a digital forensic investigator. If you have no digital forensic expertise or have avoided going to training because you don't see a need, then you will fail when it goes to court. Digital forensic investigators need to stay current on their discipline; they need to stay involved in the community providing information in and taking information away. Where do you get such information? You get the information from blogs, forums, articles, and periodicals following the industry trade magazines on the latest and greatest technologies that are coming out so that you are prepared and aware of the tools that are being used by the average computer user in the environment you may end up having to investigate. Make sure to keep your certifications current. It is very easy to forget to update your certifications and let them expire or become too outdated to be of any use. It can be very embarrassing for an investigator to be testifying only to have the defense attorney bring out your expired certification. Preparation of the investigator is critical in the collection process; this is one step that cannot be overlooked.

I want to add into the preparation stage the preparation of your equipment. Far too many investigators find no need or do not apply the simple policies of validating their equipment on a routine schedule. We talked about verification earlier in this chapter and that it is critical for an investigator/operator to perform the verification of their equipment routinely. If your tool is not working correctly, how can you say in court that you have collected evidence correctly? A good example is the need to have clean-working capture media. This process takes time as you must wipe the hard drives prior to the first initial use of capturing data to the drive. This can be a timely function and is most certainly something you do not want to do when you arrive at the objective or the crime scene. This is a prime example of why preparation of your equipment is very important.

Collection

The collection step involves the collecting of data from the scene. Simply stated, data collection is the processing of evidence in a manner that would be acceptable in any judicial venue in the world. It is at the collection point that the investigator has to be extremely careful to follow the policies and procedures that have been outlined for that investigator by their unit or department. At the stage of collection is where the majority of evidence is likely to be lost in a judicial venue. The evidence more than likely will not be lost when it gets to the lab environment as the lab environment lends itself to legitimate policies and procedures that have been worked over time, and unless the investigator makes a stupid mistake with regard to the evidence, he/she should never be questioned at the lab. The collection at the crime scene or objective is the place that poses the greatest threat of contamination. If the investigator follows policies and procedures that have been developed by the department or the unit correctly, the investigator should not have to worry too much about losing evidence at this step. If the investigator decides to do their own collection and collect evidence outside of the policies and procedures, then that evidence more than likely will not make it to the judicial venue. That makes this step extremely important. So, who is to write these policies and procedures? Hopefully, you will engage someone who has been writing or using the digital evidence process to help you write your policies and procedures for your unit organization. Another method is to reach out to another agency that is or has been using established policies and procedures. Their established policies and procedures can act as a framework to build your own policies and procedures from. The use of flow charts is extremely helpful; as we will see as we proceed through the drives in this chapter, it allows us to identify a step-by-step method that the investigator can follow at the scene.

Examination (This is the first step in the DTF process)

When examining the media, we must maintain the four pillars of computer forensics. We cannot change or manipulate the data of the suspect medium. In this step, we ensure that you are following your policies and procedures. So when you do end up at any judicial venue, you can very easily and quickly settle any arguments that may be used to accuse you of changing the collected evidence to produce a result that is not in the best interest of the individual you are investigating.

Analysis (This is the second step in the DTF process)

So now you have accomplished the first three steps, which are realistically some of the hardest steps to accomplish. You now have the job of analyzing the data that have been brought back to you. The data is raw 1s and 0s that exist on the digital media that you have recovered. We have to process that data and turn it into something that is usable, which we call information. The information is then processed so that we can identify actionable intelligence and inculpatory and exculpatory findings. The analysis should follow a set of procedural policies. The analysis should be conducted the same way in every investigation. By doing this, the investigator/operator can help prevent any accusations of bias. For example, if in every investigation you search the Windows directory, and then on this investigation you do not search the Windows directory, a good defense attorney is going to ask why you changed your procedure and did you not look in the Windows directory and if you were afraid of finding things that may set the client free. These are things that the defense attorney, or whoever is defending your suspect, is going to be looking for to help his/her case.

Reporting

The final step is the reporting of your information in a language that is understandable and readable by the common person. The report cannot be written in such a manner that it is not understandable by the layperson. While adding a lot of techno-garble or techno-speak makes you look very impressive, it yields or provides no information to the panel or review entity that has to look at your report. Try to keep your reported results in a language form that is easily readable and flows in a manner that is identifiable. The use of categories is a good idea to consolidate things such as graphics, multimedia, documents, etc. You will also find that people place greater weight on graphics than on written text. It is human nature to place greater emphasis on things that we see than on those which we read about.

The five steps mentioned earlier are simply a skeleton framework for you to build your policies and procedures on. This is not a definitive set of guidelines and should not be looked at that way. What you would want to do is build your policies and procedures and then ensure that you have incorporated all the steps above into your more detailed policies and procedures. If you include these five steps in your policies and procedures, then you likely have policies or procedures that will hold up in any judicial or panel venue.

BRIEF OVERVIEW OF DIGITAL STORAGE CONCEPTS

In this book, we are not going into depth of the file structure or how the file structure is made up or the several different types of file structures. This section is simply designed to give the investigator/operator a quick overview of the basic concepts of file storage and file storage structures.

The first thing that the investigator/operator should recognize or know is that there are two basic structures that make up the digital media storage container. Those two parts are the physical drive and the logical drive.

- The physical drive is exactly what it sounds like. This is the physical hard drive or the actual device that you hold in your hand: this is the physical structure.
- The logical drive is the virtual structure that is placed on top of the physical structure.

When I explain this in testimony, I try to use an example that everyone can understand. The way I like to explain the physical and logical structures that make up a disk drive is by elaborating its similarities to a library. When you look at a library, you see the brick-and-mortar walls that make up the physical structure of the library; these walls are not movable and are of a fixed known size. Inside the library, we can make or construct storage areas or rooms, or we can simply leave an area unused. The walls would represent the physical structure of the drive and the rooms inside would represent the logical drive or partitioning of the storage container.

If you took the top off of the physical drive and looked at the actual architecture within a hard drive, you would not see the logical partitions because the logical partitions are elements of size and location: in other words, they are not visible. With the Windows operating system, once I tell the system what geographic space I want to use and how much space I want to use on the physical drive, Windows will assign that area an identifier. If it's the first drive or bootable drive on the system, it will be called the C drive unless I force it to be called something else.

The logical drive is made up of two components:

- The system area, which is the place that holds all the administrative information for the partition.
- The data area, which holds all the actual data stored by applications on the drive.

I am going to continue to use the library analogy, as it is very easy to explain this way. The system area is like the Dewey decimal system in which the librarian sits controlling the library. The system area, like the Dewey decimal system, can have the directory for all the physical locations on the hard drive. For example, in the Dewey decimal system, you have a card that's in a drawer. The card contains the name of the book, the date of publication, the author of the book, the last date that book was checked out, etc. The same thing happens in the system area or in the directory (newer operating systems no longer maintain the directory in the system area because of the size of the directories for them). Like the Dewey decimal system, the directory maintains pointers that will allow us to go down the shelves of the books and find a specific book to read. The place in this bookshelf or where all the books are actually placed is known as the data area. To recapitulate, we have a logical partition called the C drive, which is made up of the system area and the data area. The system area holds the administrative information for the partition. The data area holds all the actual data.

Let us do a little hands-on work to cement the physical and logical drive concept. You can do these steps on your home computer. If we click on the "My Computer" icon in a Windows-based operating system, you will see a window showing numerous logical drives available. These logical drives are all represented by icons as seen in the Figure 4.3.

Use My Computer in Figure 4.4. How many physical drives are located on this system? _____ The answer is 1 (see Figure 4.4).

A B. Floppy Disk Drive Icons Image A - As in Icon View Image B - As in List View	Removable Storage Drive. Normally this means that some type of media be inserted and/or removed from the computer. Any drive can be made to appear as a removable drive. The advantage to this as an investigator is that by labeling as removable, windows will not try to write to it during normal housekeeping operations
Hard Drive Icon	The logical drive is symbolized by a small computer hard drive icon
CD ROM Drive Icon	CD ROM Drive which is identified by the icon showing a CD on top of a hard drive
napster on 'tanika' (F:)	Network Drive. These are displayed as hard drive icons with an upside down T protruding from the bottom. This particular picture shows the network drive in a disconnected status
HTCI Access Database	Internet Drive – The drive is identified by a piped folder (pipe coming from underneath the folder) with a globe placed in the middle of the folder. This folder icon is a shortcut link to offsite storage location
atck on 155.9.226....	Internet Drive Document Repository – The drive is identified by a piped folder (pipe coming from underneath the folder) with a globe a half fed paper in the folder. This folder icon is a shortcut link to offsite storage location specifically used for the storage of online documents. This type of folder will also usually be shared

■ **FIGURE 4.3** Logical drive list.

■ **FIGURE 4.4** Sample My Computer view.

The average person will normally say two drives, because they are seeing two logical drives. Remember that our library can have multiple rooms, but there is still only one physical drive.

The My Computer screen has several shortcomings; for example, you will not be able to answer the questions below:

- How many different operating systems are supported on this drive and where are they?
- Do we have a Windows-only machine or do we have a mixture of Windows and Linux? Just like DOS, Windows does not recognize that partition without special software being installed.
- What is the true size of the physical drive?

How do you then determine whether we have a physical drive or logical drives? Instead of looking in My Computer, we must look at a different application in Windows and that is the "Disk Manager." To access the Disk Manager on a Windows XP system you will do the following:

1. Click on Start.
2. Move your mouse over the My Computer label and right click on the My Computer label.
3. When the option window appears, scroll down and select manage.

4. The manage window will appear and offer you several different choices in the left-hand column; move your cursor down to Disk Management and click.
5. In the right-hand screen, the Disk Management window will open.
6. From the Disk Manager window, we will really see the physical hard drive and the partitions that are on the physical hard drive. This is the only true way, without removing the hard drive, to know exactly what is inside the system.

RULES
Digital Rules
One keystroke of any key on the keyboard is equal to 1 byte.

Eight bits make 1 byte.

Two nibbles (hex values) make 1 byte.

A sector is made up of 512 bytes.

A cluster is made up of one or more sectors based on the file system of the media.

As an investigator/operator, you should not use the My Computer screen, as it is not designed to give the detail that the Disk Management program does. Take a few minutes to look at the Disk Manager window and see if you can recognize the physical drive, which is the bootable drive.

Binary in one easy paragraph

We are going to talk about hex very quickly. The discussion and study of hex and binary can honestly fill an entire volume on its own. We are simply going to introduce the concept of hex so that you have a basic understanding of what you are seeing when you're using your tools to gather data from digital media. What you must remember is that the English language to the computer is nothing but symbols. The computer speaks one language and one language only, and that's the language of binary: On or Off. We have to come up with some method or way that the computer can assign a character to a number that then makes sense to us, the human element in front of the computer. So let us jump in and see how we do (see Figure 4.5).

BIT 128	BIT 64	BIT 32	BIT 16	BIT 8	BIT 4	BIT 2	BIT 1
0 or 1	0 or 1	0 or 1	0 or 1	0 or 1	0 or 1	0 or 1	0 or 1
NIBBLE 4 BITS (41 = A)				NIBBLE 4 BITS (41 = A)			
8 BITS = 1 BYTE OR ONE KEYSTOKE (65 = A)							

■ **FIGURE 4.5** Binary table.

The computer itself can be in one of two states. ON (1) or OFF (0). In Figure 4.5, 8 bits equals 1 byte or a single keystroke. Looking at the figure and looking at the bits that make up the byte, you will notice that a numeric value is assigned to each of the bit levels. If you add up the values across the numeric value row, you will find it will add up to 256. (If you add all the numbers you get 255. The 0 is a valid value so it is added to the number 255. So 255 + 0 is 256 possible values.) This means that we have 256 combinations that will make letters, numbers, etc. We will use the chart in Figure 4.6 to decipher the symbol to number the correlation. Notice that every character that we use in the English language is represented here; take a moment to scan over the chart and see if you can recognize the upper case and lower case alphabet characters (see Figure 4.6).

Now, let us see if we can do some basic hex to symbol correlations; take a look at the ASCII chart in Figure 4.6. If I want to spell the word "dad" and I want to see what that word would look like on the computer, after spelling the word "dad," I will have to change the characters into numbers. To do this, I can use the ASCII chart in Figure 4.6. In the chart, I see that the uppercase letter D equals 44 and that the uppercase A equals 41. So the word DAD in hex would be 44 41 44. In Figure 4.7, I have given you three words; see if you can convert those three words to hex.

Congratulations! You are now writing like a computer and hopefully you were able to convert each of the words without any problem. More information on binary and hex as well as the uses of binary and hex can be found on the Internet in many different tutorials.

Cluster what?

Now that we have a basic understanding of how data is stored in hex values, we should understand the basics of how that storage occurs on the drive itself. The smallest unit of storage that we will discuss in this book will be the byte. We learned in the last section that a byte is a single keystroke and can be everything from pressing the spacebar to pressing the zero key. Each time I do this and save the data to the hard drive, they take up one allocation or byte on the drive. These bytes are grouped together. The rule of the road on a computer is that 512 bytes grouped together equal one "sector." The sector is the smallest unit of combined storage that we will talk about. Now if you stored everything in sectors, you would end up with a management nightmare for the computer. If you think about an 80 Gig hard drive, the number of sectors is quite large (see Figure 4.8).

To make this storage a little more manageable, we group the sectors as well into the next storage structure called a "cluster." The cluster is a

DEC	HEX	Character	DEC	HEX	Character	DEC	HEX	Character	DEC	HEX	Character
0	00	Null	32	20	Space	64	40	@	96	60	`
1	01	Start of Heading	33	21	!	65	41	A	97	61	a
2	02	Start of Text	34	22	"	66	42	B	98	62	b
3	03	End of Text	35	23	$	67	43	C	99	63	c
4	04	End of Transmit	36	24	#	68	44	D	100	64	d
5	05	Enquiry	37	25	%	69	45	E	101	65	e
6	06	Acknowledge	38	26	&	70	46	F	102	66	f
7	07	Audible Bell	39	27	'	71	47	G	103	67	g
8	08	Backspace	40	28	(	72	48	H	104	68	h
9	09	Horizontal Tab	41	29	)	73	49	I	105	69	i
10	0A	Line Feed	42	2A	*	74	4A	J	106	6A	j
11	0B	Vertical Tab	43	2B	+	75	4B	K	107	6B	k
12	0C	Form Feed	44	2C	,	76	4C	L	108	6C	l
13	0D	Carriage Return	45	2D	-	77	4D	M	109	6D	m
14	0E	Shift out	46	2E	.	78	4E	N	110	6E	n
15	0F	Shift In	47	2F	/	79	4F	O	111	6F	o
16	10	Data Link Escape	48	30	0	80	50	P	112	70	p
17	11	Device Control 1	49	31	1	81	51	Q	113	71	q
18	12	Device Control 2	50	32	2	82	52	R	114	72	r
19	13	Device Control 3	51	33	3	83	53	S	115	73	s
20	14	Device Control 4	52	34	4	84	54	T	116	74	t
21	15	Neg. Acknowledge	53	35	5	85	55	U	117	75	u
22	16	Synchronous Idle	54	36	6	86	56	V	118	76	v
23	17	End Trans Block	55	37	7	87	57	W	119	77	w
24	18	Cancel	56	38	8	88	58	X	120	78	x
25	19	End of Medium	57	39	9	89	59	Y	121	79	y
26	1A	Substitution	58	3A	:	90	5A	Z	122	7A	z
27	1B	Escape	59	3B	;	91	5B	[	123	7B	{
28	1C	File Separator	60	3C	<	92	5C	\	124	7C	:
29	1D	Group Separator	61	3D	=	93	5D	]	125	7D	}
30	1E	Record Separator	62	3E	>	94	5E	^	126	7E	~
31	1F	Unit Separator	63	3F	?	95	5F	_	127	7F	

■ **FIGURE 4.6** ASCII table.

English		Hex	
Mom			
Bob			
120			

■ **FIGURE 4.7** Hex table.

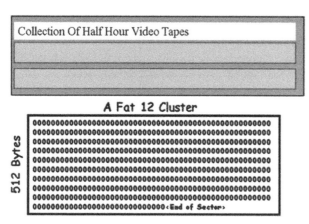

Collection Of Half Hour Video Tapes

A Fat 12 Cluster

512 Bytes

0000000000000000000000000000000000000000000000000000
0000000000000000000000000000000000000000000000000000
0000000000000000000000000000000000000000000000000000
0000000000000000000000000000000000000000000000000000
0000000000000000000000000000000000000000000000000000
0000000000000000000000000000000000000000000000000000
0000000000000000000000000000000000000000000000000000
0000000000000000000000000000000000000000000000000000
0000000000000000000000000000000000000000000000000000
0000000000000000000000000000000‹End of Sector›

■ **FIGURE 4.8** Cluster as a video tape.

grouping of sectors to form a single combined storage container. The cluster, like the sector, can only hold one item at a time. So, an example would be, if I have a file that is 100 bytes long and I store it to a cluster that holds 512 bytes, 512 bytes will no longer be available because that entire cluster has been used by the 100 byte file. The same thing happens with larger cluster sizes; for example, a common cluster size for a Windows operating system is 4096 bytes per cluster or eight sectors per cluster, so if I store a 100-byte file (see Figure 4.9) to this cluster, I will lose 4096 bytes on the drive. In some cases, this is a very efficient system; in other cases, this can be very inefficient and waste a lot of space, and it all depends on how the computer is used and what the computer is used for. Imagine saving hundreds of small notepad files to the computer. You can imagine how inefficient the system would be. If I was storing a lot of large files, then the system would be very efficient. It really depends on what I am doing with the data.

Partition size	Recommended file system / cluster size
1-16M	FAT-12 / 4K
16-256M	FAT-16 / 4K
256-512M	FAT-16 / 8K
512M-1G	FAT-16 / 16K or FAT-32 / 4K
1-8G	FAT-32 / 4K
8G and up	FAT-32 / 8K

■ **FIGURE 4.9** Files on the digital media.

Modified, accessed, and created dates

The "Modified, Accessed, and Created," dates also known as the MAC times, are very important to the investigator, as they can tell a story all their own. The biggest thing to remember here is that the dates are not based on some central clock that makes sure that accurate dates and times are being used on the computer system. The reality is that the dates and times rely on the computer's clock or BIOS clock. If the BIOS clock is set to a date in the past, then the dates on all the files being created will have the date from the past. With this in mind, look at the rules that control the MAC date and times below:

File creation date: The date the file was created on the device is stored. Remember that this is the first time that the file is created and not an attribute that is copied from another device. In other words, if I copy a file from the hard drive to the floppy, the date that will be used for the file creation date will be the date on which the file was created on the floppy drive. In the Windows operating system, just reading the directory will not update the directory.

Modified date: The date on which the file was last modified by a "save" or "save as" type command, or any time the file is changed by a process that changes any byte. This file attribute did not exist in the old DOS file structure. When modifying a folder, this attribute will change when the directory is created or when the directory is copied. Anytime the directory appears in a new volume, it will have a new created date.

Accessed date: The date the file is created or the date that the file is read or executed by any program such as a file manager or paint program. The file date will also change during the copy process. For Windows 98SE and ME, only the file will be changed any time the files properties are viewed. In DOS 7.X, there will be no access date on any type of removable media. The time stamp that is used will come from the BIOS of the system. On the folder, this attribute will be modified when the directory is created and when the directory is copied.

Let us do a little exercise to help understand what we are talking about (for this exercise, you will need a USB thumbdrive or floppy disk drive):

1. Close any open applications.
2. Double click on the "Time and Date" in the bottom right corner.
3. Note the current date and time.
4. Now adjust the date to 2 years in the past.
5. Move your cursor back to the desktop and right click on the desktop.
6. From the option menu select> New.

7. Then select> Text Document.

8. When the file name appears, change the name to "DATE."

9. Now right click on the file "DATE" and select> Properties.

10. Note the date of the MAC Dates. Note the dates are all 2 years in the past.

11. Double click on the time and date in the bottom right corner.

12. Now adjust the date to 1 year in the past.

13. Move your cursor back to the desktop.

14. Insert the floppy disk or the thumbdrive and let them install.

15. Right click on the file "DATE" on the desktop and select> Copy.

16. Paste the file to the floppy drive or the thumbdrive.

17. Now right click on the file "DATE" and select> properties.

18. Document the date and time. Notice that all the dates are now 1 year in the past.

19. Double click on the time and date in the bottom right corner.

20. Now adjust the date to 6 months in the past.

21. Access the floppy drive or the thumbdrive that you are using.

22. Double click on the file "DATE."

23. When the file opens, add the word "test" to the document.

24. Now save and close the document.

25. Now right click on the file "DATE" and select> properties.

26. Document the date and time. Notice that the modified date has been changed and the accessed date has been changed to 6 months in the past.

27. Double click on the time and date in the bottom right corner.

28. Now adjust the date to 3 months in the past.

29. Access the Floppy Drive or the Thumbdrive that you are using.

30. Double click on the file "DATE."

31. When the file opens, do not make any changes, just close the document.

32. Now right click on the file "DATE" and select> properties.

33. Document the date and time. Notice that the accessed date has been changed to 3 months in the past.

34. Double click on the time and date in the bottom right corner and adjust the date back to the current date.

This exercise should have reaffirmed your understanding of how the computer bases its dates off of the BIOS clock, not off of any central time standard. This is why in forensic examinations it is imperative to find out the BIOS date and time from the computer being analyzed, as this can tell the investigator whether the files on the disk have been stored correctly or whether the investigator needs to adjust the date and time in the forensic software to accommodate the BIOS date and time.

There is one exception to the rules above and that is when we start looking at older file systems that do not have the same amount of space for the MAC attributes. For example, the older DOS file structure did not keep the same number of file attributes as the FAT 32 does. So what happens when I copy a file from one device to another with different operating systems? If I have a disk created by DOS 3.1 and I copy the files from that disk to my hard drive, which is running Windows 2008, the modified date and the accessed date are the same. This is because the system needs an entry for the modified attribute as the DOS 3.1 file structure does not have that attribute, and so it creates it from the accessed date. This could be confusing to you as the investigator if you were trying to prove when the file was actually last worked on. It is important then to make sure you know what type of operating system you are dealing with.

Let us do one more exercise to help cement this fundamental rule set. You are a detective in the computer crime squad. The date is November 21, 2001. An individual states that he bought a computer the day before yesterday at a yard sale. When he got home, he started looking around the system and found numerous pictures of child pornography. He tells you that the computer is a Windows 98 operating system. The person tells you that he copied the pictures to the floppy disk he just gave you using the Windows file manager. He further states that after doing this he came straight down to the station to report this. You examine the floppy disk using your Windows 98 operating system and find the dates listed in Figure 4.10.

Using a blank piece of paper, note what discrepancies, if any, are there with these file dates.

File Name	Creation Date	Modification Date	Access Date	File Size
Img29.bmp	01/20/2001 10:20:01	11/20/2000 13:20:01	11/20/2001 13:20:01	231
Img30.bmp	01/20/2001 10:20:03	11/20/2000 13:20:11	11/19/2001 12:20:11	230
Img31.bmp	01/20/2001 10:20:07	11/20/2000 13:20:21	11/20/2001 15:20:21	228
Img34.bmp	01/20/2001 10:20:11	11/20/2000 13:20:41	11/20/2001 16:20:41	229

■ **FIGURE 4.10** Attribute chart.

What other questions may you want to ask the person that gave you the floppy disk based on the file dates presented here?

Try not to look at the following answers before you answer the questions:

Answer 1—There are no discrepancies with the file dates. If you do not understand the reason for the answer, reread the MAC date and time rules to see why.

Answer 2—What type of camera was used?

Where is the original computer equipment?

Why is he lying about when he copied the files to the floppy Disk? These are the questions that I would be asking of this person. Take a couple of moments to see if you understand why I might ask these questions. If the dates and times are confusing you review the MAC time rules and the exercise that you just completed.

Remember that the dates of the files will be based on the time of the BIOS on the computer not real time even if it is correct.

Hiding in plain sight

The file system itself can be used to hide valuable data from the investigator/ operator. The file attribute "Hidden" allows us to hide a file or directory from the user without actually moving or deleting the file or folder. In fact, the hidden file or folder is still completely accessible from the file system by any application as long as the user knows the direct path to the file or folder. This attribute also shows how attributes effect files in the file system.

Let's do an exercise to cement this idea solidly in your mind. Before we can continue, we need to make some changes to our operating system. We need to change the way the operating system reads the file attributes. (If you are using the XP system, please make sure you read the special notes.)

1. If you have not already done so, start your computer.
2. Once you are at the main desktop screen, move the cursor to the bottom left-hand corner over the start button. Right click one time.
3. Select explore: this will open the windows file manager.
4. Move the cursor to the menu bar and select tools.
5. From the tools menu, select folder options.
6. In folder options, move the cursor to the tabs at the top of the screen and select view.
7. In the files and folders category, look for hidden files section. Ensure that your setting is set to "do not show hidden files." If is set differently, select the option "do not show hidden files."
8. Select OK.

9. Once you have been returned to the main file manager screen, find the root directory for "C:" you should be able to find the root directory by both its symbol and the letter C:.

10. Click on the root directory: this will highlight the root directory.

11. Move your cursor to the right pane. In the open space, right click once, and choose the option "New" and then "Folder"; when a new folder appears, enter the name "hiding" for the folder and press "enter."

12. Once you have saved the name and saved your entry, right click on the new folder.

13. Select properties.

14. Once you've entered into the folder properties, document the following dates:

*(*Note*: *XP* users, click on the Folders button on top (below the Toolbar) and then on the lower left of the explorer window, click on Details). To be able to view the Modified dates, select View on the Toolbar and then select Details. This will show you the modified date and several other attributes.

    a.   Modified: _____

    b.   Created: _____

    c.   Accessed: _____

15. Now find the attributes block and choose "hidden," then choose "apply" and then OK.

16. Notice that the folder is now slightly dimmed as opposed to the other folders in the directory; now press the F5 key on your keyboard. Document what happens here.

17. Move your cursor to the start button; left click on the start button once. Move your cursor to the Find or Search and select search for Files or Folders.

    a. *(*XP*: Move your cursor to the start button; left click on the start button one time. Click on the Search button.)

18. Once the find block appears in the named block, type the word "hiding" or the name of the directory that you just created in the file manager.

    a. *(*XP*: Click on "All files and folders")

19. Make sure the look in directory is set to the C: drive click on find now. (*XP*: Click on Search.) Document your results:

    a. *(*XP users*, skip to number 27.)

20. After documenting your results, minimize the find block to the task bar and return to the main file manager screen.

21. Choose Tools from the menu, then choose Folder Options, and then choose the tab View.

22. Change selection in the files or folders category from "Do not show all files" to "Show all files."

23. Once you have selected "Show all files," choose Apply and then OK; you should return back to the main file manager screen.

24. From the main file manager screen, choose the C: drive and look for the folder that you created "hiding."

25. If you do not see the folder, press the F5 key to refresh the screen and you should now see your hidden folder.

26. Move your cursor to the task bar and maximize the find block. In the named file, put in the name of the hidden directory. Make sure it is set to the C: drive. (Go to number 28.)

27. *XP Users*: In order to find hidden files or folders, all you need to change on your search is the following: Click on the Start button and then on "All files and folders." From here click on "More advanced options." Check the box "Search hidden files and folders."

28. Once you accomplish this, press find now (*XP*: Search). Document your results.

During this exercise, we have learned some fundamentals about the Windows-based file system. This exercise has shown us that before we can do any investigations on a live computer system, we must change the file attributes so that we can view or see all the files and not just the ones someone may want you to see. Remember changing file attributes, which should be your first step in any cursory exploration of a computer system. Also remember that this should not be done on a system that is being seized, as the forensic software will identify these hidden partitions to you.

Digital evidence destruction

This section is extremely important for you to understand as it is the basis for a lot of what we do in digital media forensics. The basic concept is that data are not deleted from the drive during a normal file deletion or format. In fact, only two significant things happen to a file when we tell the operating system to delete it.

First—the first letter of the filename is replaced by the hex code E5 (Decimal 145) in DOS: this is represented as a "?" The rest of the directory and the rest of the file are unaffected.

Second—all FAT entries beginning with the starting cluster of "?" or E5 are changed from allocated to unallocated space or from the cluster identifier to 0 as you see in Figure 4.11.

Let us use the library analogy again. The deletion process is something that happens in the system area, not in the data area. Remember the system area is like the Dewey decimal system card catalog in the library and the data area is the shelves that are holding the books. So when we delete a file from the system, it is like taking the card in the card catalog and

File Allocation Table		Root Directory				Double Density	
Cluster	Status	File	ext	Size	Date	Starting	Attrib
2	D	?oster		1000		2	
3	D	Memo		200		4	
4	EOF	Letter		1500		5	
5	B						
6	7						
7	EOF						
8	D						
9	D						
10	D						
11	D						
12	D						
13	D						
14	D						

■ **FIGURE 4.11** FAT table.

removing it from the active card catalog. The user no longer sees the card and cannot find the book. The book is still on the shelf and can be found by using an undelete program or forensic software. The file will still be intact initially but maybe degraded over time as documents or other files are written to the deleted space on the drive, as the computer sees this as open space now.

Deleted files can be restored back to their original state by using any one of a number of file undelete programs. Programs such as File Recovery Pro for Windows will allow us to go onto a disk drive and recover files that have been deleted but not overwritten.

What happens when I format the digital media?

Even when a drive is formatted, the data is not overwritten on a non-removable media device such as the hard drive. When formatting the drive, the computer does a couple of things but does not remove the data from the hard drive. The type of format you use will also determine what happens to the data and system area.

- Quick Format—The Operating System removes and rebuilds the two file allocation tables showing that the drive has no readable data. That is, the data area is not touched by the operating system at all. Forensic tools can easily bring back the data from a freshly Quick Formatted drive.
- Full Format—This time the Operating System deletes both of the FAT tables as it does on the quick format but it then performs a diagnostic on the physical drive looking for bad sectors. That is why you get the percentage of format bar or digits in DOS. The operating system again does not delete any of the data from the data area on the disk.

One exception to the format rule occurs when dealing with a removable medium such as a floppy disk. If you are using an operating system such as Windows 2000 or any Windows system later than Windows 2000, a full format of the diskette actually writes over the data area, placing the value F6 in each byte. This is known as Wiping a disk, which we will discuss later in this chapter.

Looking at the rules of how the format takes place, you can see easily that the data area of the hard drive is not affected by the format in any way. Therefore, the data area can be recovered using the appropriate forensic software. Using the library example again, we can say that formatting the hard drive would be like taking the card catalog and burning it to the ground, this will functionally destroy all the pointers to the books on the shelves of the library. What has happened to the books? Nothing, the books are all still there. The librarian then rebuilds the card catalog with a fresh blank card set waiting to get its first book. This is why we cannot use the format to clean an evidence drive initially, as the residual data still remains on the hard drive. To clean a hard drive, you must use a wiping utility, which is covered later in this section.

We will use an exercise to help cement this concept for you. You will need a floppy drive (internal or external) and a floppy disk as well as the demo program of Directory Snoop, which is available for download at http://www.briggsoft.com/dsnoop.htm (if you like the program, please purchase a copy as it is a great program).

1. If you have not already done so, turn on your computer, plug in the floppy drive, and launch Windows. Now place the Floppy Disk into the Floppy Disk Drive.
   Before we begin the exercise we need to format the floppy drive. Open "My Computer" on your computer. You should see the Floppy Disk Icon. Right Click on the Floppy Disk Icon and select Format from the options menu. Do not change any settings. Select Start to begin the format. Allow the format to finish before continuing with this exercise.
2. Select Start, then (XP USERS—All Programs) Programs—Accessories—Notepad.
3. In the notepad main screen, type in the following: "This is a test to see how well data is deleted."
4. Once your note is typed, select "File" from the toolbar at the top of the screen. Select "Save As" from the File menu. In the "Save As" box, select the drive drop-down menu at the top of the screen and select the "3 ½ Floppy Drive."
5. In the file name block, type in "test.txt."
6. Once the file is saved to the "3 ½ Floppy Drive," close Notepad.

7. Select on the desktop (XP USERS—Go to the Start Menu)—My Computer—3 ½ Floppy Disk, and verify that the document you just created is on the floppy disk.

8. Right click on the document and select "delete" and then select OK.

9. Press F5 to refresh the screen and verify that the file has been deleted.

10. Close the Floppy Drive window.

11. Close the My Computer window.

12. Go to Start—Programs (XP USERS All Programs)—Directory Snoop.

13. If the program asks for a company name, enter in "HTCI"; if not skip to the next step.

14. Select the A: icon from the select drive list.

15. Look in the file list window and document your results.

16. Now select the second ?est.txt file and look at the data block at the bottom of the screen and document your results.

17. Close Directory Snoop.

18. Select on the desktop (XP USERS—Go to the Start Menu)— My Computer—3 ½ Floppy Disk, and verify that the document is still gone.

19. Right click on the A: drive and select format. Check the option Quick Format then select OK.

20. Wait until the formatting process is completed.

21. Open the A: drive, Press F5 to refresh the screen and verify that there are no files on the floppy disk.

22. Close the Floppy Drive window.

23. Close the My Computer window.

24. Go to Start—Programs (XP USERS All Programs)—Directory Snoop.

25. Enter the company name (HTCI).

26. Select the A: icon from the select drive list.

27. Look in the file list window and document your results.

28. Now select cluster 2 from the File Allocation table located at the bottom right of the directory snoop window and document your results.

29. Close Directory Snoop.

30. Select on the desktop (XP USERS—Go to the Start Menu)—My Computer—3 ½ Floppy Disk, and verify that the document is still gone.

31. Right click on the A: drive, select format and select OK.

32. Wait until the formatting process is completed.

33. Open the 3 ½ in. Floppy drive. Press F5 to refresh the screen and verify that the file has been deleted.

34. Close the Floppy Drive window.

35. Close the My Computer window.

36. Go to Start—(XP USERS All Programs) Programs—Directory Snoop.

37. Enter in the company name HTCI.

38. Select the A: icon from the select drive list.

39. Look in the file list window and document your results.

40. Now select cluster 2 from the File Allocation table located at the bottom right of the directory snoop window and document your results.

41. Close Directory Snoop.

42. What was the difference between the three tasks that you just performed?

(a) Delete

(b) Quick Format

(c) Format Remember that this type of format (wipe) will only happen on the floppy disk. All other removable media will follow the rules of the computer and not wipe the container.

Drive slack

So what about all the books that are left on the shelf after the deletions and formats? You still have the opportunity to retrieve all the data from a storage device, as we talked about in the previous section, after files have been deleted or formatted. After a time, more files will be written over the area that contained the old files. If the file is not larger than the file that was originally there, then you will have a file residue or file slack left over on the disk. File slack is best explained as clusters or sectors that have been overwritten by other data on some type of storage device. The cluster or sector is not completely overwritten though, leaving partial traces of information. An investigator/operator can use special software to go in and collect this leftover information in the file. As clusters/sectors are overwritten on the hard drive, all the sectors or clusters are not covered by the new bytes. This allows the investigator/operator to use software to collect the slack. We are going to look at this process through the example of video tapes (see Figure 4.12).

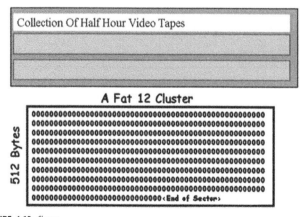

■ **FIGURE 4.12** Cluster.

If you were to purchase two 1-hour videotapes and then record several shows to them, you would be able to go back in and review those shows. If we were to reuse those tapes to record new information, we would overwrite the previous information. Any information that was not written over by the new segment show or movie we were watching would be left intact on the videotape. The computer works in much the same fashion. If the files are left intact on the hard drive and the space has not been completely reused, you may be able to obtain enough information from the file slack to put a document or some other file back together (see Figure 4.13).

The file slack can also be data that is purposefully stored there. For example, I want to hide data in a specific cluster on the hard drive. Using the Hex Editor, I can move to that cluster and append text in the last few bytes of that sector. For example, maybe I want to pass a password on or some other small bit of information. Since the file system does not read past the EOF tag, and as long as I place the data between the EOF tag and the end of the cluster, the data will be stored safely from prying eyes. Most digital forensic software applications are designed to find and retrieve this file slack. This is done automatically when the forensic software is run, which sorts the data found in the image file.

Wiping utilities

Wiping files or hard drives is the process of overwriting the byte on the hard drive with a character. As we have discussed, simply deleting and/or formatting drives are not going to get rid of the data on the hard drive. If I am hiding data, for example, from law-enforcement officials in the

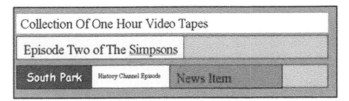

■ FIGURE 4.13 Video tapes.

hope that I will evade prosecution, I can set up and use an evidence eliminating program or a wiping program to help overwrite the data.

If I am going to use this type of program, I am going to ensure that it allows me to configure it to my specific needs. For example, if I am doing credit card fraud, I would want the ability to be able to wipe away any possible files that would incriminate me. I would probably want to set up the program to wipe out a specific directory or specific files. Why would I want to do this instead of wiping the entire drive? The biggest reason is time. It could take up to 18 hour to completely wipe out a modern hard disk drive. So, how could I use a wiping program to help me hide evidence daily? For example, I may set up my wiping program as follows:

Daily wipe the following areas:

> Temporary internet cache
> Temporary files folder
> Favorites folder
> History folder

Emergency wipe (Here come the police!) would be executed with a Hot key combination:

> My Documents\My Illegal Porn Directory
> My Documents\My Illegal Credit Card numbers

After executing the emergency wipe, do a daily wipe.

Once these files have been wiped from the drive, it will be almost impossible for any type of law enforcement to be able to find and recover files. The wiping program is truly the only real way to ensure that all the data has been removed from the hard drive. One medium that you cannot trust to a wipe is the thumbdrive or flash medium, as there is no way to verify that the wipe has been completely successful. The flash medium does not allow me as an investigator to be able to go into the data area and validate that the data area has been truly wiped; so I have to rely on the flash media controller that tells me that the flash medium has been wiped. Until a process is found to ensure that the flash medium has truly been wiped, it is recommended not to use flash medium as an evidence container. This does not include external hard drives, as they can be independently tested by putting them into a computer system and verifying the hard drive as being wiped by using a Hex editor.

The rest of this chapter will deal directly with the DTF process and how you can use the DTF process to gather intelligence, evidence, and actionable intelligence.

PROCESSING DIGITAL MEDIA USING THE DIGITAL TRIAGE FORENSIC MODEL

The processing of the digital medium is a process that should be procedural in nature; in other words, the same thing I do to this medium should be done to all media, showing the consistency of my examinations. By using a standard procedure, I will also lessen the likelihood of mistakes being made. The skeleton for the process that we are going to use is as follows:

1. Connect the external evidence drive.
2. If this is the first capture made to this external evidence drive, then we must wipe the evidence drive, preparing it to receive evidence.
3. Create an evidence partition if one is not present.
4. Activate or connect a write block tool to collect the digital medium.
5. Collect an image of the digital medium.
6. Process the data in the write-protected container with a triage tool.
7. Process the drive using P2 Commander forensic application.

Connecting the external evidence drive

If you are using the EDAS system or another forensic system, you will need to use a collection or target drive for the cases and images that will be stored during the investigation. The drive will need to be wiped initially, and a report showing that the drive has been wiped needs to be maintained. The wiping of the drive is extremely important, as it gives you a clean starting point and follows the pillars of forensics. To wipe the drive, we will use an application called Forensic Replicator (Paraben Corporation). Do not use the computer system that you are conducting the investigation with to house the evidence data files as this will turn your computer into an evidence container itself. Always save the evidence files to an external storage container. This is a very important rule to remember.

Connecting the external drive:

1. We recommend that you use at least a 1 TB drive external drive.
2. Try to stay away from unpowered external drives, as they draw significant power from the system and can be unreliable.
3. Connect the external drive to the USB cable.
4. Switch on the power to the external drive.
5. Connect the USB cable to the laptop.
6. Continue to follow these steps if this is the first time that you are using the external drive or if the drive needs to be recycled. *Note: You only have to wipe the drive when using it for the first time or resetting the drive to be reused in future investigations.*

1. Open Paraben Forensic Replicator.
2. Find the icon on the desktop for the Forensic Replicator.
3. Double click on the Forensic Replicator icon.
4. The Replicator application will launch.
5. In Forensic Replicator, click >File.
6. On the File Menu, click >Erase all data from a physical drive.
7. On the popup dialogue box, choose the radio button >Do a slow DOD 5220-22m wipe.
8. Click "Yes" on the write blocker warning that is displayed.
9. From the "Select a physical hard drive" to fully erase the dialogue box, choose the physical drive you wish to wipe. If you do not know which drive it is, you can refer back to the MMC on the previous pages to get that info.
10. Once you have chosen the drive to wipe, click > Finish.
11. A final warning will be displayed: click > OK.
12. Once the drive has been fully wiped, you have the option to run a checksum.
13. Run the checksum option.
14. Once the drive has been wiped, print the report and keep for your records.
15. Your evidence drive is now ready to be partitioned for use.
16. To do this, we must use the Disk Management application. This application is included with every Windows operating system.
17. To access the Disk Management application click on the Start button in the bottom left of your Windows desktop screen.
18. From the start menu, find the My Computer link.
19. Right click on the My Computer link.
20. Select the menu option "Manage."
21. From the Manage screen, find the selection for "Disk Management."
22. Click on "Disk Management."
23. When you open the Disk Management screen, a dialogue box will pop up asking you to activate the drive that you just wiped. If this screen does not appear, you may need to reseat the external hard drive.
24. Turn the power off, and then turn the power back on.
25. This should cause the dialogue box to appear.
26. Check the box next to the drive and activate the drive.
27. Once the drive is activated, the display will change to show the physical drives.
28. Find the external drive and click on the unallocated space in the drive window.
29. Right click the unallocated space area and Select create > New Partition.

30. Select > Primary Partition.

31. Select > NTFS or FAT 32 from the File Type options.

32. Select > the size of the drive. You do not have to use the maximum size. If you are sharing the drive with other investigators, you may want to create multiple partitions. Remember that 1024 is 1 K so a 2-Gig Drive would be 2048.

33. Create the size of the drive and select quick format.

34. Select > Finish to create the Partition.

35. Repeat these steps to make as many partitions as you need.

Connecting the write block solution

Which device type you intend to image from will determine what write blocker to use. There are two basic types of write blockers:

■ Hardware write blocker—The hardware blocker is a device that is installed that runs software internally to itself and will block the write capability of the computer to the device attached to the write blocker.

■ Software write blocker—The software blocker is an application that is run on the operating system that implements a software control to turn off the write capability of the operating system. If you are using a software write blocker, ensure to attach the external evidence collection drive prior to activating the software blocker as this will allow the external drive to be written to.

If you are collecting data from a USB device such as a thumbdrive, you need to activate the software or hardware blocker prior to connecting the device to the collection system. Importantly, make sure that you have already connected the external evidence collection drive and prepared it. If you have not connected it, connect it now (see Figure 4.14).

The hardware write blocker solution we are going to use is the Single Bay imaging station. The imaging station is a USB 2 device that will allow us to connect a Notebook, IDE, or SATA drive to the system to be captured. To set up the single bay imaging station, follow these steps:

1. Place the analysis station on a dry surface (see Figure 4.15).

2. Connect the AC power to the back of the analysis station and plug the station in (see Figure 4.16).

3. Plug the USB 2 cable into the EDAS laptop or the forensic computer (see Figure 4.17).

4. To install a hard drive into the analysis station, pull back the silver tab on the drive inserted into the analysis station (see Figure 4.18).

■ **FIGURE 4.14** Connect Single Bay imaging station.

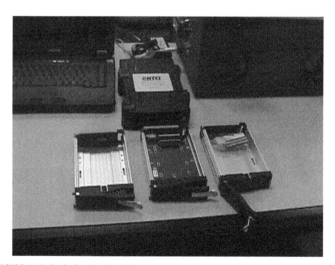

■ **FIGURE 4.15** Single Bay imaging station.

5. This will expose the key hole. Place the key into the keyhole and turn it to the six O'clock position (see Figure 4.19).
6. This will unlock the drive (see Figure 4.20).
7. Pull the drive door backwards (see Figure 4.21).
8. Once the door is extended, you can now pull the drawer out. Be careful not to drop the drawer (see Figure 4.22).

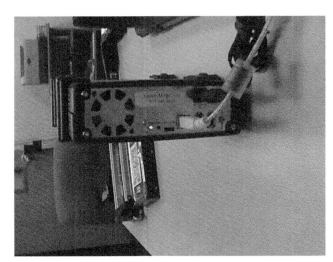

■ **FIGURE 4.16** Connect analysis station.

■ **FIGURE 4.17** Connect to the EDAS.

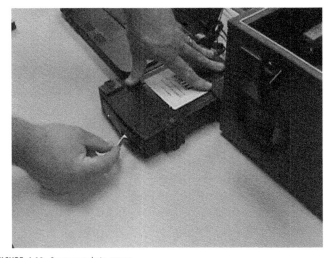

■ **FIGURE 4.18** Connect analysis system.

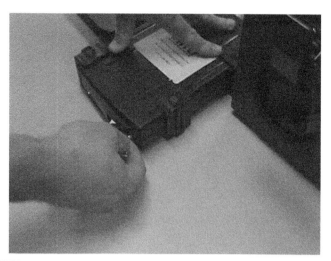

■ **FIGURE 4.19** Key turn.

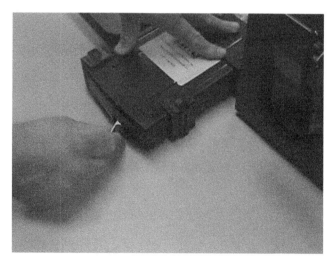

■ **FIGURE 4.20** Unlock drive.

9. Place the drawer on the table; push down the open tab on the top of the drawer (see Figure 4.23).

10. Pull the top part of the drawer backwards, exposing the drive cavity (see Figure 4.24).

11. Place the hard drive into the cavity and connect it to the cabling inside of the drawer. If your drive requires it, make sure to connect the

■ **FIGURE 4.21** Open drive.

■ **FIGURE 4.22** Pull the drawer out.

power to the back of the drive. It should be keyed so the power cord can only be inserted in one direction (see Figure 4.25).

12. Seat the drive into the tray and make sure the drive is not binding any cables or that the cable became unseated after installing (see Figure 4.26).

13. Replace the cover back on top of the tray and close the tray (see Figure 4.27).

■ **FIGURE 4.23** Remove the drawer.

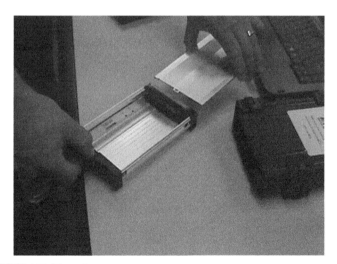

■ **FIGURE 4.24** Drive cavity.

14. Close the drawer cover back over the inserted tray (see Figure 4.28).
15. Replace the tray back into the analysis station (see Figure 4.29).
16. Close the tray lock (see Figure 4.30).
17. Close the silver tab to cover the keyhole (see Figure 4.31).
18. When operating the analysis station, the drive must be turned on (see Figure 4.32).

■ **FIGURE 4.25** Remove the Hard drive.

■ **FIGURE 4.26** Insert the Hard Drive into the tray.

19. Turn the key to the 9 o'clock position, this will turn the drive on. If the key is turned to the 7 o'clock position; this will put the drive into the traveling position. This will not turn the drive on.
20. To ensure that the single bay analysis station is working properly, you will need to enter the disk management application.
21. To access the manage applications, do the following:

■ **FIGURE 4.27** Replace the tray cover.

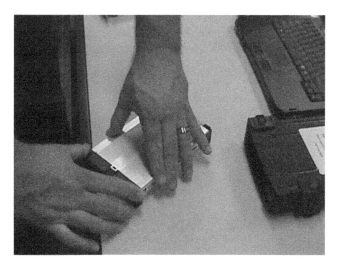

■ **FIGURE 4.28** Close the tray cover.

22. Click on the "Start" button at the bottom left of your Windows desktop screen.
23. From the Start menu, find the My Computer link.
24. Right click on the My Computer link.
25. Select the menu option Manage.
26. From the Manage application, find the selection Disk Management (see Figure 4.33).
27. Click on Disk Management (see Figure 4.34).

■ **FIGURE 4.29** Insert the tray into the Single Bay Imaging Station.

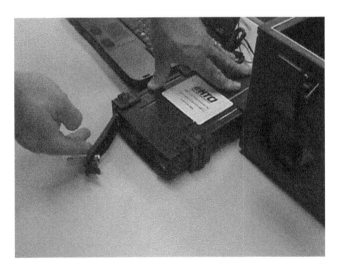

■ **FIGURE 4.30** Close the tray cover on the Single Bay imaging Station.

28. The drive that you have inserted should appear in the disk management window as a physical drive.

29. The disk management window will show all the valid partitions (see Figure 4.35).

30. The drive is ready to be used by your forensic applications. If the drive is not recognized, you can do the following:

a. Ensure the drive is turned on.

■ **FIGURE 4.31** Open the keyhole cover.

■ **FIGURE 4.32** Lock the tray into place.

    b. Ensure the USB cable is attached to the EDAS laptop.
    c. Reseat the drive into the single bay analysis station.
    d. Reseat the drive in the drive tray and replace the tray into the single bay analysis station.
    e. If the above does not allow the drive to be found, try a known good drive in the single bay analysis station and repeat the preceding steps to ensure it is functioning correctly.

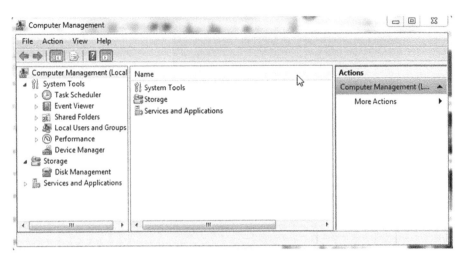

■ **FIGURE 4.33** Microsoft Management Console (MMC).

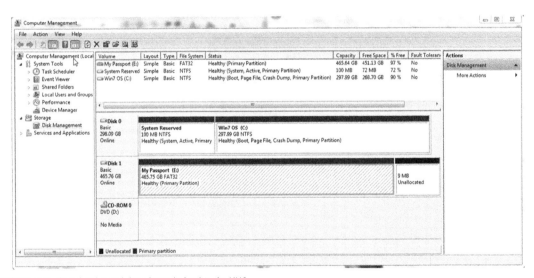

■ **FIGURE 4.34** Physical and Logical drives being displayed in the MMC.

Using field search to perform digital triage forensics or live scan

Now that we have the evidence drive connected and protected, we can use a DTF tool to do a quick analysis of a collected digital media. The DTF tool that we will use is Field Search. Field search is an example of the true need for DTF tools. Field search was written with DTF in mind. The DTF model being provided was developed for law enforcement but

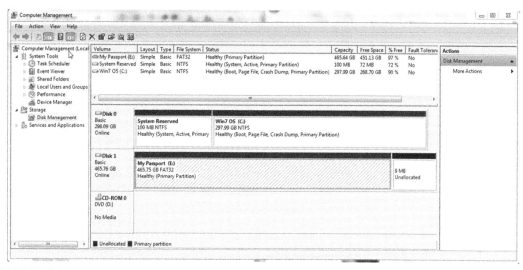

is adaptable to operators around the world performing DTF. The following is the intent of the software as envisioned by Dr Tanner. It has been modified from his original text to be presented here.

Field Search software was designed to be used as part of an overall strategy to gather computer use information to diagnose, treat, monitor, and manage the offender in the community. Recently, it has been adopted as a tool for First Responders and government agencies for use during 'Knock and Talk' and consent warrant searches. We have adjusted the tool to better accommodate this usage. Our goal remains to produce a tool for nontechnical users, which allows simple, effective examination of computers in the field. Field Search was first released in August of 2006. Its approach was based on a model of computer management developed during more than 1200 examinations of convicted sex offenders' computers using standard forensic tools (EnCase®, X-Ways Forensics®, FTK®, and various flavors of Linux tools). In brief, Field Search was designed for use by the majority of line staff officers who have limited to no technical training in forensics. It runs live in a native Windows® environment and provides a fast, powerful, yet easy method of examining and monitoring computer use. In essence, Field Search blends preview functions with evidence gathering and reporting functions. Since 2006 we have updated Field Search 4 times, making it more powerful in each successive version. InSeptember of 2008, we introduced a second application which runs live in the Mac OS X® environment and allows officers to examine MacIntosh products in the field. Currently, the two Field Search products are called FSWin (Windows® version) and FSMac (MacIntosh® version).

*As FSWin's use grew among probation and parole agencies, local law enforcement began to examine it as a potential tool for first responders and case investigators. FSWin began to be added to the 'jump kits' used by local law enforcement. In brief, it is generally considered as **ONE** of the tools available under specific circumstances (e.g., 'Knock and Talk' and/or consent searches). This trend—movement from probation and parole's use, to being used by first responders and case investigators in situations where its results might wind up as an element in new criminal charges—has brought about a discussion regarding live box examination. The discussion was at first held among forensic examiners and RCFL staff. It is beginning to expand beyond this small circle of extremely knowledgeable individuals. Dr. Jim Tanner has opined that live box examination poses no problem for forensic labs and informed prosecution.*

Tanner concludes a careful examination of the elements involved will lead jurisdictions to the conclusion [that] controlled live-box exams with Field Search during nonformal phases of case management are overwhelmingly positive with little to no adverse impact on a case. He further states a careful examination of the situation will lead to the realization that not implementing live-box exams generally results in case stalls or complete collapse of a case through inactivity.

Field Search was developed to fill the gap in case investigation and management. We will continue to improve Field Search and hope the justice system finds it valuable as one of the tools available to them.

So what can Field Search do for the operator? One of the biggest aides is that it allows nontechnical operators to perform technical tasks:

1. Search for logical images and videos (items which still exist as files on the computer).
2. Search logical text (text in files which still exist on the computer). *Note:* This function can be used to search for a wide variety of items, see Keyword Search Options below.
3. Search logical URL and Cookie histories (listings of places Web browsers have gone).
4. Examine the recycler (recycle bin) to see what has been recently deleted.
5. Retrieve a list of Links to files on the computer.
6. Retrieve a list of most recently used (MRU) files for many of the applications on the computer (occurs automatically at program launch).
7. List the media available to the user on the system.

8. Quickly seize evidence and copy it to removable medium.

9. Easily produce an exportable report which contains system configuration and all evidence seized (with associated path and MAC dates).

10. Export exhaustive information into an Excel® worksheet for further examination when time allows.

11. Extract browser (URL) histories from file slack space and volume free space (listings which have been deleted but remain on the drive). This requires significant additional time.

12. Field Search will have the ability to scan entire drives and external media (when attached), or drill down to scan single folders.

If you are the operator gathering data on a potential suspect, this tool provides you the ability to surreptitiously gather data. An example of its use might be as follows: You are watching a suspect at an Internet café. He has been using the computer for an hour. You have watched him create a couple of documents and browse through several Web sites. He leaves the café. You immediately sit down at the same computer plug in your thumbdrive and, from your portable applications screen, launch Field Search. Field Search recovers web links and history and the names of files the suspect was working on. I am sure as an operator you can see the immediate value of this tool.

Creating a portable drive to run field search

Field search can be run from a USB flash drive or a CD. We are going to create a USB drive that is based on portable applications. This will allow us to add Field Search to the menu so that we can run the application directly. The portable application menu also allows us to add other programs that will come in useful if we do not have our own computer with us. The portable application USB can be run from any computer that allows USB access. You will need the following files from KB Solutions:

- FSWin.exe (Main program)
- FSWin.xml (sets image filter parameters for Field Search)
- config.xml (sets other parameters for Field Search)
- FSWin.frx (report template for NTFS-FSWin-FAT.frx is for FAT systems)
- libmcl.dll (a library file needed to play videos inside Field Search)
- sqlite3.dll (a library file needed to examine Mozilla browsers version 3 and higher)
- In addition, there may be several optional files that appear in the folder:
- FSWin.log (an optional file which contains the activity log)

- paths.xml (an optional file created when folder level searches are conducted)
- keywords.xml (an optional file which contains predetermined keyword search lists)

To begin, we need to download a couple of files:

Download the latest standard suite portable applications file from http://www.portableapps.com. Once you have downloaded the files install them onto the USB drive that you wish to use as your portable investigator drive.

Download the latest copy of Field Search from http://www.kbsolutions.com. Fill out the request form to get the program (The program is an NIJ project and is free to operators and law enforcement officers). Make sure to read the Eula, and understand it.

Once you have gotten the program from KB Solutions, you will need to unzip them from the archive. One folder will be called FSWINDOWS, the other one will be FSMACINTOSH. We will copy the FSWINDOWS folder onto the USB drive into the portable applications directory. To create the portable applications USB drive, follow the steps below:

1. Download the latest portable applications standard suite from http://www.portableapps.com.
2. Install the portable applications to a USB thumbdrive that is at least 4 GB in size.
3. Plug in the thumbdrive that you want to set up into the computer.
   Find the portable applications file that you have downloaded. Open the application to begin the install.
   Select the Accept Terms box and select continue.
   Install the program to the root directory of the thumbdrive you want to use. Example would be F:\
   After the portable applications have been installed to the USB thumbdrive; we will add the other programs.
4. Unzip the file that you received from KB Solutions and copy the FSWIN folder onto the USB thumbdrive into the folder Portable Applications (see Figure 4.36).
5. Email support@gohtci.com and request a copy of the HTCI USBToggle tool and the HTCI SIM Card Analysis program. It is a freeware tool provided by HTCI. Copy the program USBToggle into the Portable Applications folder. This is a freeware application provided by HTCI. USBToggle is a program provided to act as a software blocker which will isolate evidence thumbdrives attached to the system.

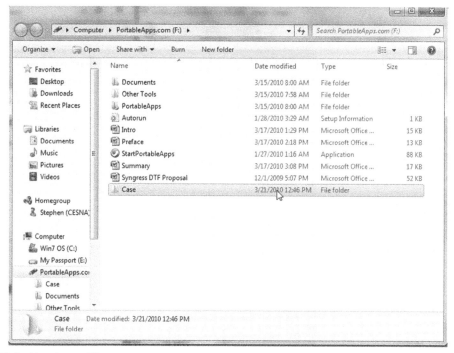

■ **FIGURE 4.36** Portable applications folder.

6. When you launch the Portable Applications, the program reads the programs available and installs the Field Search application. Field Search is now ready to run from the Portable Applications menu. To learn about the other applications found in the Portable Applications suite, get to the Web site and read about each of the programs (see Figure 4.37).
7. On the thumbdrive, create a folder called Case.
8. Create a folder called Other Software Tools.
   a. Drivers for the thumbdrive to work on Windows® 98.
   b. Copy fsutil.exe from the windows System 32 directory into this folder. fsutil.exe is a DOS tool used to turn off last access date function if necessary.

Launching field search

1. If you are going to scan a USB device such as an external hard drive or thumbdrive device, make sure to run the USBToggle tool (to get this free tool, send an e-mail to Support@gohtci.com and request the

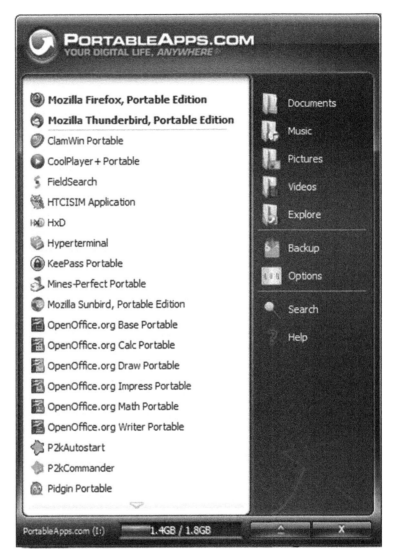

■ **FIGURE 4.37** Portable applications menu.

USBToggle. Make sure to say you are reading this book). If you want to block all new devices being installed to be Read Only, then select Read Only. If you want to Disable all unused ports, the Select Disable Ports option should be selected.

2. Launch the tool from the USBToggle from the portable applications menu.

■ **FIGURE 4.38** HTCI USBToggle.

3. When you launch the USBToggle tool, an icon will appear in the right-hand lower toolbar. The toolbar icon will be in different colors to represent different functions (see Figure 4.38).
   a. Green—All USB drives are open;
   b. Yellow—New USB devices inserted will be write-protected;
   c. Red—All USB ports are disabled.
4. You can now plug in any device.
5. With the portable applications menu, open select Field Search and click on it one time. This will bring up the End Users License Agreement page for field Search. DO NOT DOUBLE CLICK on the menu. If you do double click, the menu item will try to load multiple instances of the application and you will receive error messages. To fix this, simply press Ctrl-Alt-Del and choose the task manager. Click on field search and choose End task to cancel the other instances of the application.
6. Click on "Accept" to continue.
7. If possible, temporarily disconnect the computer from the Internet; reconnect after gathering your intelligence/evidence.
8. The main screen will appear (see Figure 4.39).
9. Run "Final Report"; Immediately run "Final Report." Look at the header data on the report to determine when Windows® was last installed (see Figure 4.40).
10. Compare the report's created date/time against your watch for current time.
11. Look at the IDE Devices table in the report. If you see that USB or removable media have been connected to the computer, you may want to look for the media near the offender's workstation.

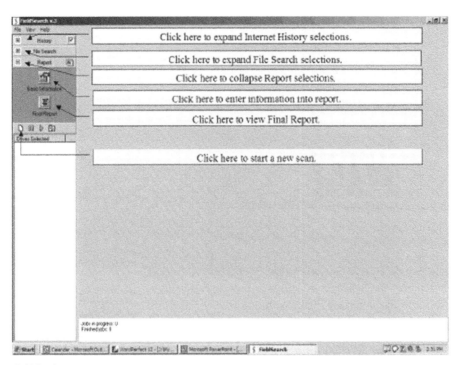

■ **FIGURE 4.39** Field Search main menu.

■ **FIGURE 4.40** Final report.

12. Select Basic Information in the comments field, and note any discrepancies in the system clock and local time. Save the report to your USB drive. Check that it actually made it to your USB drive. [*Always* check after each save to ensure the report is where you think it is (see Figure 4.41).]

13. Select MRU Sort the Most Recently Used by Last Access Date. This will give you a quick understanding of how the offender uses the computer. It may also give you an idea of drives or folders for closer scrutiny. Look for drives not physically present on the computer at the moment. This may reflect previous connection of USB or Firewire external media (see Figure 4.42).

14. Start "New Scan"; click on the "blank page" icon or select file "New Scan" (see Figure 4.43).

15. Select the drive to be scanned.

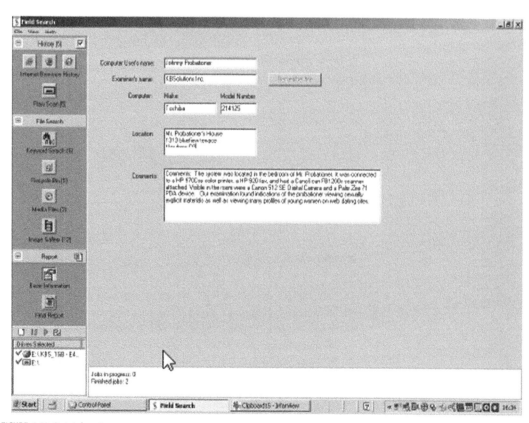

■ **FIGURE 4.41** Basic information screen.

■ **FIGURE 4.42** MRU screen.

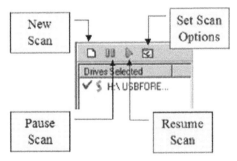

■ **FIGURE 4.43** Start new scan.

16. Select which drives you want to scan by checking the appropriate boxes.
17. Click on the "Options" tab to select scan options (see Figure 4.44).
18. Select the scan options you want. We recommend you begin with "Collect Images," "Collect Internet History," "Scan in ZIP archives," "Collect link files," and "Perform keywords search." Be sure to enter the video file formats you wish to search for. Field Search will default to searching for
    a. AVI
    b. MPG

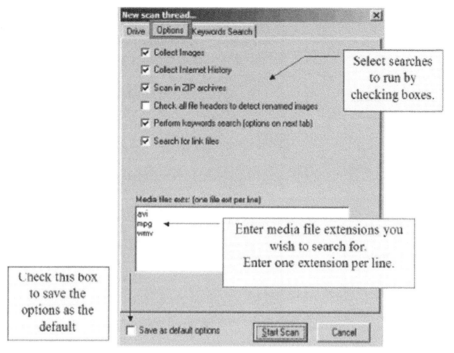

■ **FIGURE 4.44** Options screen.

    c. MOV

    d. WMV

19. Click on the "Keywords Search" tab (see Figure 4.45).

20. Select the keywords to search for.

21. Enter any keywords or phrases or select predefined sets.
You might add other terms or terms of importance to the local
area or investigation. Make sure that after you create the keyword
list you save the scheme so that you do not have to retype the
keywords again.

22. Enter the file types to be searched (more file types add more time to
the search). We recommend searching TXT, HTM, HTML, and LOG
files at a minimum.

23. Click "Start Scan" to begin Scan.

24. The scan will start immediately. You can click on the drive letter *after
about 30 s* and see the scan's progress.

25. The scan progress is displayed at the bottom of the screen. *Note*: It will
appear that Field Search is doing nothing for about 30 s. Wait
patiently; it is scanning the drive's directory tree. If you attempt to do

■ **FIGURE 4.45** Portable applications folder.

anything while the directory tree is being scanned, you will get the dreaded "hour glass." While the directory tree is being scanned, collect the information you need for the Basic Information section (e.g., computer type, model, etc.)

26. After approximately 30 seconds, you can begin to fill out the basic information. Describe the computer, giving a serial number if possible, and note any attached equipment. The comments field can be used to report findings as well as equipment.

27. To avoid formatting issues in the final report, it is best to limit your text entry so it fits inside the boxes as they first come up (see Figure 4.46).

28. You can now begin the process of digital triage forensics. Begin reviewing results and select items for inclusion in your report.

29. The order in which you review results is personal preference. DTF suggests you review the Image Gallery first and then the Keyword

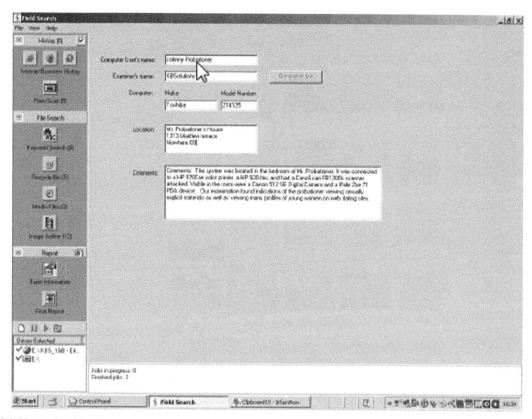

■ **FIGURE 4.46** Basic information screen.

Search. *Note:* Do not review media or images until you see a green checkmark next to the drive letter (Field Search has finished scanning). Doing so could cause memory problems.

30. Check items for inclusion in the report by checking the box next to the item you want to include in the report (see Figure 4.47).

31. If you found Mozilla®-based browser Internet Histories and there were indications it was used to surf suspect sites, you may choose to conduct a second search with the "Check all file headers..." option selected.

32. Focus this search on the Documents and Settings folder only.

33. If you believe a Mozilla®-based browser may have text strings saved in the cache that contain important information, you may choose to conduct a second search with the "Search in files..." pane left empty. This will search every file in the folder for the keywords (see Figure 4.48).

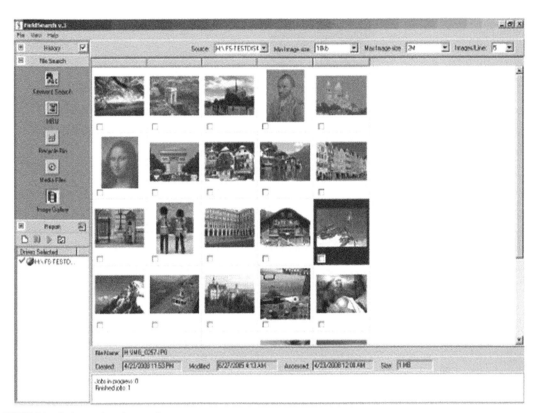

■ **FIGURE 4.47** Check items for inclusion to the report.

34. Caution: choosing to do a second search on Mozilla®-based browsers can increase the amount of time Field Search requires to complete its task. You should do this only if it is warranted.
35. Run the report to see how it looks. Generally, you should have no more than 2-4 pages in the report. If you have more, you may have included too many examples of the suspect's computer use. Decide which elements best represent the suspect's usage and remove the remainder.
36. You can go back to the individual result pages and simply uncheck the boxes to remove items from the report.
37. To expedite review of selected images, URL records, Word Search findings, or Raw Scan records, change the Source to "Selected."
38. To expedite the review of URL history records, click on the "checkbox" in the History tab.
39. Save Report when viewing the report: click on the small disk icon at the top of the page to save the report to removable media.
40. Select a report type: (see Figure 4.49)

■ **FIGURE 4.48** Mozilla browsers.

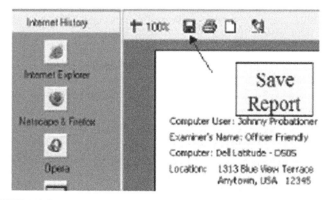

■ **FIGURE 4.49** Report types.

    a. Rich Text File (*.rtf)—this can be opened in Word® and edited.
    b. Adobe Acrobat Document (*.pdf)—this cannot be edited, but can be read by almost any computer.

41. *Make sure* you save the report to your removable media.

42. Export information to the Excel® spreadsheet (see Figure 4.50).

43. We recommend you always export the Excel® spreadsheet. It takes only a few seconds and provides you with an extensive back-up set of data.

The above steps are suggested for the collection of intevidence. You can see from using this program that it is possible to capture intevidence from the suspect drive. This tool is a great step forward in the world of DTF tools. The operator can take complete control of the drive to be captured using the filters provided in the tool.

■ **FIGURE 4.50** Excel export.

The next section will allow us to use a more powerful DTF tool to gather and perform analysis of digital media.

Creating a suspect image to be analyzed by P2 commander using forensic replicator

Earlier, we talked about the single bay imaging station and the USBToggle to write-protect any digital media. Depending on which type of media you are going to use, employ the tool required.

■ Hard drives—SATA, Notebook, and IDE, use the single bay imaging station.
■ USB devices—Thumbdrive, SD card, and portable USB hard drives, use the USBToggle tool.

Now that you have protected the suspect drive, you can gather an image from the drive (an image in the digital forensic world is not a graphic; it is a compressed capture of the suspect drive into a file). We are going to use Forensic Replicator to create the image file. You can download a demo of the replicator application from the Paraben Corporation. The link to this program is http://www.paraben.com/programs/demo.html; you can also download the P2 Commander demo application which will be used later.

1. Find the icon on the desktop for the Forensic Replicator. Double click on the Forensic Replicator icon (see Figure 4.51).
2. The Replicator application will launch (see Figure 4.52).
3. In Forensic Replicator, click >File.
4. On the file menu, click > Create a physical drive image (see Figure 4.53).
5. A dialogue box will appear telling you that you will be creating a suspect drive image. Click > Next (see Figure 4.54).
6. A dialogue box will appear asking which physical drive you would like to image (See Figure 4.55).

■ **FIGURE 4.51** Forensic Replicator icon.

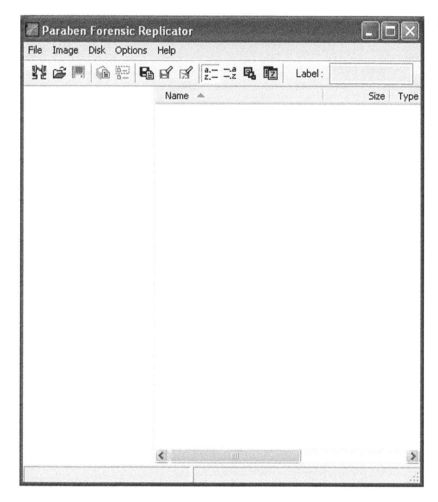

■ **FIGURE 4.52** Forensic Replicator.

7. The Select > File to Write dialogue box will appear. Choose the path
   to where you would like to store the image file. Make sure to store it to
   your external drive; never store data to the internal storage
   (see Figure 4.56).
8. Click > the radio button Save in Raw Format (this is the most
   common format to use and the most compatible format).
9. Select > Next, the Report Wizard Dialogue Box will be displayed
   (see Figure 4.57).
10. Choose > Text file.
11. Choose > Image information.
12. Choose > Time and date of acquisition.
13. Choose > Export partition structure.

■ **FIGURE 4.53** Replicator file menu.

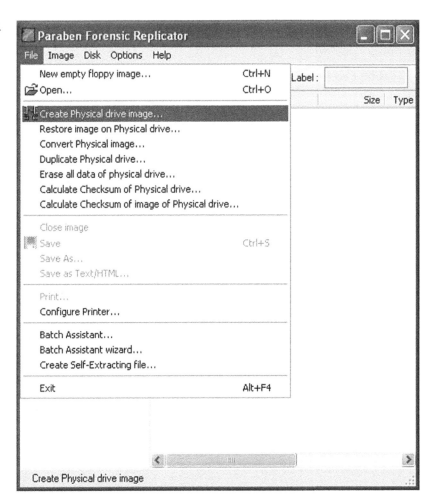

14. Choose > Add report header (see Figure 4.58).
15. Click > Next; the report header dialogue box will be displayed.
16. Fill out the rest of the form with any relevant information.
17. Select > Finish and choose where to save the report. Save the report to the same location as your image file.
18. The image file will be created and a progress dialogue box will be displayed to show you the progress of the image.
19. When the image is completed, make sure to print the text report and save it with your case file.
20. When the Checksum dialogue box appears, run the Checksum to ensure file integrity.

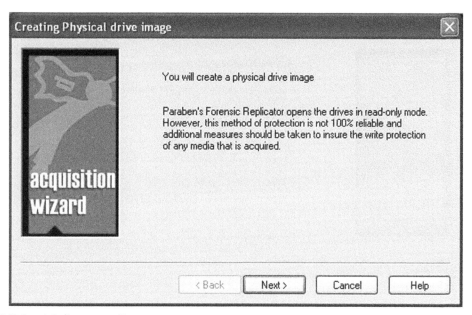

■ **FIGURE 4.54** Forensic Replicator suspect drive.

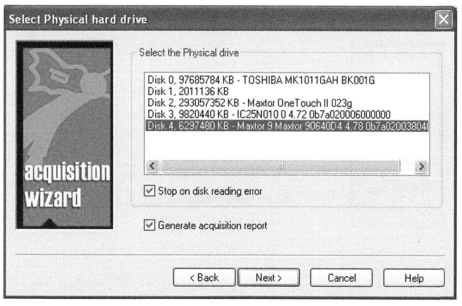

■ **FIGURE 4.55** Select Physical Drive to image.

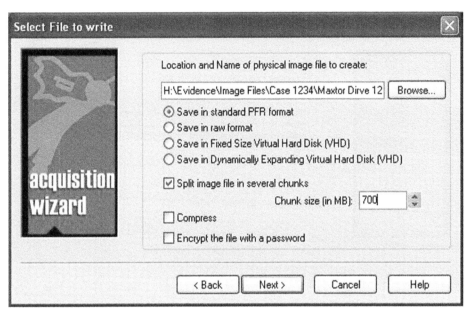

■ **FIGURE** 4.56 File destination.

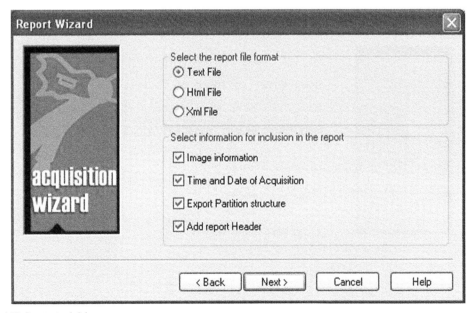

■ **FIGURE** 4.57 Report wizard dialogue.

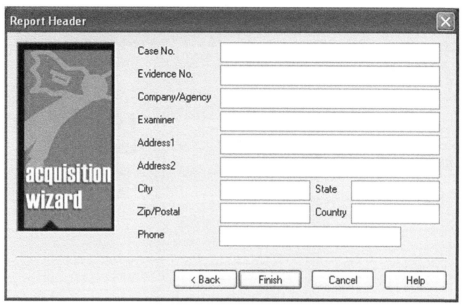

■ **FIGURE 4.58** Add Report header.

21. You will be able to find the file as it will show up with a red icon identifying it as a replicator file (see Figure 4.59).
22. You should also print and keep the report with your other report files. This report that is generated by Replicator is a part of the case file (see Figure 4.60).
23. Make sure to remember where the file is, as we will open it in the next set of steps.

Replicator is an extremely easy program to use that allows the investigator/operator a set of tools to create or wipe the digital media files. Every investigator/operator will need these tools to be able to accomplish the replication and wiping tasks.

Processing the suspect image using P2 Commander

P2 Commander can open all known forensic image formats. The steps below will allow you to open any image file including the raw image file that was just created. You can download the demo file from the Paraben Site at http://www.paraben.com/programs/demo.html. Remember, we are conducting digital triage forensics, so we are not going to process the entire image file immediately. If you have time after doing the DTF analysis, you can continue to process the image file, as P2 Commander has full-featured

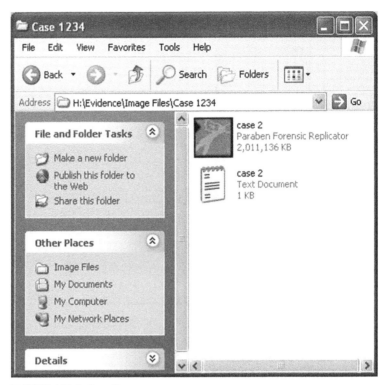

■ **FIGURE 4.59** Replicator file.

digital forensic capability. Initially, we are going to use the automatic wizards to categorize the data on the drive into containers that will allow us to quickly find actionable intelligence or to identify digital media of importance. We are using the stock help files provided in P2 Commander to describe the initial analysis of the image file for the purposes of this tutorial. Modifications have been made to meet the DTF process. Follow the steps below to begin the DTF process using P2 Commander:

1. Find the icon on the desktop for P2 Commander (see Figure 4.61).
2. Double click on the P2 Commander icon.
3. The P2 Commander application will launch.
4. When the program opens, you will have the option to open a case or create a new case (see Figure 4.62).
5. Select > Create a New Case (see Figure 4.63).
6. The New Case wizard will appear.
7. On the Case Properties tab, enter the case name. Make sure to use alphanumeric characters; do not use any special characters in the file name or the folder name. The case name field is a required field (see Figure 4.64).

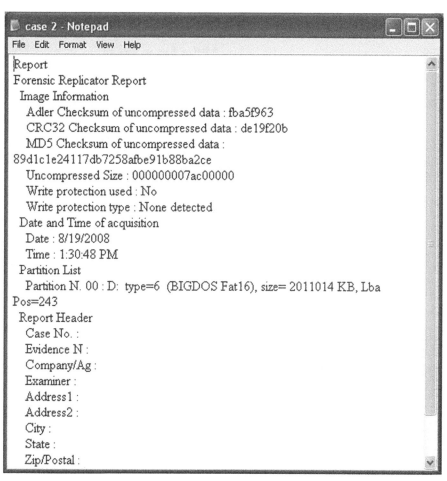

Report
Forensic Replicator Report
 Image Information
   Adler Checksum of uncompressed data : fba5f963
   CRC32 Checksum of uncompressed data : de19f20b
   MD5 Checksum of uncompressed data :
89d1c1e24117db7258afbe91b88ba2ce
   Uncompressed Size : 000000007ac00000
   Write protection used : No
   Write protection type : None detected
 Date and Time of acquisition
 Date : 8/19/2008
 Time : 1:30:48 PM
 Partition List
 Partition N. 00 : D: type=6 (BIGDOS Fat16), size= 2011014 KB, Lba
Pos=243
 Report Header
  Case No. :
  Evidence N :
  Company/Ag :
  Examiner :
  Address1 :
  Address2 :
  City :
  State :
  Zip/Postal :

■ **FIGURE 4.60** After replication report.

8. Uncheck the image analyzer, as we are not going to be using the image
analyzer; this will also help speed up the program.

9. Select the Additional Information tab, enter the investigator
information on it, and click on the Finish button. *Note*: Once the
entered information is saved, it will appear in a drop-down list for
future cases (see Figure 4.65).

■ **FIGURE 4.61** P2 Commander icon.

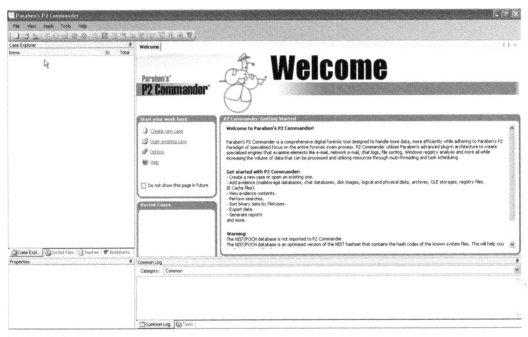

■ **FIGURE 4.62** P2 Open screen.

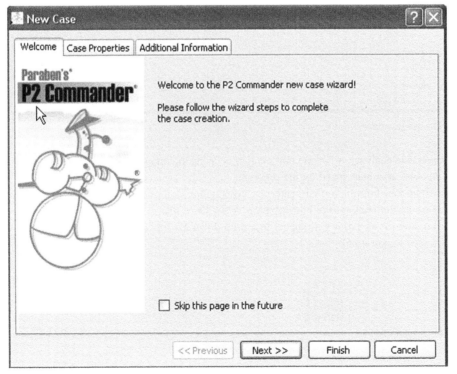

■ **FIGURE 4.63** New Case wizard.

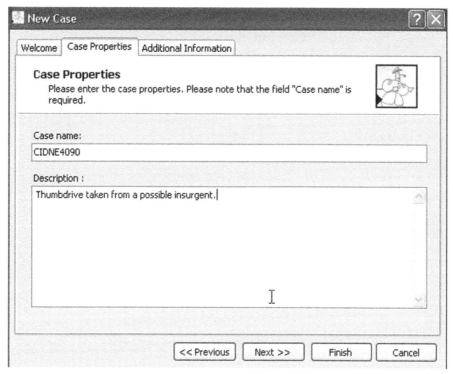

■ FIGURE 4.64 Case properties.

10. Select the folder in which the case will be stored.
11. The new case is created. The "Add New Evidence" wizard opens.
12. If the Add New Evidence wizard does not open. Select > File-Add Evidence or click on the Add New Evidence quick tool button or press CTRL+A or right-click on the case and select Add New Evidence in the context menu.
13. The Add New Evidence wizard opens (see Figure 4.66).
14. Select the image file category in the source type list (we can use any of the other categories depending on what it is we are trying to capture) (see Figure 4.67).
15. Click on the Autodetect option in the right pane.
16. Browse to the location where the image file is located (this is the file you created using the replicator application earlier).
17. A dialogue box will open to enter the evidence name. This name is used to identify the image file in the Case Explorer (see Figure 4.68).

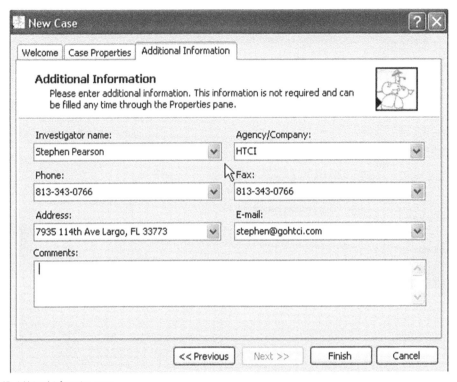

■ **FIGURE 4.65** Additional information screen.

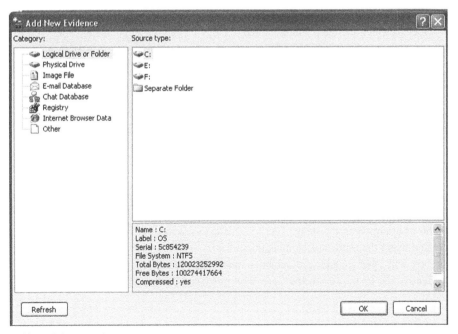

■ **FIGURE 4.66** Add New Evidence wizard.

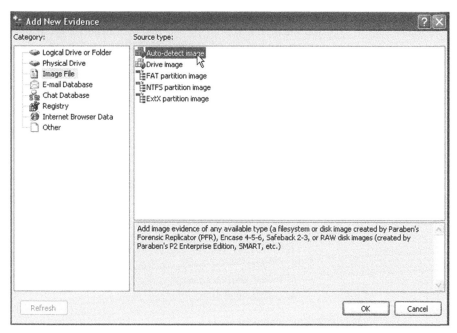

■ **FIGURE 4.67** Image File category.

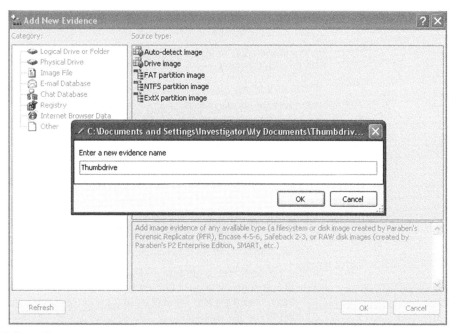

■ **FIGURE 4.68** Enter evidence name.

18. Click OK, and the image will be added to the Case Explorer.
19. We need to sort all the data into the categories we talked about earlier. P2 Commander's wizard will sort the data into 15 categories:
    a. Documents
    b. E-mail
    c. Chats
    d. Spreadsheets
    e. Graphics
    f. Databases
    g. Executable
    h. Compressed
    i. Multimedia
    j. Text
    k. XML
    l. Encrypted
    m. Others
    n. Image analyzer results
    o. Unallocated files

IMAGE ANALYZER

We do not use image analyzer for digital triage forensics. It is a very useful feature, so I want to cover it in this sidebar. Parabens's definition and use of the image analyzer follows:

The image analyzer feature allows you to find images that potentially include pornography.

This illicit image detector scans all images to determine attributes that indicate the image may be of a pornographic nature. It uses sophisticated, analytical processes consisting of thousands of algorithms. These include 11 different detection methods to provide enough information to reliably distinguish between pornographic and nonpornographic images.

To run the image analyzer, check the "Use Image Analyzer" checkbox on the general options page of the P2 Commander sorting engine wizard.

After sorting, the graphic files will be sorted into three categories in the sorted files pane: Highly Suspect, Suspect, and Low Suspect (these folders are subfolders of the image analyzer results folder).

Note: For large files (larger than 10 MB), image analyzer checks whether there is enough memory to load and analyze them. If there is not enough memory, then these files are skipped and the corresponding information is added to the common log.

You can define the options of the image analyzer on the Image Analyzer options page of the P2 Commander sorting engine.

The following options are available:

Engine sensitivity: The larger the value of the engine sensitivity, the more images will be put in the "Highly suspected" and "Suspected" categories. Keep in mind that increasing the sensitivity will also increase the number of false positives (nonpornographic images placed in the wrong category).

Use file filter: If this checkbox is checked, then only files of the defined size will be checked by the image analyzer.

Use resolution filter: If this checkbox is checked, then only images of the defined size will be checked by the image analyzer.

Note: Files that were not checked by the image analyzer, owing to filtering options or because they are too big, are stored in the graphics folder.

20. Expand the case node by clicking on the + sign next to the case.

21. Expand the node next to Partition Parser.

22. Expand each partition to identify the type of format that each partition is using (see Figure 4.69).

23. Right click on the format name such as FAT or NTFS. From the dropdown menu, choose the sorting command.

24. Repeat the above step until all the containers are sorting. *Note:* As you execute more sorts, the system will process each sort more slowly, as the system is using resources for each sort. It is sometimes better to run one at a time.

25. If there are hash databases attached to the case and the "Calculate MD5" option was selected before sorting, then after sorting you'll be asked to link sorted files to hash databases. Click OK to start linking. *Note:* Linking can be done any time after sorting.

26. Sorted files/folders are marked in blue after refreshing. Sorted and linked files are marked in purple.

27. The results of sorting can be seen in the "Sorted Files" pane. Files are sorted by categories according to their file types. *Caution:* If a folder's contents have changed (data was added to it), you should clear sorting and then sort the folder again to get all its data indexed properly (see Figure 4.70).

28. Now that the sorts are running, you can select the Sorted tab under the "Case Explorer" pane. This will show the categories that data will be placed into. Double click on the graphics category. The sorted

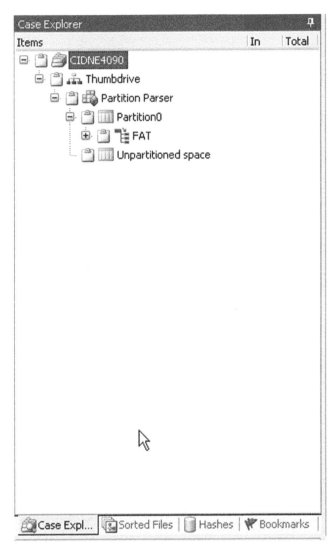

■ **FIGURE 4.69** Partition view.

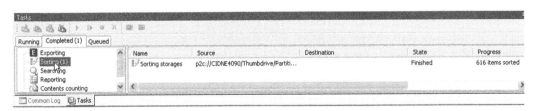

■ **FIGURE 4.70** Sorting pane.

graphics will appear in the left-hand pane within a minute or two. This is not the comprehensive or complete list yet. You will not get the comprehensive list until you have allowed the program to finish sorting. You can immediately, though, begin the process of reviewing the graphics. You will want to press the F5 key every 35-40 s to see the new files found. *Note*: When you press the F5 key, it will take you back to the beginning and refresh the entire listing. Once the sort has been completed, an entry will appear in the completed window of the tasks tab at the bottom of the screen (see Figure 4.71).

29. Now we can move onto bookmarking files that we have found of interest.

Bookmarking found files

When you find a file of interest such as a graphic, multimedia file, or text document, you can save the file or text to a bookmark. This allows the operator to save pointers to the suspect drive, which will allow you to include them later in reports or an export file to an Excel spreadsheet.

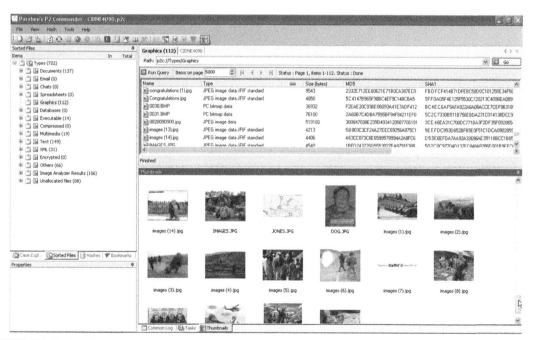

■ **FIGURE 4.71** Sorted graphics screen.

This is the easiest way to remember where you found the evidence on the suspect drive.

To begin bookmarking, select the bookmark tab in the bottom set of tabs under "Case Explorer." You will have no folders in the pane initially. We want to create a couple of folders so that we can further categorize the files we find.

1. Let us create two folders: one called Graphics and one called Multimedia (see Figure 4.72).

■ **FIGURE 4.72** Bookmarks screen.

2. To create the folders, right click in the open area and select New Folder and call the folder "Graphics." Repeat the process and call the folder "multimedia."

3. Now let us look at the case and select some files of interest.

4. Click on the Sorted tab.

5. Select the Graphics tab: all the graphic files will populate the right-hand window.

6. To bookmark files in the graphic pane, right click on the file. A set of choices will appear.

   a. Copy URL: Copies the selected result URL to the clipboard.

   b. Add bookmark: Adds a bookmark pointing to the selected result.

   c. Bookmark search results: Adds a bookmark to the results of the currently finished search.

   d. Navigate to URL: Navigates to the selected results in the Data View pane and Case Explorer pane.

7. Click on Bookmark (see Figure 4.73).

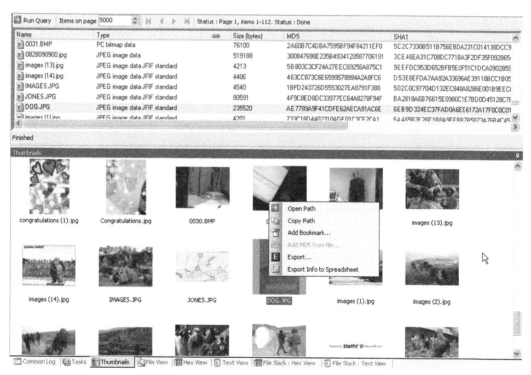

■ **FIGURE 4.73** Bookmark the file.

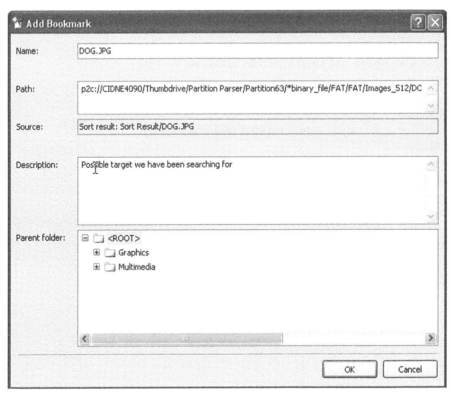

8. Do not select Bookmark Search, as this will bookmark the search not the file. But, we want to bookmark the file.
9. Once you select bookmark, a screen will appear which will allow you to enter a name for the bookmark and select under which folder to save the bookmark (see Figure 4.74).
10. Make sure to add a description for the bookmark that you are about to create.
11. Now select the OK button to save the bookmark.
12. Continue to repeat these steps through the other tabs in the sorted container until all the files that you want bookmarked in the case have been bookmarked.
13. When you save the case, all the bookmarks will be saved as well.

Saving and renaming a case

To save the currently opened case, you can do one of the following:

1. Click on the Save Tooltip in the menu bar.

2. Select File-Save.
3. Press CTRL+S.

To rename the currently opened case, you can proceed as follows:

1. Click on "File-Save As."
2. The standard Windows "Save File As" window will open.
3. Select the location and the new name of the file that will be used to save the file.
4. Click the "Save" button.

Closing the case

1. To close the currently opened case, click File—Close Case or press CTRL+X.
2. The program will ask if you want to save the case if any changes were made since the previous save.

Searching the sorted data

The File Search allows the user to search sorted files using different Boolean search parameters. To perform a file search, proceed as follows:

1. Click on the Search button, which looks like a magnifying glass in the toolbar, or select Tools Search.
2. The search pane opens (see Figure 4.75).
3. Click on the "Browse" button to specify the subfolders of the selected folder in which search will be performed.
4. Enter your keywords to search for in the block for keywords. This will search through the sorted files.
5. Search parameters can be added at this point by clicking on the radio buttons.

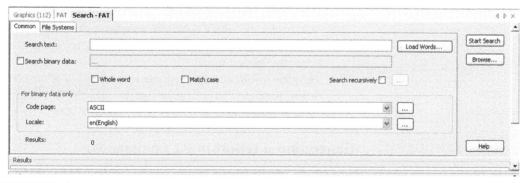

■ **FIGURE 4.75** Search pane.

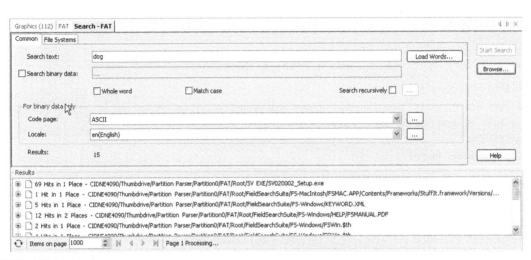

■ **FIGURE 4.76** Search results pane.

6. Click the "Run Query" button. To find all sorted files, leave all fields empty and click on the "Run Query" button.
7. The search starts. Its status is shown in the Tasks pane and can be stopped, paused, and started from there. Please note that the results of the finished searches are saved. They will be stored until the task is removed from the Task Pool.
8. Search results are shown in the bottom part of the search pane (see Figure 4.76).
9. After double clicking on the search result, it will be opened in the data viewer pane and can be viewed.
10. The results area of the search pane has the right-click context menu, which contains the following commands:
    a. Copy URL: copies the selected result URL to the clipboard.
    b. Add bookmark: adds a bookmark pointing to the selected result.
    c. Bookmark search results: adds a bookmark to the results of the currently finished search.
    d. Navigate to URL: navigates to the selected results in the "Data View" pane and "Case Explorer" pane.
    e. Save to XML: saves the results of the search to XML.

Generating a report in P2 Commander

1. Save the case. *Note*: It's highly recommended to sort the data before generating a report (see Figure 4.77).

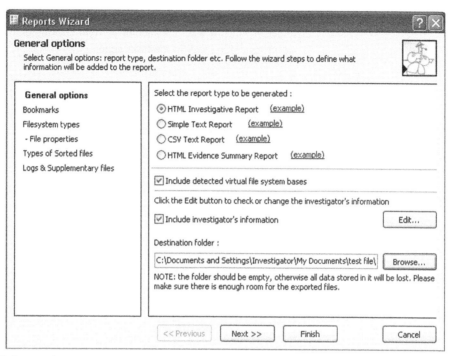

■ FIGURE 4.77 Generating the report.

2. Check the data that you want to add to the report. It can be any of the following:
   a. Evidence or the part of the evidence (it can be selected in the Case Explorer pane or in the Data Viewer pane);
   b. A category of sorted files (it is selected in the Sorted Files pane);
   c. Bookmarks (they are selected in the Bookmarks pane). *Note:* If you want to add all evidence of any type, it's not necessary to check them all (it will be enough to select the corresponding option in the Reports Wizard).
3. Click on the "Generate Report" button or select "File-Generate Report."
4. If the case is not saved, you will be prompted to save it. The report cannot be generated for the unsaved cases.
5. The "Reports wizard" opens.
6. Move between the Reports wizard pages and select the necessary information.
7. When all necessary selections are made, click on the "Finish" button to generate a report.
8. The report's generating process is shown in the Tasks pane.

9. When the report is generated, you can open it either directly from the folder in which it was generated or by right-clicking on the completed report generating task in the tasks pane.

Creating the Comma Separated Value (CSV) output

To generate a CSV file that can be uploaded in many different applications, you will need to generate a CSV report.

1. Click on the "Generate Report" button or select "File-Generate Report."
2. If the case is not saved, you will be prompted to save it. The report cannot be generated for the unsaved cases.
3. The Reports wizard opens.
4. Choose the CSV file output from the Report wizard screen.
5. When all necessary selections are made, click on the Finish button to generate a report.
6. The report generating process is shown in the Tasks pane.
7. When the report is generated, you can open it either directly from the folder in which it was generated or by right-clicking on the completed report generating task in the tasks pane.

Using P2 Commander to gather intelligence/evidence is very straightforward. In four easy steps, the operator can begin to gather actionable intelligence for the battlefield commander. The true power of P2 Commander is its ability to run multiple tasks and queries at one time, providing immediate results. When the operator is done, he/she can generate a CSV report that is usable in any application supporting CSV imports, which is just about every application in the battlefield environment.

SUMMARY

The digital media of the future are going to become more and more complex. The computers of the future will be connected 24 h a day 7 days a week in a cloud computing environment. Investigators/operators are going to be versed in technology that they may never have thought would be an important part of a criminal investigation. A day will come where it will be a requirement to have Internet connectivity to allow the system that you are working on to be able to function. The level of complexity of the social media sites and the growth of the social media sites will dwarf the storage containers that we call standard today. The social world will one day be online in many aspects and the ability to disconnect from it will not be so readily available.

Sadamm Husein said it best in the late 1990s that America's Achilles heel is the technology that we have come to trust in so much. The terrorist of tomorrow will not speak English or Arabic, but they will speak binary and they will come and go at lightning speed. If we are not prepared for this battle, we will lose. Now is the time for the investigator/operator to learn how to gather and collect the intevidence.

This chapter has dealt with the challenges posed in collecting digital media in the battlefield environment. As with investigations conducted in the United States, barriers exist that can make the collection and processing very difficult. The tools and equipment required to process the scene are available to the operator in the field. It will come down to the policies and procedures employed.

Chapter 5

Using the DTF model to collect and process cell phones and SIM cards

The cell phone is quickly becoming one of the most important pieces of evidence found at the battlefield objective. The terrorist or insurgent has found that the flexibility in using the cell phone makes it an invaluable tactical tool. Therefore, it is important to be able to exploit the cell phone quickly and efficiently. With the concept of digital triage forensics (DTF), you will also want to be able to get to the actionable intelligence that resides on the body of the cell phone or the SIM card. This chapter will discuss methods and procedures that will allow you to gather data from a cell phone or SIM card and then apply the DTF processing methods to gather data.

CELLULAR DEVICES ARE REPLACING THE LAPTOP

As we talked about earlier, computer storage is moving away from the fixed system and toward more flexible systems and portable storage. With the growth of the cell phone as a necessary accessory, people have demanded more and more conveniences be combined with it. The cell phone has become a datebook, to-do list, video console, social media connector, and many more things. In the mid-2000s, a camera became a standard installed accessory and an Secure Digital (SD) card was thrown in for extra storage, which then became the standard. People started using the cell phone to take pictures, foregoing the need to buy a camera. The cell phone was then connected to the Internet, and the portal device was born. People saw the convenience of using the cell phone, which they carried every day to store data on. The cell phone was quickly becoming a repository for all types of data. With the invention of portable office tools, such as Microsoft Office for the Windows-based mobile devices and Open Office on the Linux-based devices, the user literally could create and review documents from their cell phones. This drove the industry to maximize the onboard memory of the cell phone. The cell phone capacity quickly increased, offering containers that can store 32 Gig of data (by

Digital Triage Forensics. Doi: 10.1016/B978-1-59749-596-7.00005-X the time this book is published the size of the data container will have grown as it is a never ending process). This much data storage rivals some laptops that one would carry for business.

In the near future, you will see the speed of the cell phone and the storage of containers increase, adding tools and functionality that are equal to the laptop but include full cellular capability. The first of these devices has already been released with the Apple iPad, kindle and cell phones that incorporate projectors or child tracking tools, remote controllers for home accessories, etc. These just-released devices are giving us a glimpse of the things to come. Investigators will need to be ready to exploit and capture data from devices that will become increasingly complex. The portal device is already giving our enemies an increased functionality by providing the capability to connect the cell phone to e-mail, external storage containers, short message service (SMS), and multimedia SMS (MMS) (see Figure 5.1). These tools all allow for the increased collaboration of a group while still maintaining a physical separation. For example, if we conduct all our meetings in a virtual reality room online and never physically get together then the current tracking methods that follows me in the physical world may fail to identify the group.

In Figure 5.1, you see the migration from the standard cell phone (Basic Phone listed to the left) that was used to make phone calls to the portal device (Advanced or Smart Phone listed to the right) that is designed to allow the user of the cell phone the capability to work outside the confines of the cell phone. This portal design provides the investigator with all new

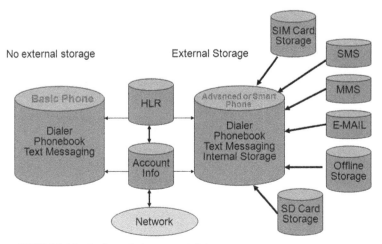

■ **FIGURE 5.1** Migration from cell phone to portal devices.

challenges, as the cell phone may yield less data and the network may yield more data. In the future it is going to be tricky finding the data we need. An example of this would be the Apple iPhone and the Vonage plug-in. If you use the Vonage plug-in to make all your calls, then the call records at your service provider will not show the calls that you made; instead, you will have to go to Vonage to get the records of calls made on the Vonage network. Some cell phones do track information about calls made with voice over Internet protocol (VOIP) applications but not all cell phones track this information. The same process works for Skype or any other VOIP provider. You can see how this one external application could cause problems when investigating the use of the cell phone. As the evidence moves away from being on the body of the cell phone the harder it will become to gather evidence. Custom VOIP applications will provide an even greater threat as we may or may not have the tools that will be able to let us see any residue of VOIP activity. This will become an ever increasing challenge to the investigator.

Like the external applications talked about earlier, the growth of cloud computing gives the cell phone user the ability to connect and run live applications or desktop applications directly from the cell phone itself. The first of these free commercial applications exists now with mesh networks (www.mesh.com). Mesh networks allow the interconnection of all your devices. In other words, you may store data on one device and share it in the cloud through the mesh network (see Figure 5.2) between all your devices.

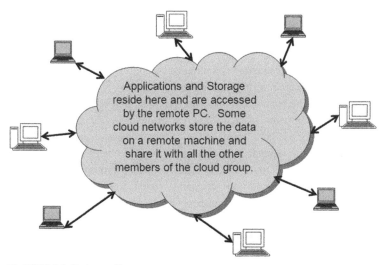

Applications and Storage reside here and are accessed by the remote PC. Some cloud networks store the data on a remote machine and share it with all the other members of the cloud group.

■ **FIGURE 5.2** Cloud networking.

Any device connected to the mesh network then has the ability to share the data. So you can connect your desktop computer, laptop computer, and cell phone all to the same mesh network and share data.

HANDS ON

Mesh Networks

To clear this point, you can try this experiment. Go to www.mesh.com from any Windows-based system. Using Internet Explorer as your browser, create a mesh network account. You will need to have your Windows Live account information, as it uses this ID for the username and password. Once you have an account, connect your desktop to the mesh network and share a folder. Now log in at another computer and redo the steps, but do not create an account; just use the one that you have already created. You should be able to see the desktop with the shared folder. You can also connect all your devices so that you can access remote desktops from your computers and run them as if they were your desktops. It is a very cool application and worth trying. Have fun in the cloud.

The use of cloud computing and cloud applications is going to present the investigator with unique and new challenges that are beyond the scope of this book but will soon need to be addressed in both training and understanding. The enemy is going to be able to use this cloud environment as a way of passing information, laundering money, and evading detection while planning and launching attacks. Cloud computing is a combat multiplier for the enemy.

PROPRIETARY CELL PHONE TOOLS VERSUS NONPROPRIETARY CELL PHONE TOOLS

A lot of new investigators are flooding the cell phone forensic world, from battlefield investigators to patrol officers, all of whom perform limited analysis of cell phones. The growing problem that we see is that the new investigators do not have the background in forensics to make informed decisions. This, combined with a purchasing department that is not well versed in forensic applications, can lead to a very bad purchasing practice. Now, of course, this is not true of everyone, but there are agencies making purchasing decisions based simply on marketing campaigns. Instead of making purchases based on thought-out capabilities matrix, organizations and agencies are buying products based on its name alone. This is a mistake as it leads to complacency with regard to future purchases as organizations are led to believe that this is the only solution when, in fact, many options are available. Organizations need to constantly review the capability matrix to ensure the program or product that they are purchasing still meets their needs and that there is no other product available. We have seen investigators purchase a commercially off-the-shelf system (COTS) only to find that they must change their entire workflow to make the product work for them. This is ridiculous; the COTS solution should be something that can be added on as a force multiplier and flow with the current work flow of the investigator. This is even more important when you are talking about deployed investigators that are in life-threatening situations at the objective or scene.

The one true and solid rule of the cell phone forensic/analysis arena is that there is no one solution that will gather all cell phones and cell phone data. Some cell phone forensic vendors will tell you that their device is the best system and gets the most data, and some will even claim to get all the data from a cell phone, but this is simply not true. Every tool on the market today has its own strengths and weaknesses and must be evaluated and used together to provide a 95% solution. If you review any of the major cell phone forensic/analysis applications, you will find that they all claim to support thousands of cell phones, but a deeper look at the listing of supported phones will yield different results. In Table 5.1 a listing of brands is presented in column 1 with columns 2–9 representing cell phone forensic applications. An example of marketing would be that the cell

Table 5.1 Cell phone comparison matrix

MSRP Kits with Cables	$0.00	$589.00	$1499.00	$1095.00	$2495.00	$3900.00	$7500.00	$12,995.00
Annual Support Fee	N/A	$299.00	$599.00	$220.00	$800.00	$1991.00	$999.00	$850.00
Number of Supported Models		551	Over 1350	Over 2200		Over 570	Over 2000	1819
Windows PC Based	Yes	Yes	Yes	Yes	Yes	Yes	No	Yes
Stand alone device required	No	No	No	No	No	Yes	Yes	Yes
Proprietary Cables	No	No	No	No	No	Yes	Yes	Yes
Acer				10		6	1	2
Alcatel		11				2	7	1
Amoi			5			3	3	1
Apple		2	4	1	1	5	2	2
ASUS		14	23	14		1	3	
AT&T			6			1		
Audiovox	1		2	8	22	4	55	
BenQ			2					2

phone company will say that they support Alcatel cell phones. This technically is correct as you can see in Table 5.1 vendor 2 (column 2) shows that 11 Alcatel phones are supported. But that is 11 Alcatel cell phones out of 89 total cell phones. So the marketing though not incorrect is misleading and the purchaser may buy the device and still not be able to access the specific Alcatel cell phone that they need. The buyer needs to be aware of this prior to purchasing any cell phone forensic product.

In Table 5.2, we show two fictitious companies that provide cell phone software. This chart is representative of what you will actually find when you begin your research into cell phone analysis capabilities. The question we have for you is this: Is Company A any better than Company B? In some things yes and some things no. So you cannot say one is better than the other. Now let us say that you need to get an MMS as a part of your investigation: which company would you go with? The answer would be easy: Company B, as it supports MMS, but now you won't get pictures that are supported by Company A's software. Does this make Company B any better than Company A? Absolutely not: what it means is that each has its own strengths and weaknesses and you as the investigator need to choose tools that support your needs. In the situation above, the real answer is that you need both of the software applications. This will allow you to get 100% of the data available. Don't be fooled by slick names and great marketing; the bottom line is that none of the vendors get all the data. A multiapplication discipline is the only true answer for complete analysis of cell phones. Make sure that you perform a needs assessment of the area that you will be operating in to determine the cell phone applications that will best support your needs.

Ok, so now you are looking at all the applications, and some are way more expensive than others. Does greater cost equate to a better tool? The simple answer is NO. Again, you need to look at your capability needs and optimize the use of available applications compared to your budget and the footprint that the cell phone tools take up. In our research of the products available on the market today, we have found that there is a direct correlation between the cost of a product and its proprietary nature.

Table 5.2 Two ficticious companies that provide cell phone software.

Cell Software Provider	Phone	SMS	MMS	SD Card	Call Logs	Email	Pictures
A	SPH A620	Yes	No	Yes	Yes	No	Yes
B	SPH A620	Yes	Yes	Yes	No	Yes	No

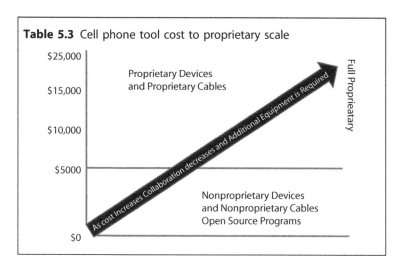

Table 5.3 Cell phone tool cost to proprietary scale

As you can see in Table 5.3, the more you spend, the less you are able to combine applications together. Why is this so important to the investigator in need of cell phone forensic/analysis software? Simple, the investigator needs to maximize the capability and footprint without a corresponding increase in cost.

Let us take a look at a battlefield investigation team or small team unit investigator, for example. The load that the team must carry has to be optimized to keep the team as maneuverable and flexible as possible. If you review the equipment that is already carried by these teams, in almost every case you will find that all of them have a laptop running the Microsoft Windows operating system in their preexisting load. This is perfect, as we can optimize that preexisting laptop device to provide an enhanced capability for the investigator without increasing weight or footprint. Since the devices can all share a single set of cables, there is a reduction in the need to have specialized cables to work with a unique appliance. If you buy the more expensive appliance and application set, you increase the amount of weight and the footprint of the investigator tools while decreasing the interoperability with other applications, as most of the more expensive proprietary devices require proprietary cabling for the devices to work. This can double the amount of cables that would be necessary to exploit cell phones. As we learned earlier none of the cell phone applications can do it all and therefore two or more tools may have to be employed. If I have to carry a device for each of the tools plus their own cables, that dramatically increases my load. Instead I should be able to run multiple tools from one device with a shared set of cables. Now I am increasing my capability without increasing my load.

HANDS ON

Compare Companies Against Your Cell Phone

To bring this to a clear point, you can try this experiment. Take your own cell phone and look it up on the major cell phone forensic software sites and search for your cell phone. See what is being reported as being supported by each vendor for your own cell phone. Now compare the costs of each application to see which one gives you the biggest bang for your budget. You maybe surprised that the less expensive devices actually do more. Even more dramatic is that the freeware may be the best choice.

There is also no guarantee that you will increase the capability by buying the more expensive solution (refer to the National Institute of Standards and Technology (NIST) report over viewing common cell phone applications http://csrc.nist.gov/publications/nistir/nistir-7387.pdf).

So, buying the most expensive as seen in Table 5.4 does not always mean you have the best solution. Proprietary appliances and applications definitely have a place in the cell phone and forensic/analysis world, but not in the small unit or team which makes up the DTF model.

FREEWARE AND SHAREWARE AS CELL PHONE FORENSIC/ANALYSIS TOOLS

So what about the freeware and open source applications that are out there? Great question. There are numerous tools available today that are completely free. So why does the investigator not just use those? The truth is they could, but the use of these tools increases the complexity of capturing data and can make the collection more time intensive. The downside to the free tools then is sometimes you have to work harder to gather the data. A Website that tracks the open source and commercial applications

Table 5.4 Proprietary versus nonproprietary

Nonproprietary Applications with common cables = No increased footprint and weight and increase the interoperability among the applications.

Proprietary Applications with Appliances = Greater cost, footprint and weight with less interoperability among the applications.

is a site called E Evidence http://www.e-evidence.info/cellular.html. This site is a great resource for you to use when building up your capabilities.

Another shift in the open source world is very recent. The military is changing its view of the open source community. In a memorandum dated October 16, 2009, David M. Wennergren who is performing the duties of the ASD(NII)/DoD CIO provided guidelines to be used by the army to employ open source software. This is a radical shift for the military but one that is long overdue. http://oss-institute.org/Govt_OSS_Policy/DoD_2009_OSS.pdf.

The bottom line for open source software is that some of the best cell phone forensic software out on the market is from the open source community. There are tools that work better and bring back much more data than any of the commercial software in the market today. Hold on! Don't start calling your lawyer to tell them we are trying to destroy capitalism: we are not. There is a need for the commercial software and the dedication by the vendor that is normally attached to a commercial product. Open source programs maybe written and then never updated or revised by the programmer again, which is the downfall of the open source community; it can be very fickle. But don't overlook the open source community, as it typically applies the same nonproprietary model that we recommend in the DTF model.

HANDS ON

Find Open Source Applications

On your computer, open your browser and then type in http://www.sourceforge.net. In the search for dialogue box, type in "Cell Phone," "Cellphone," and "SIM Card"; read through the programs that are returned to you. You will find very quickly that there are a lot of applications out there in the Open Source world. Always make sure to give back to the developer if you are going to use the open source programs. Usually the donation amount is minimal.

One example of a freeware tool that has become a standard law-enforcement tool is Bitpim. This program can be found in Sourceforge, which provides links to the Bitpim Web site and also a place to download the latest application files. We would recommend checking the open source sites monthly or quarterly: you may be pleasantly surprised by what you find (make sure to find Bitpim and TULP 2G in sourceforge). Bitpim is software only— you will need the cable to go with the software and the cell phone driver to be able to access the cell phone.

Cross validation is not a nicety; it is a requirement for the investigator. It is the only way that the investigators will ever be sure that they have retrieved all of the data from the cell phone or device that they are searching.

USING CROSS VALIDATION WITH YOUR TOOLS

Cross validation means that we will use two tools to validate the results being gathered from a single device. In other words, if you wanted to validate your forensic tool, such as a hard drive copying tool or a hard drive analysis tool, you would use two similar tools to run exactly the same analysis. After conducting the analysis, you should find exactly the same information from both extractions. This lets you know that the first tool is working correctly and gathering all the reported data. This is the process of cross validation. By doing this, you will know quickly whether your tool is working correctly to gather data. We cannot guarantee that the vendors have not just done a great job of advertising and that the tool actually works. There is a genuine lack of understanding of cross validation in the cell phone collection investigation world. Investigators are all ready to fall on their swords over the results provided by a manufacturer. The saying "you don't know what you don't know" applies directly here. In this book, we will use four different tools: Device Seizure, Deployable Device seizure (DDS), Secure View, and the HTCI SIM Analysis tool to conduct cross validation of a single device. A combination of any of these tools against another will show or support the validity of the other tools' findings. Remember, cell phones are not like hard drives: you can't take the disk head, put it at the beginning of the drive, tell it to copy everything across the drive, and receive a readable report at the end. Instead, the cell phone forensic software has to send commands into the phone to retrieve data from each of the containers it wants data from. Therefore, a cell phone is more like a bunch of paint cans lined up in a row. Every time we want information, we request the appropriate paint can to be opened and extract the data that is in the can. If the command is not sent requesting the data from the paint can, then the data is simply skipped and not gathered. This concept is a big reason why cell phone forensic/analysis applications can produce different results even though they say they support the same cell phones. You should at the this point understand why we recommend having multiple tools in our cellular collection toolbox. We have to be able to verify that what we are collecting is truly the total amount of data available. Thomas Eskridge, the COO of the High Tech Crime Institute provided a prime example of this recently when he was collecting data from a cell phone. The first application pulled 25 pictures from the cell phone. Tom ran a second tool against the cell phone which retrieved 85 pictures from the same cell phone. It was clearly evident that the first tool was not getting all the data from the cell phone. Without running this second tool we would have never seen the 60 pictures that were not gathered. Remember Sourceforge can provide some very nice cost effective tools for you (www.sourcefourge.net).

TRIAGE PROCESSING OF CELLULAR DEVICES

Over the next few sections, we will use the DTF flow charts to perform analysis of cell phones (see Figures 5.3 and 5.4).

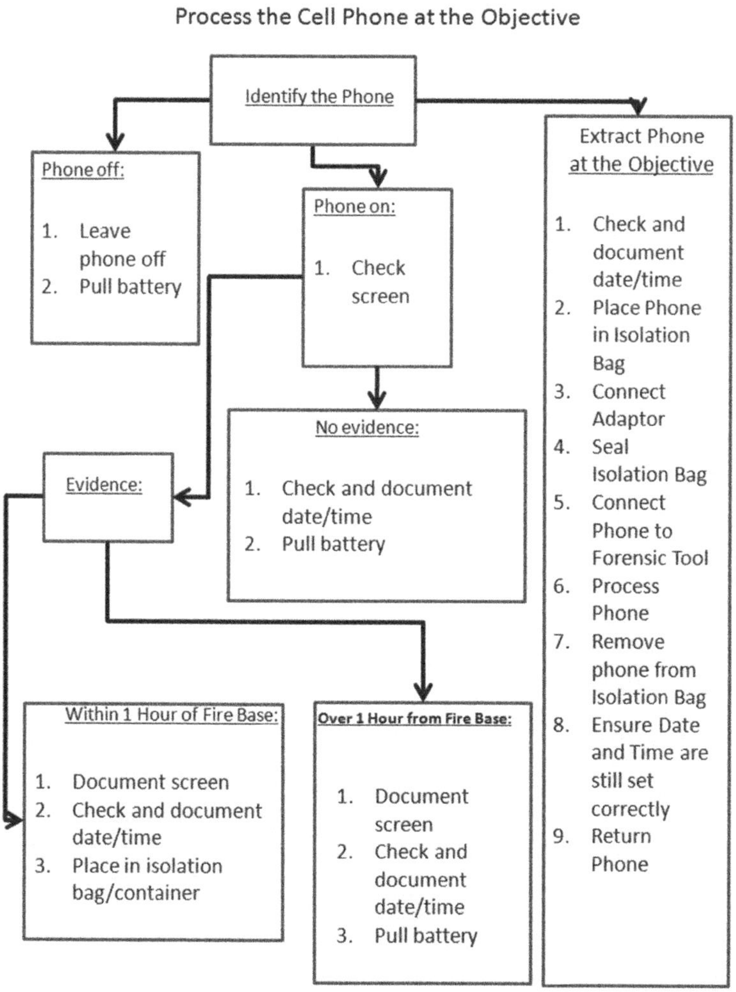

■ **FIGURE 5.3** Objective flowchart.

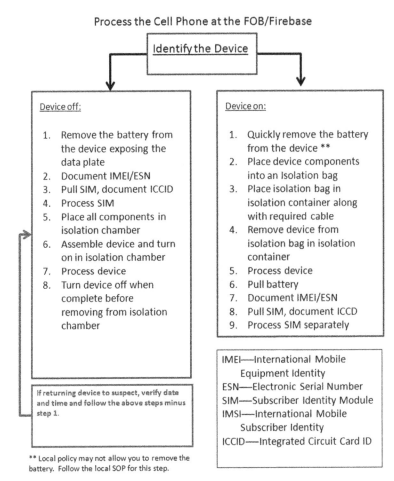

Process the Cell Phone at the FOB/Firebase

Identify the Device

Device off:

1. Remove the battery from the device exposing the data plate
2. Document IMEI/ESN
3. Pull SIM, document ICCID
4. Process SIM
5. Place all components in isolation chamber
6. Assemble device and turn on in isolation chamber
7. Process device
8. Turn device off when complete before removing from isolation chamber

If returning device to suspect, verify date and time and follow the above steps minus step 1.

** Local policy may not allow you to remove the battery. Follow the local SOP for this step.

Device on:

1. Quickly remove the battery from the device **
2. Place device components into an Isolation bag
3. Place isolation bag in isolation container along with required cable
4. Remove device from isolation bag in isolation container
5. Process device
6. Pull battery
7. Document IMEI/ESN
8. Pull SIM, document ICCD
9. Process SIM separately

IMEI—International Mobile Equipment Identity
ESN—Electronic Serial Number
SIM—Subscriber Identity Module
IMSI—International Mobile Subscriber Identity
ICCID—Integrated Circuit Card ID

■ **FIGURE 5.4** FOB or firebase flowchart.

The flowcharts shown in Figures 5.3 and 5.4 are used together to show the proper flow in the DTF collection process. The charts are designed around the process of safety of the investigator first and secondly the time it takes to collect the data. As you will see in the flowcharts that there may be times when small amounts of data are lost using the flowchart, but the safety of the operator will always outweigh the risk of transactional data loss. It is also not a certainty that the data will be lost, but it is a certainty that the operator will be put at risk if the flowcharts are not followed. As new tactics appear in the battlefield arena or new theaters of operations appear, the enemy will begin to use cellular devices with new methods, forcing the change of the collection tactics. There will be a constant cat-and-mouse game played between the investigator and the enemy. The flowcharts above should not be seen as something written in stone but rather as a living, growing document, flexible to the theater and the available technology.

USING THE MFC TO IDENTIFY THE CELLULAR DEVICE

If you have an internet connection, an extremely useful tool that can be used is the Mobile Forensics Central (MFC) Web site http://www.mobileforensicscentral.com/mfc/. The MFC Web site will allow you to conduct an initial review of the specifications of the device to be analyzed. This can be very helpful when trying to figure out what is available to be retrieved from a cell phone.

The MFC is a free site that is operated and maintained by Teel Technologies. The site does not advertise within the MFC to maintain its unbiased stance. The site is completely funded by Teel Technologies. For this incredibly useful site to be maintained into the future, donations are encouraged.

HANDS ON
Alternate Site to MFC
If you cannot connect to the MFC for some reason or if the MFC does not have the cell phone you are searching for, you can try a backup site called "Phone Scoop" at http://www.phonescoop.com. This site does not contain the magnitude of specific information that the MFC provides, but it does have a wealth of information on cell phones. It is certainly a site worth bookmarking.

Once you have typed in the URL for the MFC, a start screen will appear (see Figure 5.5). This start screen will provide some basic information about the MFC and its capabilities. You will find a link to the Telegraph newsletter as well as links to new cell phone analysis technologies (see Figure 5.5).

Look at the top of the start screen and you will find the "Start Here" (new user) or Sign In (already a user). If you are a new member, click on the link "Start Here." If you are an already existing member, select "Sign In." The next screen will allow you to sign in or sign up for the MFC (see Figure 5.6).

If you have an account already, simply fill in your account username and password and select login. If you are new to the site, select the contact form button from the right-hand window which will take you to the next

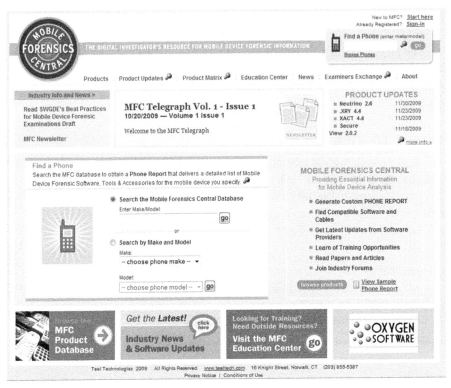

■ **FIGURE 5.5** MFC start screen.

■ **FIGURE 5.6** MFC login and contact form screen.

screen (see Figure 5.6). Fill in all the information requested on the screen. In the description block, put in a note that you saw the site from this book. Select the "Submit" button (see Figure 5.7). You will receive an e-mail with your user information. (If you do not receive the information in 24 h, check your Junk Mail: sometimes it gets sent there.)

Once you have logged in, you will be presented with the cell phone search screen (see Figure 5.8).

Type in the model of the cell phone that you are looking for. In the example, we are using a Samsung SPH-A620 cell phone (see Figure 5.8). You can also use the drop down menu to select the cell phone from the vendor list and choose the make and model of the cell phone your are looking at (see Figure 5.9).

If the cell phone is in the database, a detail screen will appear showing a graphic of the cell phone in the upper left of the screen. If the cell phone is

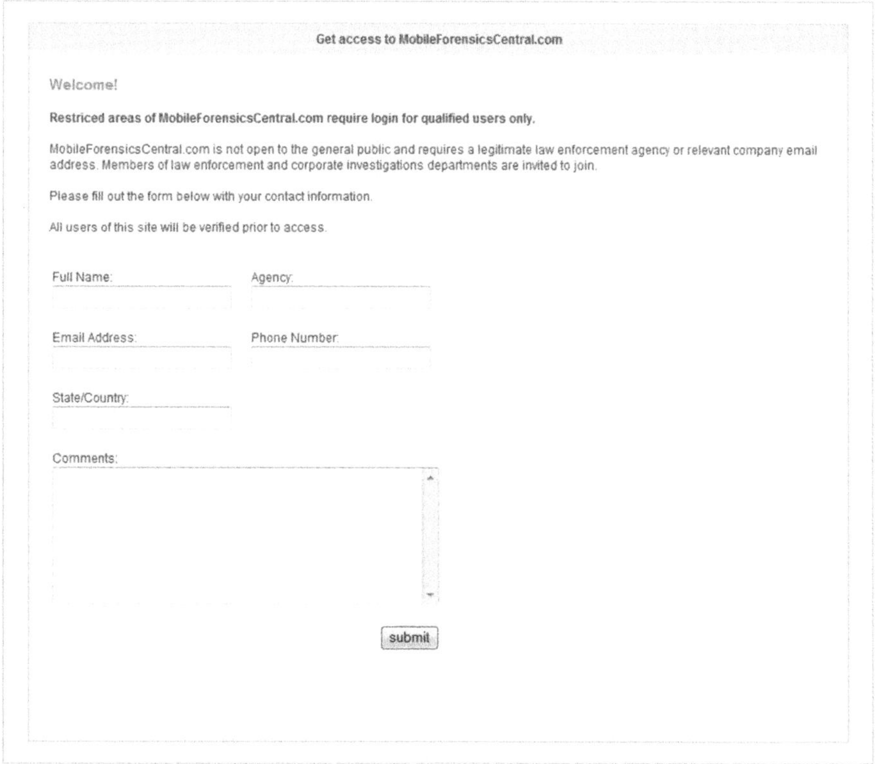

■ **FIGURE 5.7** Contact form.

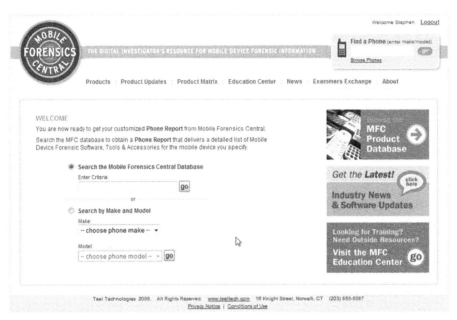

■ **FIGURE 5.8** Cell phone search screen.

■ **FIGURE 5.9** Vendor-identified search screen.

not found, a screen telling you to reneter your search requirement will be presented. After the cell phone has been found, the first screen or first tab page that will be shown is the software screen. If you look at the top of the page you will notice that there are four tabs across the top.

- Software—The software tab is used to identify those cell phone applications that will work with the cell phone. The screen will also tell you what you may be able to gather from the cell phone.
- Tips—The tips screen will identify the iGO tip that can be used to power the device.
- Phone Specs—Detailed phone specifications can be found on this screen. This is one of the most important pages, as it will identify what you can expect to recover from the cell phone that you are trying to perform analysis on.
- Examiners Exchange—The examiners exchange allows examiners to share their experiences when conducting a cell phone analysis. This can be very useful if an investigator finds a unique issue with a specific cell phone acquisition. We encourage you to use this exchange anytime you acquire a cell phone to document your experiences. The more information that is provided by examiners, the better off the community will become.

The software tab will tell you which cell phone forensic tools can be used to gather data from the cell phone (see Figure 5.10).

This is a very important tab, as it can save you literally hundreds of hours of trial and error. The only flaw that we have found with this page is that the results are based on the manufacturer's stated results, which at times have been found to be slightly overrated. For the most part, the results provided are very accurate. Even with this one flaw, this page is still extremely useful and powerful for the investigator.

The Tips tab is used to display the power tips that can be used with the cell phone. The tips are part of the Teel Technology power tips package. If you have Teel technologies tips set, then this page will be very useful in selecting the correct power tip (see Figure 5.11).

For information on the Teel Tips, go to the Teel Technology Web site and order the tips directly.

The Phone Specs tab is designed to show the investigator the details of the cell phone such as how much storage the cell phone has and whether or not the cell phone has a camera, etc. With this information, the investigator will be able to determine the potential amount of evidence that can be gathered from the cell phone. For example, if you wanted to know how

■ **FIGURE 5.10** Software tab.

many contact records the cell phone can potentially hold, you can go to this page and look up the cell phone you are working on. Once the cell phone is displayed, you can click on the phone specs page and review all the data about the cell phone (see Figure 5.12).

This page can save you hours of looking for data that is not there or this page can make you look deeper or try another solution if the results found do not match up.

Last but certainly not least is the Examiners Exchange page. This page when utilized is a direct link to other investigators. The Examiners Exchange page allows investigators to leave remarks or problems that they faced when dealing with a certain cell phone (see Figure 5.13).

Other investigators can then comment back or leave their own experiences. This page, if used correctly, is a great way to help investigators from making mistakes or wasting time trying to connect to a cell phone incorrectly. We would encourage everyone to take advantage of this very unique tool.

■ **FIGURE 5.11** Tips tab.

By putting all of these resources together under one roof, the investigator has a very powerful set of tools. If the community takes advantage of Teel Technology's very hard work, the MFC portal can grow to be a resource that will serve the investigative community for years to come.

Using the MFC to conduct research is a very important part of the cell phone analysis process. You now have the ability to do some research prior to the investigation, which will provide you with valuable information prior to performing the actual acquisition. Over the next few sections, you will see how the use of the MFC is invaluable.

COLLECTION CONCERNS WITH CELLULAR DEVICES

When processing a radio-frequency (RF) device such as a cell phone, the investigator has to be extremely careful. One of the biggest mistakes that can be made by the investigator is that they forget the device is a two-way communication device. So what does this mean to you? Simple, it means

Welcome Stephen. Logout

Find a Phone (enter make/model)

Browse Phones

THE DIGITAL INVESTIGATOR'S RESOURCE FOR MOBILE DEVICE FORENSIC INFORMATION

Products   Product Updates   Product Matrix   Education Center   News   Examiners Exchange   About

Phone Report: Samsung SPH-A620   print

Click the **TABS** below to see support and information for the **Samsung SPH-A620**

Software (8)   Tips (1)   Phone Specs   Examiner's Exchange (1)

Samsung SPH-A620 Phone Specifications and Features:

NETWORKS	AMPS 850 / CDMA 850 / CDMA 1900
OS	(N/A)
MEMORY	?
HARD DRIVE	-
WEIGTH	4.48 oz (127 g)
DIMENSIONS	3.54" x 1.90" x 1.00" (90 x 48 x 25 mm)
FORM FACTOR	Clamshell Stub / Extendable Antenna
BATTERY LIFE	Talk: 2.90 hours (174 minutes) Standby: 168 hours (7 days)
BATTERY TYPE	LiIon
DISPLAY	Type: LCD (Color TFT/TFD) Colors: 65,536 (16-bit) Size: 128 x 160 pixels TFT
BLUETOOTH	-
INFRARED	-
USB SUPPORT	-
PHONE BOOK CAPACITY	300
CALCULATOR	Yes
CALENDAR	Yes
TODOS	up to 20 items
CAMERA	with flash / picture wallet feature

Examiner's Exchange

Analyzed the Samsung SPH-A620?

Read what examiners are saying about the Samsung SPH-A620.

read comments / reviews

Find Another Phone
(enter make/model)

Enter Criteria:

■ **FIGURE 5.12** Phone Specs tab.

that the device can be used against the investigator as easily as the investigator will try to use data against the suspect or target.

Let us talk about cell phone spyware. Go to http://www.google.com and type in "cell phone spyware" as your search. Several pages of results will come back. Take a few minutes and look at the services provided by the paid for and free cell phone spyware. With this spyware application you can use the cell phone to collect the following information:

Tracking—The spyware in conjunction with Google Maps becomes a great resource for tracking, allowing the cell phone to update a map that you can read with any Internet-connected browser.

Silent Ring—The cell phone can be set not to ring, but immediately turn on the microphone allowing you to listen to all of the conversations in the immediate area. Think of all the conversations that you have behind closed doors or riding back in your vehicle that would be very useful to the enemy.

■ **FIGURE 5.13** Examiners exchange.

Visual Tracking—The cell phone can have the camera function turned on, streaming a constant video of your ongoing activities.

SMS Message Tracking—If the cell phone is used to send any text messages as the person that installed the spyware, you would get a copy of the text message on your computer by e-mail or instant messenger depending on the chosen spyware application. Just these reasons alone should be enough to make the operator want to maximize the protection afforded by isolating the RF signal.

For example, an iPhone that has spyware properly emplaced on it can be used as a remote camera to follow an individual wherever he/she goes; it can be used as a listening device so that someone can call the phone without the phone making any noise; turn the speakerphone on, and allow the person on the other iPhone to listen to your entire conversation without you knowing that your phone is on; and the phone can also be tracked by GPS on Google maps providing approximately a 5-min delay in your location, which can be extremely dangerous to the investigator performing operations in theaters outside of the United States. For example, someone could place spyware onto the cell phone that you're collecting and you don't perform the isolation steps and the insurgent follows the operator back to the forward operating base tracking the trail of the operator the entire time. This can then used as a tool for setting up insurgent ambushes on the operator in the future as they are familiar with the track the operator takes back to the FOB. Using the GPS would allow the insurgents to know exactly where the cell phone was being analyzed by the investigator, which could be extremely useful in setting up some type of attack.

So how do you prevent Spyware from being used against you and protect the cell phone from the network? Simple, apply the isolation procedures that we will be talking about to prevent the manipulation of the device and to prevent the cell phone from being able to participate on the network.

DON'T PUSH THAT BUTTON

Let us look at the average person who picks up a cell phone. What does the average person do? Their first tendency is to start pushing buttons, looking for something! I think if you asked them what they were looking for, they probably would tell you that they do not know what it is they are looking for; they are just being curious. And we all know what happened to the curious cat. In a normal situation this is not a problem, as you probably don't care if you lose data or corrupt the container. In a situation where you're collecting cell phones as evidence or intelligence, this can be extremely destructive for the investigator. A very simple tactical training plan (TTP) that could be employed by an insurgent would be to set up a dummy or decoy phone for an investigator to collect. Knowing that when the investigator collects the cell phone and by there known procedures turns off the cell phone, I could key remap the power off button to perform a quick dial function. Why not use this against the investigator? Here a snippet from http://reviews.cnet.com/cell-phones/samsung-gravity-sgh-t459/4505-6454_7-33399109.html "You can remap the messaging key to point to the inbox, the instant-messaging application, or a new e-mail as well." If someone can remap the key to the inbox, how about remapping it to speed-dial a phone number as stated above. This number would be connected to the phone number that is setup on the secondary improvised explosive device (IED) set to explode under your feet. Someone could, in effect, let you blow yourself up.

ISOLATING THE CELLULAR DEVICE

Currently, three methods exist that will allow the operator to accomplish the safe collection of the cell phone.

Method 1—Don't push any buttons and provide a wave bubble (http://www.ladyada.net/make/wavebubble) or electronic countermeasure (ECM) shield that can isolate the cell phone by producing an RF bubble area around the cell phone which will prevent RF communication. The problem with this method is that you will be limited to the length of time that the ECM or wave bubble can be employed for. As soon as the ECM or wave bubble is turned off, the cell phone will begin to communicate with the network.

Method 2—Don't push any buttons and place the phone immediately into a Faraday bag or isolation bag. The isolation bag will prevent the cell phone from being able to communicate with the network, thereby providing local isolation. Two problems have been identified when using the isolation bag.

First, if there are any tears or breaks in the bag, it will not be able to prevent the device from communicating with the network. Newer, more powerful phones may still be able to communicate even though the cell phone is properly sealed in the isolation bag.

Second, when the cell phone is placed into the Faraday or isolation bag, the cell phone immediately begins to increase its transmitter power, attempting to communicate with a tower. This will cause a more rapid drain of the battery, and if the battery is low, will shut the cell phone down. If you have undocumented evidence on the screen, it will be lost when this happens. The call logs may also be lost when the battery depletes.

Method 3—Don't push any buttons and remove the battery from the back of the cell phone then place the cell phone in an isolation bag. Unfortunately, when you pull the battery from the back of the cell phone, you may lose some transactional data that has not been written to the flash memory of the cell phone such as the last numbers called or received. This loss of data has been noted on most phones but not all phones. Some phones still write the data to the flash memory due to the way they process transactional data swaps. The investigator must weigh the safety of his team with the need to gather intelligence. If the investigator is looking for photographic evidence or text messages on the cell phone, as we do in the DTF model, then the last numbers dialed may not be as important and safety would dictate removing the battery from the cell phone.

The investigator in the field will have to make this decision whenever collecting cell phones using the DTF model.

The only time that the cell phone should not have the battery removed is if evidence appears on the screen that has not been recorded or sent, such as a composed text message. In this instance, the message can be collected by transcription or a photograph, and then the battery can be removed.

Using Method 3 is the safest method for gathering the cell phone from the objective for the operator. It is also the only proven method that ensures that the cell phone cannot communicate with the cell network.

USING THE HTCI ISOLATION CHAMBER

In the previous sections, we talked about the need for isolating cell phones and that the investigator should not push the buttons on the cell phone as they could potentially lead to disastrous results. We also talked about three methods for protecting the cell phone to prevent the operator from becoming a victim or for allowing the evidence to become corrupted. As with all the processes in the DTF model, the best method will depend on the circumstances that the investigators find themselves in.

No matter which method is used the cell phone is returned to the forward operating base (FOB) in a Faraday or isolation bag. This should be a requirement for the protection of the evidence and the operator. If the cell phone is not properly protected, you may want to think twice before analyzing the cell phone. While the cell phone is in the isolation bag the cell phone is protected. Remember the cell phone cannot be removed from the isolation bag without exposing it to the possibility of connecting to the network. To ensure the cell phone cannot connect to the network we will use the HTCI isolation chamber to continue the Faraday process. But the isolation chamber will allow us to connect the cell phone to our cell phone analysis software while maintaining the isolation of the cell phone.

Advantages of the HTCI isolation chamber are

- Light weight design
- Does not require power
- User friendly
- Inexpensive
- Rugged construction
- Combat-theater tested

The HTCI isolation chamber is made for HTCI by the Ramsey Corporation, a long-time RF isolation company. The isolation chamber can be reviewed and purchased from http://www.forensicstore.com/product_p/htci-sb-01.htm.

The HTCI isolation chamber is made up of five significant components (see Figure 5.14):

- Lid
- View screen
- Bottom container
- Faraday glove inserts
- RF-shielded USB ports

The isolation chamber includes its own power source internal to the chamber and its own light source internal to the chamber provided by an LED bar just below the view screen. A more advanced version of the isolation chamber incorporates a video camera directly into the lid of the chamber that allows the user to be able to videotape and record the complete analysis inside the chamber.

SUGGESTED ADD ON

Add a stylus to the Isolation Chamber

While using the isolation chamber, you will run into situations where a small piece will need to be opened or the SIM card will need to be removed. This is very difficult with the large gloved hands. To help with this, you can place a hard stylus into the chamber, which will allow you manipulate the items in the chamber. A stylus with a rubber end is preferred as it grabs a little better.

■ **FIGURE 5.14** HTCI isolation chamber.

To use the isolation chamber, the investigator can follow these simple steps:

1. Place the isolation chamber on a flat surface large enough to hold the isolation chamber.
2. Unlatch the two latches on the front lid of the isolation chamber (see Figure 5.15). The isolation chamber automatically lifts up with the compressed air shocks inside the isolation chamber.
3. Once this is done, the internal container is exposed, allowing the investigator to be able to place the Faraday or isolation bag with the evidence cell phone into the lower container (see Figure 5.16).
4. Place the isolation bag into the isolation chamber (see Figure 5.17).
5. Find the cable that will be used to acquire the cell phone in your cell phone analysis kit. Place the cable into the isolation chamber.
   Note: When the cell phone first arrives, it will be in a Faraday bag and you may not be able to identify the cell phone. To remedy this problem, insert the cell phone into the isolation chamber following the steps outlined. Remove the cell phone from the Faraday bag. You should now be able to identify the cell phone. Find the cable in your cell phone kit, place the cell phone back into the Faraday bag, and make sure it is sealed. Now, open the isolation chamber and insert the cable.
6. Connect the male USB end of the cable into the female USB connector inside the lower container of the isolation chamber.
7. (Optional) Plug the charger for the cell phone into the power strip of the isolation chamber.

■ **FIGURE 5.15** Two latches on the lid.

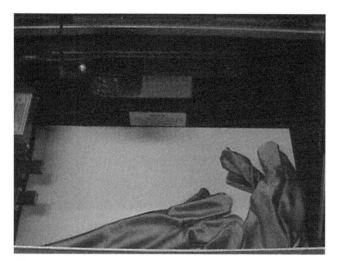

■ **FIGURE 5.16** Internal chamber.

■ **FIGURE 5.17** Internal container with isolation bag, cable, SIM card reader, and SIM card evidence holder.

8. To process a SIM card, place the SIM card reader into the isolation chamber.

9. Place the SIM card evidence holder into the isolation chamber.

10. Do not remove the phone from the Faraday or isolation bag at this time.

11. Plug the isolation chamber into a power source so that the internal power strip and lights will work.

12. Turn the lights on in the isolation chamber by using the small switch on the LED bar directly below the view screen (see Figure 5.18).
13. Once all the components have been placed carefully into the isolation chamber and the lights turned on, simply close the lid.
14. Verify the seal around the lid of the isolation chamber.
15. Once the lid is sealed, latch the two front latches by securing the lid to the top of the isolation chamber (see Figure 5.19).
16. The isolation chamber is sealed and ready to be used to process the cellular evidence inside.

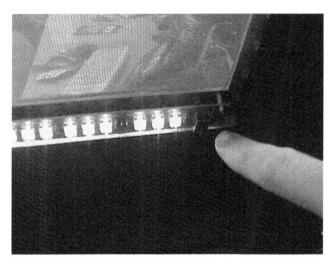

■ **FIGURE 5.18** Turning the lights on in the isolation chamber.

■ **FIGURE 5.19** Close and seal the lid.

17. Take the gloves that come with the isolation chamber and put them on. Never place your hands directly into the isolation chamber's Faraday gloves, as the oils from your fingers can damage the gloves.

18. With the plastic gloves on your hands, place your hands into the Faraday gloves. You are now able to manipulate the items inside of the isolation chamber (see Figure 5.20).

19. With your hands in the Faraday gloves, you can now open the isolation bag containing the cell phone. The cell phone may or may not come with the battery attached to the back of the phone (see Figure 5.21).

■ **FIGURE 5.20** Cover your hands with gloves.

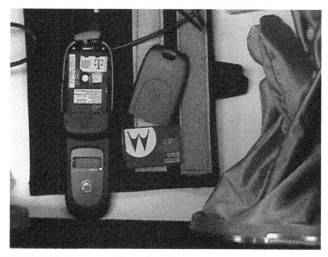

■ **FIGURE 5.21** Cell phone removed from isolation bag.

If the battery is not on the back of the phone, we will take this opportunity to document the data plate on the back of the phone.

20. The data plate will provide us with our initial information to start the DTF analysis (see Figure 5.22). The information that we would like to gather is as follows:

   a. Electronic serial number (ESN) on CDMA cell phones;
   b. International mobile equipment identifier (IMEI) on GSM cell phones;
   c. Integrated circuit card identification (ICCID) from the installed SIM card. You may need to pull the SIM card out to view the numbers (see Figure 5.23). Make sure to place the SIM card back into place after documenting the SIM card;
   d. Any additional numbers on the data plate such as Model number or serial number.

21. Hold the cell phone as close as possible to the view screen in the lid of the container.

22. Document the numbers listed above. Transcribe the numbers or take a photo through the view screen.

23. At this point, place the battery back onto the cell phone. If the battery was left on the cell phone, you will be able to get the data off of the phone after the analysis (see Figure 5.24).

24. With the phone battery connected, take the end of the data cable that you placed in the isolation chamber previously and connect it to the cell phone.

■ **FIGURE 5.22** Cell phone GSM data plate.

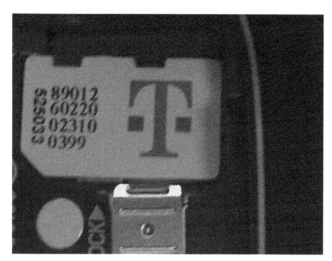

■ **FIGURE 5.23** ICCID on the SIM card.

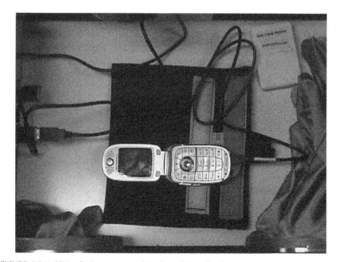

■ **FIGURE 5.24** GSM cell phone connected to the isolation chamber.

25. Ensure that the data cable is still connected to the USB connector inside of the isolation chamber.
26. Once you have done this, the phone may require you to turn the phone on at this point (see Figure 5.25).
27. Once the cell phone has been turned on, the cell phone may require you to manipulate the settings to allow the cell phone to be connected by USB. The cell phone may also need to wait until after the isolation

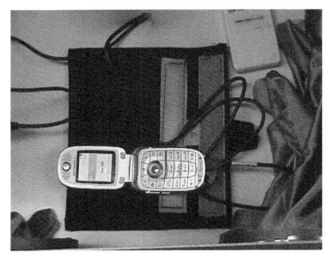

■ **FIGURE 5.25** Cell phone turned on.

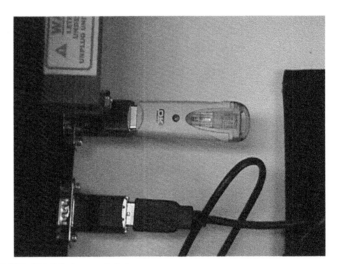

■ **FIGURE 5.26** Cell phone manipulation.

chamber has been connected to the electronic discovery analysis system (EDAS) (see Figure 5.26).

28. Make the necessary changes to the cell phone.

29. Plug the USB connecting cable connector to the isolation chamber's outside USB connector (see Figure 5.27). Make sure to connect the cable to the connector that corresponds with the connector on the inside of the chamber (see Figure 5.26).

■ **FIGURE 5.27** Connect to the external connector.

■ **FIGURE 5.28** Connect to the EDAS.

30. Connect the other end of the USB connecting cable connector into your EDAS (see Figure 5.28).
31. The EDAS's new hardware wizard will activate and load the drivers for the specific cell phone or SIM card reader that you placed into the isolation chamber.
32. Once the appropriate drivers have been installed and the new hardware has been recognized, you can run any cell phone analysis software on the EDAS to gather the data from the cell phone or SIM card.

33. To connect the SIM card reader to the isolation chamber, first place the SIM card you wish to perform analysis on into the SIM card reader (see Figure 5.29).

34. Plug the USB reader into the second USB connector in the isolation chamber (see Figure 5.30).

35. Plug the USB cable connector to the isolation chamber's outside USB connector. Make sure to connect the cable to the connector that corresponds to the connector on the inside of the chamber.

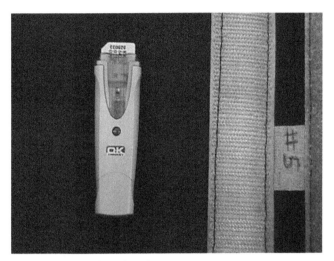

■ **FIGURE 5.29** Insert SIM card into the reader.

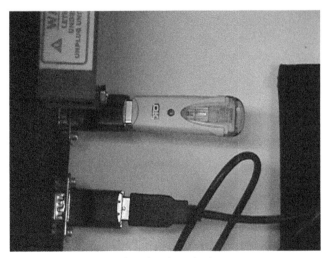

■ **FIGURE 5.30** Connect SIM card reader to the isolation chamber.

36. Connect the other end of the USB cable connector into your EDAS.

37. The EDAS's new hardware wizard will activate and load the drivers for the specific SIM card reader that you connected in the isolation chamber.

38. To disconnect the isolation chamber, remove the USB connecting cable from the EDAS.

39. Once you have disconnected the isolation chamber from the EDAS, you can then disconnect the cell phone or the SIM card reader from the cable or USB inside of the isolation chamber. Remove the battery from the back of the cell phone.

40. (Optional) If you did not collect the data plate information in the previous steps, you can now collect this information as described above.

41. Place the cell phone back into the isolation bag.

42. The SIM card should be removed from the SIM Card reader and placed into the evidence container that you placed in the isolation chamber earlier in these instructions (see Figure 5.31).

43. Once the isolation bag has been sealed inside the isolation chamber, it is safe to unlatch the lid and extract the cell phone or SIM card from the chamber.

Using the isolation chamber, you were able to process the cell phone and SIM card. At the same time, you were able to also protect the evidence and keep it as pristine as possible by not allowing the cell phone to be connected to any outside network or persons. If you do not use the

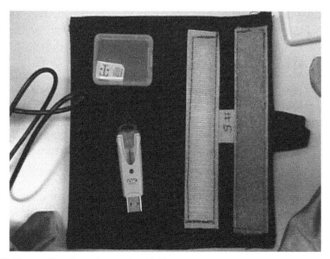

■ **FIGURE 5.31** Place SIM card into evidence holder.

isolation chamber, you must employ some other mechanism to keep the cell phone isolated, as this is critically important to ensure the credibility of the evidence. The worst thing that can happen to an investigator performing an analysis of a cell phone is for the phone to begin receiving more e-mail messages, text messages, or phone calls, or the device be wiped by an external agent. If any of these were to happen, it could be disastrous to your investigation. Using the HTCI isolation chamber, you can prevent these risks from happening during the analysis.

PROCESSING THE CELL PHONE

When the cell phone is brought back from the objective, it will be in an isolation bag, as was discussed earlier. The isolation bag is placed into the HTCI isolation chamber, and the chamber is sealed following the instructions given in the HTCI isolation chamber instructions. You will now remove the cell phone from the isolation bag within the isolation chamber. The cell phone should have the battery already removed from the back of the cell phone (if it does not, leave the battery on the back of the cell phone).

If the battery is off the cell phone, hold the cell phone close to the view screen of the isolation chamber so you can read and document the numbers that are on the data plate of the phone. Make sure to annotate or take a good digital photo of the data plate through the view screen window. The most important information to gather from the data plate is the following:

- ESN—Electronic serial number (CDMA or Hybrid cell phones only)
- IMEI—International mobile equipment identifier (found on GSM cell phones or hybrid cell phones
- ICCID—Integrated circuit card identification (found on the SIM card in GSM cell phones)

Once the battery has been placed back on the cell phone, you will not be able to read the data plate. It is important to gather these numbers as you will want to verify the information on the data plate with the information in the cell phone to ensure the cell phone has not been modified. You can also get this information after the cell phone has been analyzed and prior to it being put back into the isolation bag in the isolation chamber.

After collecting the information from the data plate, reconnect the battery back onto the cell phone (make sure not to disturb the possible fingerprints on the back of the battery) and connect the cell phone to the internal compartment connector of the isolation chamber. Once the cell phone is connected, you can now connect the isolation chamber to your EDAS laptop. Once you've connected your cell phone to the EDAS laptop, a new hardware Wizard should appear. If the drivers are installed correctly for the cell phone you are trying to acquire, the New Hardware wizard will state that new hardware has been found and that the drivers have been installed correctly. If the new hardware is not installed correctly, you need to verify that you have the correct drivers for the cell phone that you are trying to acquire and that the cell phone forensic software supports the cell phone to be analyzed. Once the drivers are installed correctly, you are ready to begin the acquisition and analysis of the cell phone.

Conducting the cell phone acquisition using device seizure

Device Seizure is a tool that will show the capability of user deep search analytics capability. Device Seizure allows the investigator to conduct a complete analysis of the data that is retrieved from cell phones. This is the first of four tools that will show the different types of data collection and analysis. You will see a common thread throughout all of the applications, as they all acquire data in the same way. It is the post analytics that will differentiate the software applications.

Before attempting to follow these instructions, download a demo copy of the latest Device Seizure application from the Paraben corporation Web site at http://www.paraben.com/programs/demo.html. (You can use the sample case provided with this book.) Follow the instructions to install the program. If you have problems installing the application, contact the Paraben Corporation for support.

After installing the application, you will have a new icon on your desktop (see Figure 5.32).

Find this icon. If you do not have this icon, then do the following:

Left click Start in the lower left-hand corner of the desktop.

1. Select All Programs
2. Select Paraben
3. Select Device Seizure

This will launch the Device Seizure application. Once the program has loaded, you will have a blank Device Seizure desktop.

■ **FIGURE 5.32** Device Seizure desktop icon.

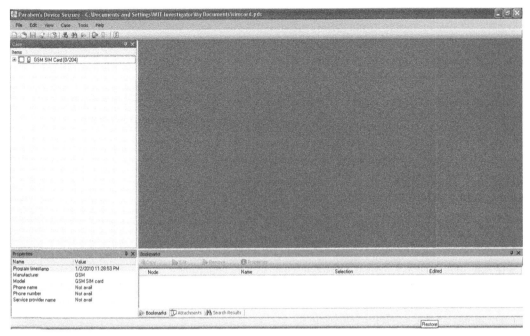

■ **FIGURE 5.33** Device Seizure desktop.

The default desktop for the application is made up of four panes (see Figure 5.33).

- Upper left pane is the case information pane.
- Upper right pane shows detailed information of whatever is selected in any of the other panes.
- Bottom left pane shows information about the cell phone or SIM card initially. This pane will also show details of items selected in the upper right pane.
- Bottom right pane will show the Bookmarks tab, Activities tab, or tasks that are performed by Device Seizure.

Utilizing these four panes, the first responder will be able to complete the full analysis of a cell phone or SIM card.

Creating the case

The following steps will take you through the steps to acquire the data from the cell phone.

If this is the first time you are using the application, you will have a quick-start screen shown in the upper right window. You will need to create a

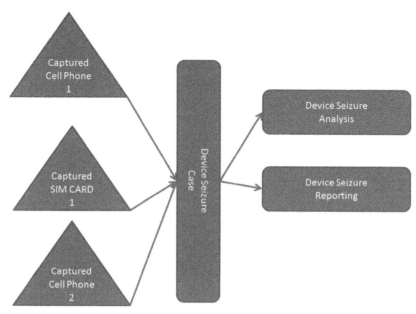

■ **FIGURE 5.34** Case topology.

new case prior to collecting the cell phone. Device Seizure uses the one to many principal when creating cases (see Figure 5.34).

In other words, you will create one case with many devices that relate to that case, all viewable from the case screen. This, for the investigator, is nice, as it allows him/her to keep all relative data involved in a case in one place. So let us begin.

1. From the quick start menu, select create New Case, or from the toolbar select File then New (see Figure 5.35).
2. A dialog box will appear; choose where you wish to save your case. Remember, the case should be saved to your external evidence drive. We do not ever want to save evidence to the local computer, as that will contaminate the hard drive that you will be using to process all of your other cases on.
   a. Give your case a file name; the file name will be in whatever format your unit organization has chosen. In Iraq you may be required to use the CIDNE number for the file name. Once you've entered the filename, select (Save).
3. Information about the case screen (see Figure 5.36).
   a. Enter the case number, which again may be your CIDNE number.
   b. The property and evidence number should be taken from your evidence bag if you are using numbered evidence bags.

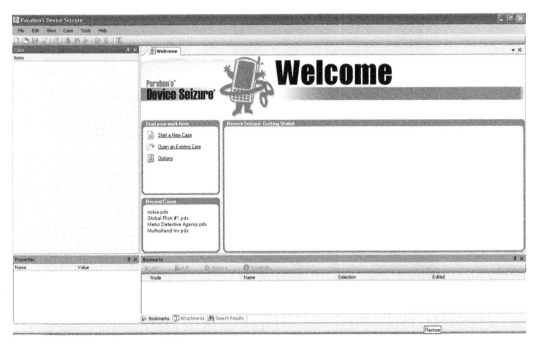

■ **FIGURE 5.35** Create the case.

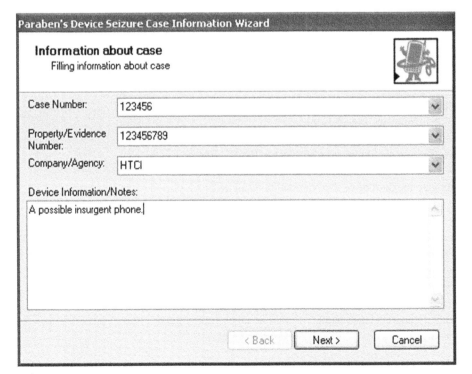

■ **FIGURE 5.36** Information case screen.

   c. Company or Agency should be a unit descriptor such as WIT Team 1.

   d. Notes field. It is always good to put in some descriptive information as to why you are creating this case. This can help you out later on when you come back and have to open the case for further investigation and don't quite remember exactly what you were looking for in this case (as you conduct cases they will start to blend together). This information can also help another investigator who has to assume your case to finish your case.

4. Once you've entered in all the information, select (Next).

5. Information about the Examiner screen is next. Here you will enter your information (see Figure 5.37).

   a. Name—Your name

   b. Address—Best address possible to the FOB

   c. Address1

   d. Country—Where are you

   e. State—If applicable

   f. Zip—If applicable

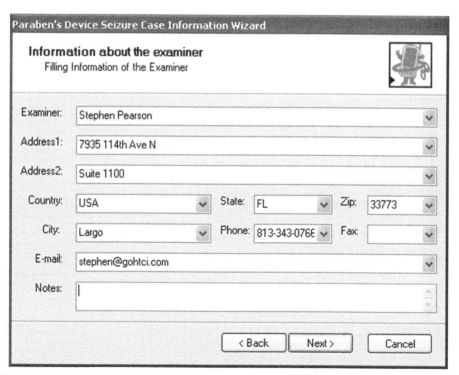

■ **FIGURE 5.37** Examiner information screen.

    g. City—Location of the FOB

    h. Phone—A contact number to you

    i. Fax—A place to FAX questions

    j. E-mail—You contact e-mail at the FOB

    Note: This information is used to contact you after this case has been sent to the next higher echelon such as the S2 or a prosecutor. This information will also be used to identify the actual examiner if this evidence should go to court.

6. Once the information has been entered, select (Next).

7. Summary of your Selection Screen will show you all the information you have entered up to this point. If there is any information in the screen that is not correct, simply press (Back) until you see the screen that has the information you wish to change. If there are no problems with the information that has been entered, simply select (Next); this will complete the case Information Wizards (see Figure 5.38).

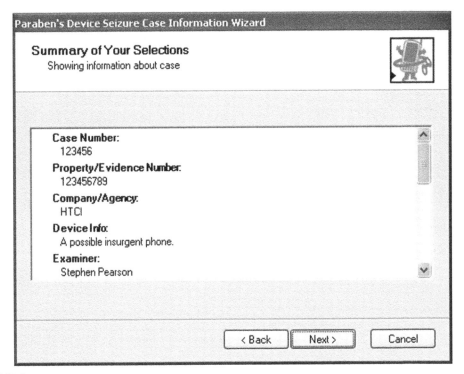

■ **FIGURE 5.38** Summary screen.

Acquiring the cell phone

You are now ready to begin gathering data into your case and performing the analysis.

Remember that Paraben's Device Seizure is a one-case to multiple-device investigation tool (see Figure 5.39). To add a cell phone or SIM card into the case container, we will use the Data Acquisition wizard. To activate the wizard, you can use two methods. The first will be from the main toolbar tools: dropdown the menu select.

Using the second method, you can simply click the Data Acquisition wizard icon tool tip on the shortcut toolbar just below the main toolbar at the top of the screen. Let us begin.

1. Connect to the EDAS laptop to the isolation chamber as discussed in the section "Using the HTCI isolation chamber."
2. Make sure to follow the instructions for connecting the cell phone into the isolation chamber.
3. Left click the Data Acquisition wizard shortcut tool icon. The device acquisition wizard immediately appears; this wizard will allow you to

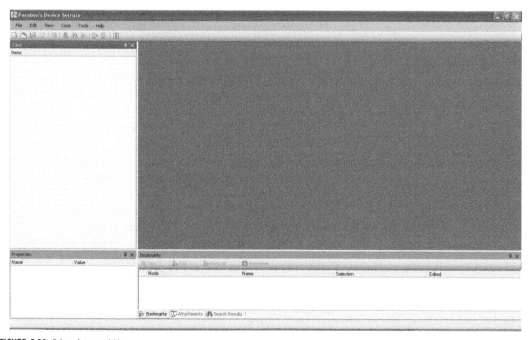

■ **FIGURE 5.39** Select data acquisition.

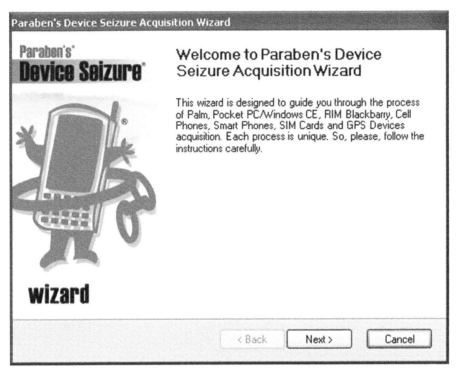

■ **FIGURE 5.40** Acquisition wizard.

connect to the cell phone that was connected earlier in this chapter. Once the Device Acquisition wizard appears, you will select (Next) (see Figure 5.40).

4. The device type selection screen will appear (see Figure 5.41).
5. From the dropdown supported manufacturers, choose the type of cell phone that you are going to acquire. For this example, you are going to use the Samsung CDMA phone (see Figure 5.42).
6. Once a selection has been made select (Next).
7. Model Selection screen will appear (see Figure 5.43).
8. The supported dropdown models should autodetect the option preselected; if the autodetect is preselected, simply select <Next>. If the autodetect is not selected, you will need to choose the model of the cell phone you are trying to connect to or a cell phone that is close to the one you are trying to connect to.
9. The connection selection screen will then appear and request the connection type from the dropdown menu. You see that you have a Samsung modem that is available for you to connect, so you will select

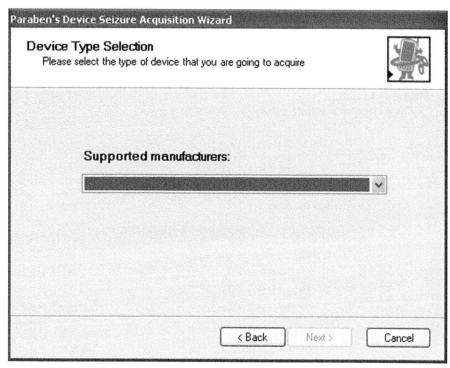

■ **FIGURE 5.41** Supported manufacturers.

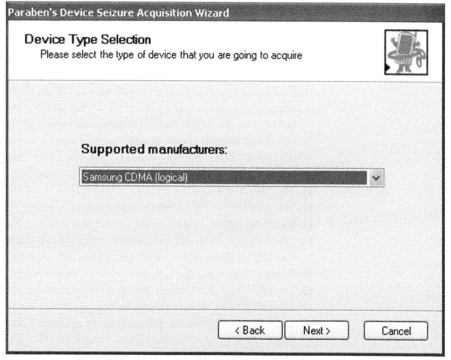

■ **FIGURE 5.42** Supported manufacturers.

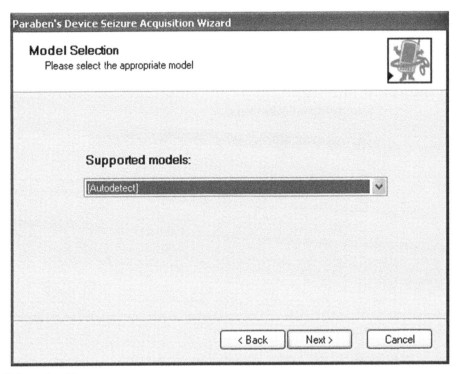

■ **FIGURE 5.43** Supported models.

the Samsung Modem, and it will show your connection type. You will then select (Next) (see Figure 5.44).

10. In the data type selection, there will be a list of data types that are available for you to capture using the device seizure program. If an option does not appear here, then Device Seizure will not be able to gather that data. You may need to use an alternate program to gather the specific items that you are seeking. Select all by clicking the blue linked <select all> at the bottom right of the screen (see Figure 5.45).

11. Then select <Next>

12. The summary of My Selection screen will now appear.

13. Verify that all the selections are correct (see Figure 5.46).

14. Check the fill sorter after acquisition checkbox. This will speed up your digital triage process after the acquisition of the cell phone.

15. Select <Next> and the acquisition wizard should begin.

16. The time to acquire a phone can be a few minutes or over 10 min, depending on the size of the phone that you wish to acquire.

17. Make sure that during this process you do not disturb the phone or the cables, as moving cables during the acquisition will cause the

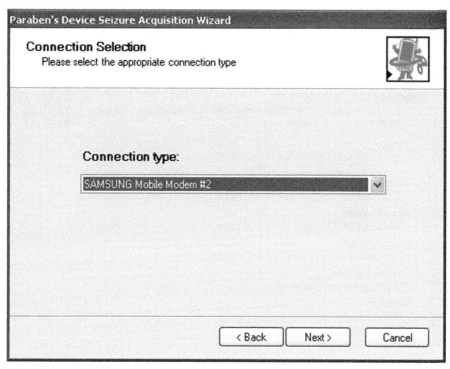

■ **FIGURE 5.44** Connection type.

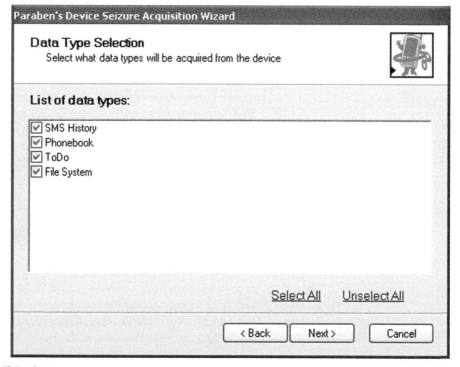

■ **FIGURE 5.45** List data types.

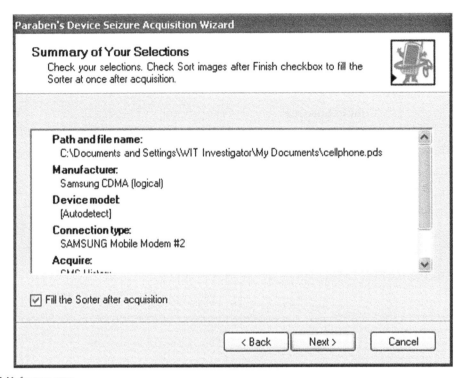

■ **FIGURE 5.46** Summary screen.

acquisition to fail. If the acquisition fails, you must repeat all the acquisition steps over again. You do not need to recreate a new case. If the phone is an older phone or the cell phone is possibly damaged, you may have to attempt to acquire the phone several different times until the phone is actually retrieved correctly. Patience is a virtue when working with cell phone forensic applications.

18. Once the acquisition wizard has completed acquiring, the cell phone acquisition result summary screen will appear. The acquisition result will show all the tasks that you requested it to perform and whether or not the task was completed successfully (see Figure 5.47). If all of the tasks were successful, this will take you to the Completing Paraben's Device Seizure Acquisition wizard screen. If you have finished, simply select the <Finish> button.

Once the acquisition has completed, you must remove the phone from the laptop to prevent any contamination to the cell phone. To do this, simply remove the USB cable that connects the laptop and the isolation chamber. Now, inside of the isolation chamber, remove the battery from the cell

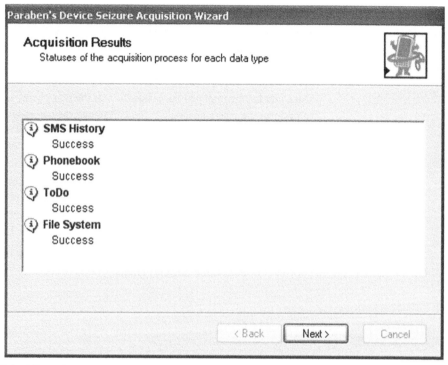

■ FIGURE 5.47 Acquisition results.

phone and place the cell phone and the battery into the Faraday bag and reseal the Faraday bag; this will complete the process of acquiring the cell phone.

Once the acquisition has completed, you will be returned to the default four-pane desktop view. You will now notice in the upper left-hand case pane that the Samsung cell phone now appears with an expand plus sign next to it.

Acquiring the SIM card

If there is a SIM card that needs to be processed, we will acquire the SIM card after we acquire the cell phone. Even though the SIM card is gathered in the initial processing of the cell phone, we are going to acquire it separately to ensure that we have retrieved all the data and that data has not been hidden from us. Use the data acquisition wizard to gather the SIM card. When prompted for a Manufacturer, select SIM card from the supported models and the card reader from the communications selection screen. The Data Acquisition should then proceed the same way as it did for processing the cell phone. Since we are using a CDMA phone as our example phone, there is no SIM card to process; therefore, we do not need to go through the SIM card acquisition steps.

Performing the triage analysis

Once you have completed the acquisition of the cell phone, it is now time to perform the triage analysis of the cell phone. In our example, we have captured a Samsung cell phone. You should be back at the Device Seizure Desktop with the four panes available to you. In the upper left corner, you will see the Samsung node. When the cursor is placed on the node, it will highlight. Your first pieces of valuable information will be displayed at the bottom of the screen. Look at the bottom left pane, and you will find the phone number that has been assigned to the cell phone. You will also be given the manufacturer, type, and model of the phone (see Figure 5.48).

The phone number is important information, so we will make sure to document or bookmark that information.

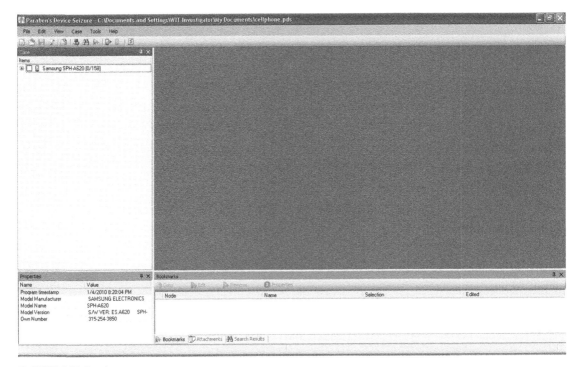

■ **FIGURE 5.48** Four data panes.

Bookmarking is the process of highlighting data within the evidence container. We will bookmark the phone number. To do this, follow these steps:

1. Select the phone number by moving the cursor over the number and left click one time.
2. The selection will turn blue; now right-click the highlighted area and select <add bookmark>.
3. In the short description, we will call this "phone number."
4. Add a description for the bookmark. Normally you will want to put something into the description that would allow you or someone else to understand why you bookmarked the item. Once you have done this, select <OK>.
5. Notice in the bookmarks pane (lower right bottom pane) that a bookmark has been entered under the Samsung node with the name of "phone number" with the value of 315-254-3850, which was the data in the phone number block (see Figure 5.49).

The next step in the triage process is to identify those items that are not interpretable—in other words, pictures on the cell phone, as you do not have to interpret those images.

■ **FIGURE 5.49** Bookmark screen.

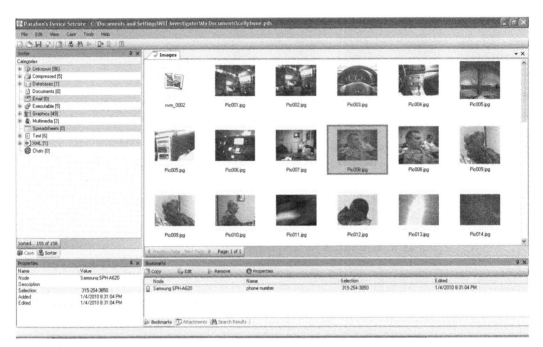

■ **FIGURE 5.50** Images screen.

To display the images from the toolbar:

1. Select Case.
2. Select Fill Sorter. This will populate the images from the cell phone in the right-hand pane (see Figure 5.50).

Notice the sorter screen has now appeared with 12 categories. If data is recognized by category, the numbers in the parentheses will indicate how many elements have been found. This process has quickly allowed us to see the images that are on the cell phone. After reviewing the images from the cell phone, you should have an idea of what the user has been doing with that cell phone; if this is an insurgent cell phone, you will probably find images that show culverts or fence lines or paths used by soldiers. This would immediately let us know that the cell phone was being used by a possible insurgent. This is actionable intelligence. If you find images of value, you can bookmark those images so that you can give them to our next higher unit for processing.

To bookmark an image, you simply highlight the image you wish to bookmark.

1. Right-click on the image and give the image a short name.
2. Select okay to save the bookmark in the bookmarks screen at the bottom of the screen.
3. Notice that the second bookmark now appears.

You will look at the other 12 categories for data that may be viewable starting with multimedia. Make sure to gather the Phone Book and any call logs that you can find. Call logs and other like items are normally found in the case pane under the file system of the cell phone. To find this, simply carry out the following:

1. Select the Case tab to left of the sorter tab.
2. Expand the cell phone node you wish to explore.
3. Once the cell phone has been expanded, scroll through each data element looking for additional information. You will notice under the file system of the cell phone that there are numerous entries such as SMS history phonebook. These are all areas we want to look at prior to closing this case.

Clicking on the SMS history will show the SMS messages that have been sent or received by this cell phone depending on the cell phone. The problem you will have is when the messages that have been used by the cell phone are in a foreign language. You may not be able to interpret those messages unless you understand that language. This completes the triage process of the phone; all we have to do now is report our findings.

Generating the report

This will depend on the theater of operations that you are working in and the format the command needs you to extract the information into. The report shows the basic bookmarks and the basic cell phone information such as phone number, etc., to create the CSV file.

1. From the File Menu, select <generate report>. The generate report Wizard will appear.
2. You will have the choice of
   a. CSV
   b. HTML
   c. Text
3. The CSV selection will produce a report that is usable or importable into a spreadsheet program. This format is very common in Iraq to import the reports into the CIDNE application.

Choosing the CSV format will allow us to use or import the data into any other application such as Microsoft Office. This format is also going to provide the greatest flexibility if none of those applications exist and you need to perform your own analysis, as you can download a free spreadsheet program to read or conduct analysis on the data with.

Saving the case

Make sure that you save your case by selecting

1. File menu
2. Select Save, and save your case file

This is as far as we go with the triage forensics process. Remember, the triage forensics process looks for information of actionable intelligence. Further examination of this phone can be conducted at the lab level by a certified forensic examiner.

DTF processing using DDS

The second application that we will use is the DDS, which is another Paraben application. DDS is brand new tool that is taking the cell phone forensics into a new direction. Amber Schroader, the president of Paraben Corporation, has agreed to allow the preview of the beta version, which debuted during the writing of this book and is now available to the public. This program is designed specifically to meet the needs of the investigator who is looking for specific actionable intelligence. The tool does not come with the full bells and whistles of its big brother Device Seizure; instead, it is designed for the newly trained investigators in stressful battlefield environments. The tool was designed and built around an easy-to-use interface that is easily manipulated by the gloved hand. The second premise of the tool is that minimal training should be required to be able to master this tool. Finally, the design allows for the rapid collection and categorization of data by the investigator at the objective using nonproprietary cabling.

The key benefits of the program are the following:

- Easy-to-use interface, providing for touch screen compatibility;
- Intuitive as it will try to recognize the device that is attached to automatically:
  - Streamlined search tool
  - Autosort of known file formats
- Ability to save and review cases.

To begin using a DDS, download the program or purchase the program from the Paraben Corporation and follow the steps for the initial setup.

■ **FIGURE 5.51** Deployable Device Seizure desktop icon.

1. After you have installed the program, a new desktop icon will appear (see Figure 5.51).
2. Find the icon on the desktop and double-click on it. This will launch the application. If you have a license, install the license by selecting as follows:
   a. Select Help.
   b. Select Registration.
   c. Then fill out the fields as directed by the Paraben Registration; this will register and license the product.
3. Once DDS has loaded, you will be shown the main DDS screen (see Figure 5.52).

■ **FIGURE 5.52** DDS main screen.

4. The screen is broken up into two basic parts.
   a. The main application buttons on the center right of the screen,
   b. Upper file menu at the top right of the screen allowing for configuration and registration choices.

Processing the cell phone

To use DDS to acquire a cell phone, follow these steps:

1. Connect the EDAS laptop to the isolation chamber as discussed in the section "Using the HTCI isolation chamber." (If you are collecting data from an objective or at the battlefield scene, make sure to use an isolation bag or portable isolation chamber while collecting the cell phones.)
2. If you are using the HTCI isolation chamber, make sure to follow the instructions for connecting the cell phone into the isolation chamber covered in the section "Using the HTCI isolation chamber."
3. Once the cell phone is recognized by the EDAS laptop or tactical acquisition device (TAD), the new hardware wizard recognizes and installs the drivers for the cell phone that you are trying to acquire automatically.
4. Make sure to give the acquisition system time to install the drivers for the cell phone before trying to launch the acquisition wizard.
5. Once you feel you are ready to begin, select the "Start Acquisition" button from the main screen. This is a large button on the right-hand side of the screen with a green arrow on top of it (see Figure 5.53).
6. The "Choose connected device" screen will appear. (Notice a picture of the cell phone is represented on the screen.)
7. If the cell phone does not automatically show up, wait for a few minutes and try again as the cell phone driver may not have fully installed (see Figure 5.54).
8. In our example, we are using a Samsung CDMA cell phone. Notice that under the picture of the cell phone, the title, "Samsung CDMA" appears (see Figure 5.55).
9. You will be given two option buttons: (see Figure 5.55)
   a. Acquire text data only
   b. Acquire all data
10. Acquiring text data only will pull out only textual information. This is the faster of the two options as it skips any graphics. For those performing DTFs though, this will skip the very items that we want the most: the graphics.

■ **FIGURE 5.53** Choose the start acquisition.

■ **FIGURE 5.54** Connected device screen.

■ **FIGURE 5.55** Choose data to acquire screen.

11. Select the "Acquire all data" option (see Figure 5.55), as this will pull both textual and multimedia from the cell phone. This option will take more time, as it is acquiring graphics as well as the text. (Remember we are doing DTFs on the battlefield, so we will want the graphics, as the graphics are truly the only data that we do not need to interpret. This will give us the best chance at gathering actionable intelligence.)

12. On this screen, there are two other options to choose from:
    a. Choose another device
    b. Cancel

13. If this is not the device you wish to work with, you can choose to use another device. By selecting choose "another device" (see Figure 5.55) option, you will be taken back to the main menu.

14. If you do not want to continue with the extraction, simply cancel the operation by selecting Cancel (see Figure 5.55): this will end the process.

15. After you select the "Acquire all" data button (see Figure 5.55), the application will automatically begin the process of acquiring the cell phone data.

■ **FIGURE 5.56** DDS processing cell phone screen.

16. At this point, the application will connect to the cell phone. A progress status screen will be shown in the bottom center of the screen (see Figure 5.56); it is important to remember at this time not to disturb the cell phone, as this may cause errors or the application to fail completely.

17. As the cell phone begins to be acquired, you will also notice that on the upper left side of the screen (see Figure 5.56) the following categories are displayed:
    a. Contacts
    b. Messages
    c. Call History
    d. Organizer
    e. Graphics
    f. Multimedia

18. The spinning circles next to each of the categories mean that the phone is processing each of those categories. The spinning circles will stop once that category has been processed and data is ready to be previewed.

■ **FIGURE 5.57** Cell phone identification screen.

19. At the bottom left of the screen, an image of the cell phone appears (see Figure 5.57).
20. Move your cursor to the bottom left of the screen just under the cell phone image and select "View Details."
21. A window will appear in the center of the screen with three tabs:
    a. Properties
    b. Bookmarks
    c. Search Results
22. Document the information in the Properties Window about the cell phone.
    a. Cell phone number
    b. Type of cell phone
    c. Manufacturer
    d. Version
23. Now click on the other two tabs to see what information is presented. You should have no results in the other two windows at this point (see Figures 5.58).
24. Now look to the upper right of the screen; you will notice that categories are being populated (Figure 5.59). As the results are pulled from the cell phone, a green check mark will appear next to the data

■ **FIGURE 5.58** Bookmark screen.

■ **FIGURE 5.59** Search results screen.

■ **FIGURE 5.60** Amount of data being acquired.

acquired and will move on to the next category. If the data was not able to be pulled from the cell phone for a specific category, then a red X and the word failed will appear instead (see Figure 5.60).

25. To see how much data is being retrieved from the cell phone, you can look to the bottom right of the screen and see the collected data in MB (see Figure 5.61).

26. Once the acquisition is completed, a message will appear in the center status message screen stating "Acquisition Completed" (see Figure 5.61).

27. Now that the phone has been fully acquired, immediately remove the isolation chamber connector (see Figure 5.62). This will complete the acquisition of the cell phone and allow us to move directly into the analysis phase.

Processing the SIM card

1. Processing the SIM card is exactly the same as processing the cell phone.

2. Connect to the EDAS laptop to the isolation chamber, making sure to follow the instructions for connecting the SIM card reader into the isolation chamber, which was discussed earlier (see Figure 5.63).

■ **FIGURE 5.61** Acquisition complete screen.

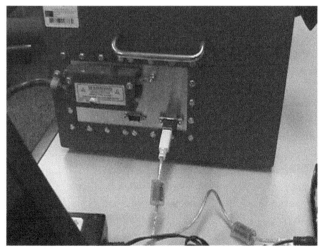

■ **FIGURE 5.62** Remove acquisition station.

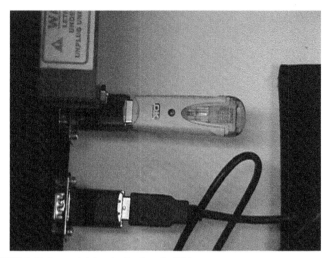

■ **FIGURE 5.63** Connect isolation chamber from the EDAS.

3. Once the SIM card reader is recognized by the acquisition device, the new hardware Wizard recognizes and installs the drivers for the cell phone that you are trying to acquire (see Figure 5.64).

4. From the main screen, select the "Start Acquisition" button. This is a large button on the right-hand side of the screen with a green arrow on top of it.

5. "Choose connected device" screen will appear. Notice a picture of the SIM card reader is represented (see Figure 5.65). This is the SIM card reader that DDS has autodetected on the system. If the SIM card reader does not automatically show up, wait for a few minutes and try again, as the SIM card reader driver may not have fully installed.

6. Continue processing this device by clicking on the SIM card reader picture itself.

7. There are two other options to choose from (see Figure 5.66):
- Choose another device
- Cancel

8. If this is not the device you wish to work with, you can choose to use another device. By selecting the "Choose another device" option, you will be taken back to the main menu.

9. If you do not want to continue, simply cancel the operation by selecting "Cancel"; this will end the process (Figure 5.67).

10. After selecting the SIM card reader, you will begin to pull all textual data from the SIM card. The application will automatically begin the process of acquiring the SIM card. The application will connect to the

■ **FIGURE 5.64** Choose the start acquisition.

SIM card and a progress status screen will be shown in the bottom
center of the screen (see Figures 5.68 and 5.69).
11. You will notice, after we pressed Acquire all data, that in the bottom
left of the screen an image of the SIM card appeared (see Figure 5.70).
12. Move your cursor to the bottom left of the screen just under the SIM
card image and select "View Details."
13. A window will appear in the center of the screen with three tabs:
   a. Properties
   b. Bookmarks
   c. Search Results
14. Document the information in the properties window about the
SIM card:
   a. Manufacturer
   b. Cell phone number
   c. Service provider
   d. Model
   e. Phone number

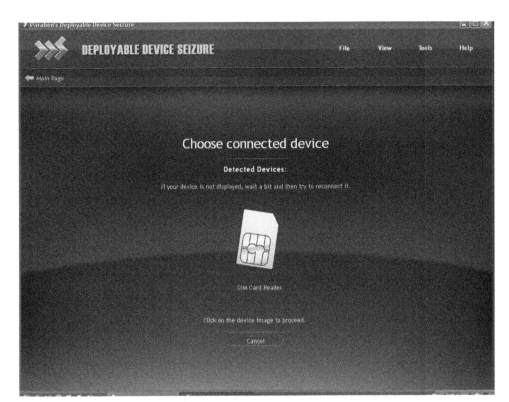

■ **FIGURE 5.65** Choose connected device.

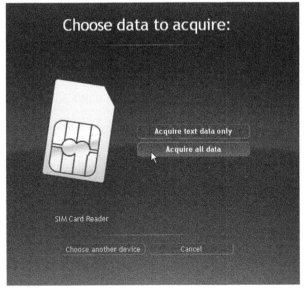

■ **FIGURE 5.66** Choose connected device.

■ **FIGURE 5.67** *Choose connected device.*

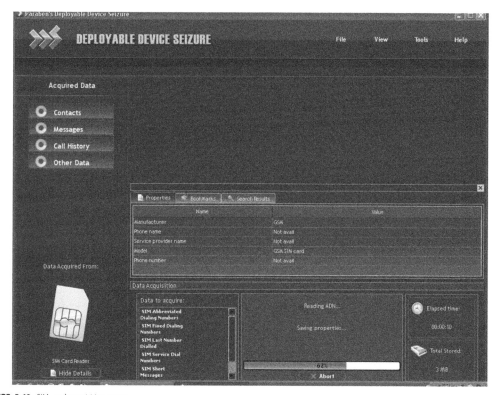

■ **FIGURE 5.68** *SIM card acquisition screen.*

15. Now click on the other two tabs to see what information is presented. You should have no results in the other two windows at this point (see Figure 5.71).
16. Now look to the upper left of the screen (see Figure 5.72). You will notice that categories are being populated and the results pulled from the SIM card. A green check mark will appear next to the data acquired and will move on to the next category. If the data was not

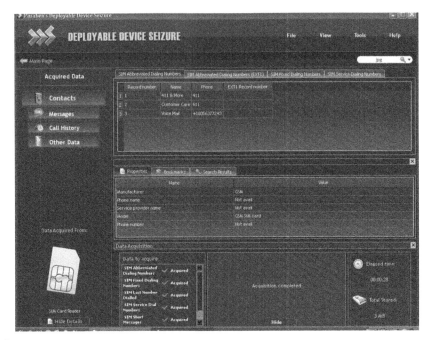

■ **FIGURE 5.69** Contact screen.

■ **FIGURE 5.70** Messages screen.

■ **FIGURE 5.71** Call history.

■ **FIGURE 5.72** Other data.

able to be pulled from the SIM card for a specific category, then a red X and the word "failed" will appear instead.

17. You will notice that you do not have the graphics or multimedia category in the upper left of the acquisition screen window. SIM cards do not contain multimedia.

18. The categories on the upper left will be (see Figure 5.73) as below:
    a. Contacts
    b. Messages
    c. Call history
    d. Other data

19. To see how much data is being retrieved from the SIM card, you can look at the bottom right of the screen and see the collected data in MB (see Figure 5.73).

20. Once the acquisition is completed, a message will appear in the center status message screen (see Figure 5.73).

21. Now that the phone has been fully acquired, immediately remove the isolation chamber connector (see Figure 5.74).

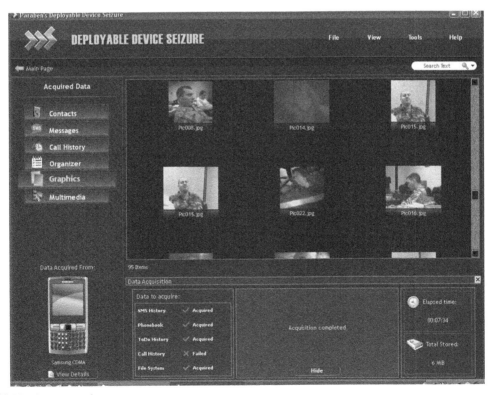

■ **FIGURE 5.73** Acquisition complete screen.

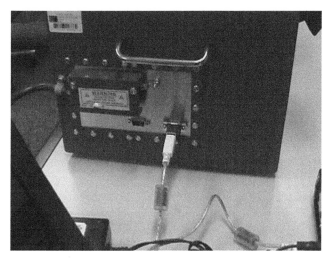

■ **FIGURE 5.74** Remove isolation chamber from the EDAS.

Conducting digital triage analysis using DDS

Once the acquisition has been conducted of the cell phone or SIM card, the analysis of the data that has been retrieved is going to be roughly the same. Remember that the process for DTF model is designed to gather as much actionable intelligence as quickly as possible. You will get to this data by looking at the graphics and multimedia category tabs of the cell phone acquisition first.

1. From the cell phone acquisition screen, click on the graphics category. Scroll through the graphics that are on the cell phone, looking for anything that might be of value (see Figure 5.75).
2. Once an image is found that is usable, right click on the image and select "Add to Bookmarks" (see Figure 5.76).
3. Name the bookmark. In the example, we name the bookmark "possible IED."
4. In the details window, put in a description of the bookmark. We will put in "Showing a possible IED" (see Figure 5.77).
5. Select "Save"; notice that you have two bookmarks in the bookmarks window.
6. Other actions you can take with the picture are the following:
   a. Double click on the image, which brings the image to the forefront.
   b. Right click on the image and export the image out as a JPEG file. You can then use another graphics application to enhance the image (see Figure 5.77).

■ **FIGURE 5.75** Select the graphics tab.

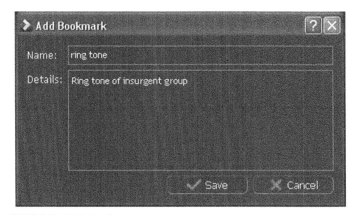

■ **FIGURE 5.76** Add bookmark.

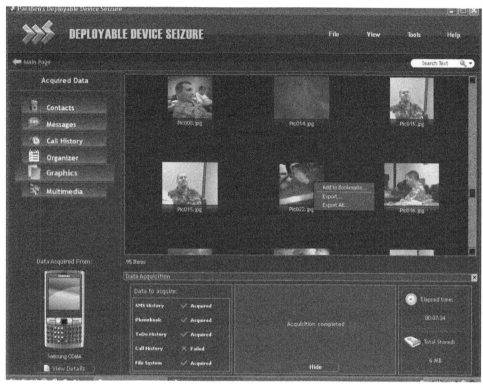

■ **FIGURE 5.77** Add bookmark.

7. Continue processing through the graphics until all of the graphics have been reviewed, selecting all the images that would be considered actionable intelligence (see Figure 5.78).
8. Select the multimedia category from the upper left side of the screen.
9. Scroll through the multimedia looking for items that may have investigative value (see Figure 5.79).
10. If you find a multimedia item of investigative value, right click on the multimedia item and add it to the bookmarks.
11. Other actions you can take with the multimedia are the following:
    a. Double click on the multimedia item brings the multimedia item to the forefront.
    b. Right click on the multimedia item and export the multimedia item in a file format that is readable by your computer's multimedia application. You may need to install an external multimedia application, or you may need to install a codec pack that supports the file type you are trying watch or listen to.
12. Continue processing through the multimedia files until all of the multimedia files have been reviewed (see Figure 5.79).

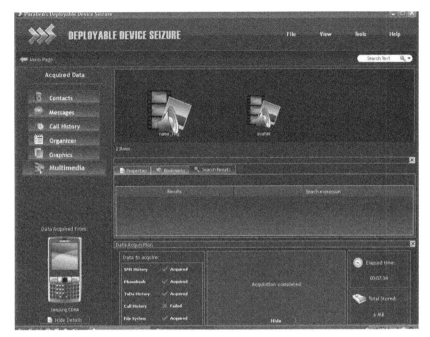

■ **FIGURE 5.78** Multimedia.

■ **FIGURE 5.79** Multimedia category.

13. There is one difference in the processing of the SIM sard. This is that the SIM card does not contain any graphics or multimedia. The SIM card is textual only, so you will not have the options to look at graphics or multimedia. When processing the SIM card, you will still go through all of the tabs, bookmarking those items of importance.

Now that you have performed the initial DTF process, you can go through the rest of the tabs on the upper left-hand side of the screen to see if there are any other items of value. If you find other items of value, you can simply right click on the item and select "Add to Bookmarks."

Processing a SIM card after acquisition is different only because the SIM card does not contain any multimedia files. To obtain actionable intelligence, the investigator will be relying on the textual data only. This can be a problem if the data is in a language other than that of the investigator. Textual data can be relayed in code as well. If you have ever watched your kids text, you know that they text in a language that is new and certainly does not follow the standards of the English language. To gather actionable intelligence from the SIM card, we will process the textual containers in a different order (see Figure 5.80).

■ **FIGURE 5.80** Call history.

■ **FIGURE 5.81** Contacts.

1. Select "Call History"
2. The call history category is displayed in the right panel. Choose the "Last Numbers Dialed" tab.
3. Highlight or select all the records in the last numbers dialed tab.
4. Right click the list and export as an Excel file.
5. Save the Excel file.
6. Now select the next tab in "Call History," which is the "Last Number Dialed (Ext1)" tab.
7. Repeat the steps to highlight and export the data to an Excel file.
8. Select "Contacts" (see Figure 5.81).
9. The contacts category is displayed in the right panel (see Figure 5.82).
10. Select each one of the tabs displayed at the top of the contacts panel.

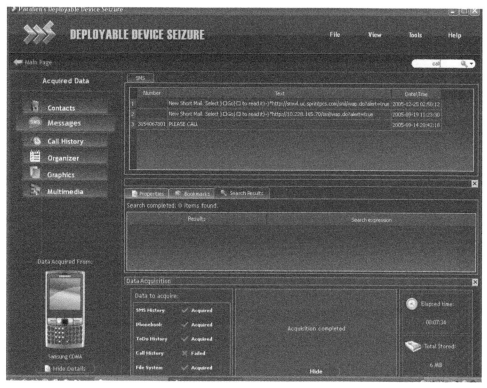

■ **FIGURE 5.82** Contacts.

11. Right click the list of contacts from each panel and export as an Excel file.

12. Save the Excel file.

13. Continue to process through all the phone book entries following the steps above.

14. Select "Messages" (see Figure 5.83).

15. The messages category is displayed in the right panel.

16. Select each one of the tabs displayed at the top of the messages panel.

17. Right click the list of messages from each panel, and export as an Excel file.

18. Save the Excel file.

19. Continue to process all the message entries following the steps above.

20. The last category to choose is the "Other Data" category.

■ **FIGURE 5.83** Search the acquired case.

21. Scroll through the other data category looking for any actionable intelligence. If you find any data, make sure to bookmark the items and if necessary export the items to Excel.

Searching the data in DDS

If you have specific information that you would like to look up such as phone numbers, names, and/or text-specific strings, do the following (see Figure 5.84):

■ **FIGURE 5.84** Export data to Excel.

1. Select the search window in the upper right side of the screen.
2. Type in the text that you are looking for.
3. In the "Search Results" window, items matching the search will be displayed.
4. If you want to select any of the items, right click on the item and select "Add to Bookmarks."
5. Enter in a name for the bookmark and enter in a description.
6. Select "OK" to save the bookmark, which will now be displayed in the bookmarks window.

Exporting to a spreadsheet

There are items that can be analyzed best in a spreadsheet format such as phone books, call logs, and SMS messages. This exporting process also gives you the opportunity to look at multiple devices at one time. To use this data in a spreadsheet, you need to export them to a "Comma Separated Value" (CSV) file (see Figure 5.85). To do this, proceed as follows:

1. Select the data that you want to export.
2. Right click on the data and choose "Export Data to CSV."
3. Choose a file name and location of where you want to store the CSV file. Make sure to store this to your external drive (see Figure 5.86).

■ **FIGURE 5.85** Save exported data.

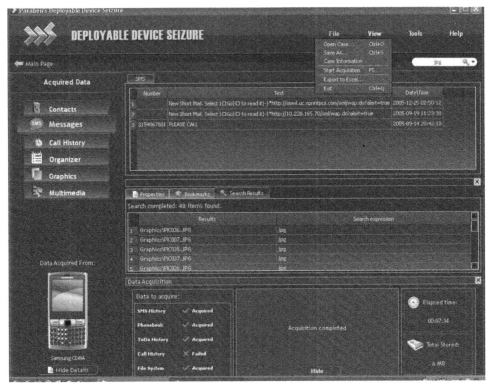

■ **FIGURE 5.86** Save case option from file menu.

4. Select "OK."
5. The file is now stored in the location chosen as a CSV file. You can open the file directly from any spreadsheet application for continued analysis.

Saving the case

To save the case, follow these steps:

1. Select "File" from the toolbar in the upper right menu.
2. Select "File" and then "Save" (see Figure 5.87).
3. Choose the location to save the case (see Figure 5.87).
4. Select "OK," and the case will be saved.

As you can see, the program is very simple to use and provides the investigator absolutely the quickest method of producing actionable intelligence. We look forward to seeing this program in prime time, and we think you will see this as a staple in the deployment kits around the world.

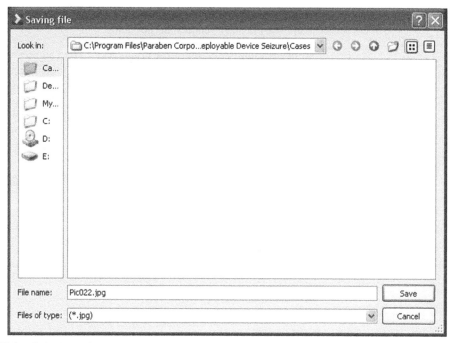

■ **FIGURE 5.87** Save the location to the case.

Conducting digital triage analysis using Secure View 2 with svProbe

Secure View 2 with svProbe (SVP) is a relatively new application. The application Secure View has been a staple in the cell phone forensic world for many years. The new power of SVP comes from its ability to do full analytics of captured data from the cell phone with scripts that even an untrained investigator can easily figure out. SVP can process cell phones, SIM cards, or SD cards (although we do not recommend using the SD card function for DTF as we have found that SD cards can be acquired much more accurately using traditional forensic media applications such as P2 Commander, FTK, or Encase). SVP is in this book because of its unique analytic capability, making it the third application that can be used to process the cellular devices. The SVP program allows you to capture the objective and process that data immediately. This can be extremely useful for small teams that are required or have a need for identifying and isolating suspects. During this section, SVP will show you how easy it can be to collect data and perform analytics at the objective. This section will also show how SVP is one of the first applications to allow the collection and interpretation of data from other vendors, which is something that the other vendors are not doing.

To begin using SVP, you must install SVP. You can download a demo version from http://www.susteen.com. Once the application has been installed on the computer, an icon will appear on the desktop.

1. Click on the icon to launch the application (see Figure 5.88).
2. The full application requires a dongle to run; so a warning will come up asking you for a dongle if one is not detected (see Figure 5.89).
3. Once the application is launched, the main menu will appear for security (see Figure 5.90).

■ **FIGURE 5.88** Secure View 2 desktop icon.

■ **FIGURE 5.89** Secure View 2 dongle warning.

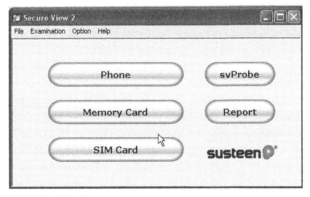

■ **FIGURE 5.90** Secure View 2 main menu.

4. Once the main menu is displayed, you will have the option to launch five different applications.
   a. Phone—Capture data from a cell phone
   b. Memory card—Capture data from a SD card or flash memory device
   c. SIM card—Capture data from a SIM card
   d. svProbe—Provides for analytics of devices that have been captured by this program or other programs
   e. Report—The ability to generate a report that is viewable in the standard browser

Acquiring the cell phone

1. Connect the EDAS laptop to the isolation chamber as discussed in the section "Using the HTCI isolation chamber." (If you are collecting data from an objective or at the battlefield scene, make sure to use an isolation bag or portable isolation chamber while collecting the cell phones.)

2. If you are using the HTCI isolation chamber, make sure to follow the instructions for connecting the cell phone to the isolation chamber covered in the section "Using the HTCI isolation chamber."

3. Once the cell phone is recognized by the EDAS laptop or TAD, the new hardware wizard recognizes and installs the drivers for the cell phone that you are trying to acquire automatically.

4. Make sure to give the acquisition system time to install the drivers for the cell phone before trying to launch the acquisition wizard.

5. Once you have allowed the cell phone to connect, click the phone button one time, which will launch the phone acquisition wizard (see Figure 5.91).

6. Once the application has been launched, "Welcome to the Phone Setup Wizard" will be activated, giving you four choices to connect the cell phone (see Figure 5.92).
   a. USB cable
   b. Serial cable
   c. Bluetooth
   d. Infrared

7. Choose the connection option that will allow you to connect to your cell phone (see Figure 5.92).

8. Choose the country from the dropdown menu (see Figure 5.93). For this example, we have chosen US as the country code.

9. Next, select a carrier that you believe cell phone was operating on. If the carrier that you are looking for does not appear or you do not know the carrier, simply select no carrier. This will allow you to connect to any cell phone regardless of the carrier (see Figure 5.94).

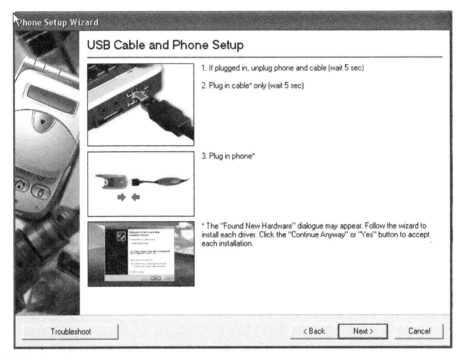

■ **FIGURE 5.91** Connection option menu.

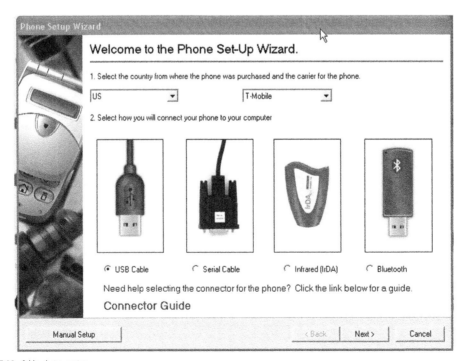

■ **FIGURE 5.92** Cable choice option.

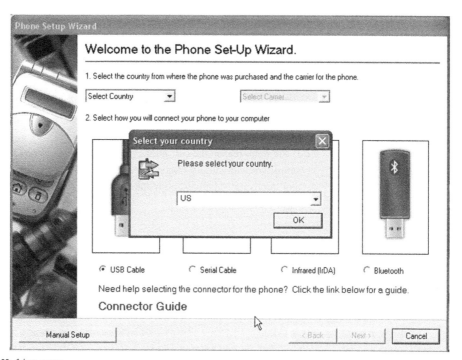

■ **FIGURE 5.93** Select country.

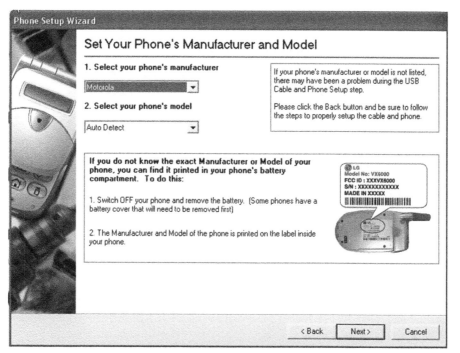

■ **FIGURE 5.94** Save case option from the file menu.

10. Once all the options have been chosen, press the "Next" button.
11. The USB cable and phone setup screen will appear (if another connection type has been selected, then the connection screen will appear for that type). If the phone is detected, the screen will tell you the status of your connection; if the phone is not detected, then a menu screen will appear with instructions on what you must do to connect your phone. Follow the directions on the screen to try and connect the phone (see Figure 5.95).
12. If for some reason the cell phone cannot be connected by the automatic setup, you can simply choose the manual setup by selecting "Back" and choosing "Manual Setup" at the bottom of the screen (see Figure 5.96).

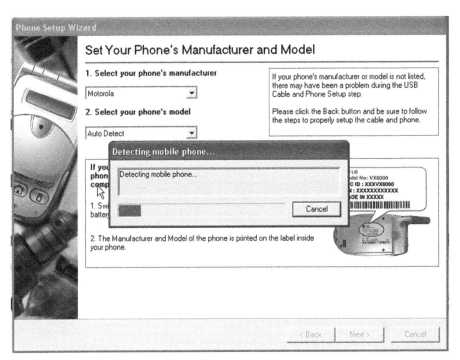

■ **FIGURE 5.95** Detecting cell phone.

■ **FIGURE 5.96** Manual setup.

13. If everything goes well, the phone setup wizard will appear showing the model of your phone.
14. The fastest way to connect your cell phone with SVP is to use the autodetect provided by SVP.
15. If you do not wish to use this option or you wish to manually select the cell phone dropdown, select "your phone's model" to access the cell phone (see Figure 5.96).
16. Once everything has been detected correctly, the cable has been connected correctly, and the program has detected the cell phone, the phone status summary will appear.
17. This will tell you what data options are available during the acquisition of the phone. If an option is not supported, the word "No" will appear in the supported status column (see Figure 5.97).
18. To continue processing the cell phone, press the "Finish" button.
19. You will be asked which data elements you wish to capture from the phone. You can select all or none of the options. This will change from

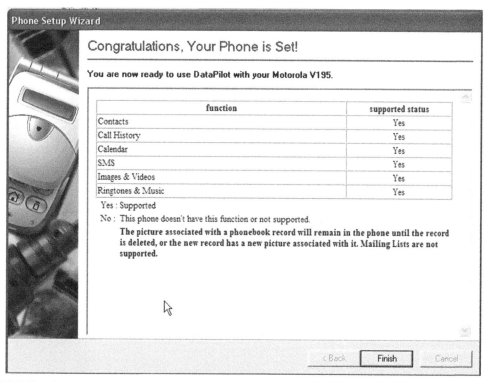

■ **FIGURE 5.97** Your phone is set.

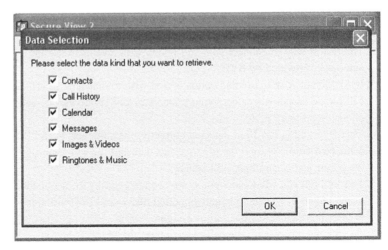

■ **FIGURE 5.98** Capture options.

phone to phone, as different options are supported on different phones (see Figure 5.98).

20. Select "OK" on the collection options box. SVP will begin to acquire the cell phone. (Do not disturb the cell phone during this process, as disconnecting the cable or shutting the computer off will cause the application to stop working and you will not receive an entire or full capture of the device.)

21. Once the application has completed successfully, a dialog box will appear telling you that the acquisition has been successful (see Figure 5.99).

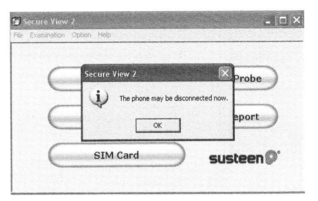

■ **FIGURE 5.99** Phone is detected.

Producing the report

22. After the acquisition has been completed, the examiner's information page will appear. Fill in all the fields, as most of them are self-explanatory (see Figure 5.100).

23. Select the logo that you wish to have displayed on the reports generated by SVP. To choose a logo, select "Browse" and take a logo from your computer.

24. Make sure to fill out the case file number as this number will be used to track the report (see Figure 5.100).

25. After filling all the information, press "OK."

26. The phone information dialog box will appear. Fill in the information, as this information will appear on the report that is created by the application. (Remember the the ESN and IMEI number can be found in the battery compartment under the battery. This information should be retrievable at this point, as there is no longer a need to have the phone attached to the acquisition device) (see Figure 5.101).

27. The generated report will appear immediately after the acquisition has been completed.

So far this has been no different from any other applications and could at this point be just lumped in with the other cell phone applications. This though is where SVP really begins to shine. SVP allows for the inclusion of multiple cell phone reports to be analyzed, read, and displayed. In other words, if you have captured data using another application, you can use SVP to include it into a single report. SVP has unlocked the proprietary code that has kept all the applications independent for years. This is fantastic as you

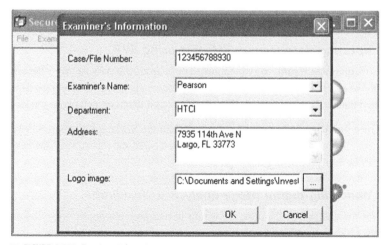

■ **FIGURE 5.100** Examiners information.

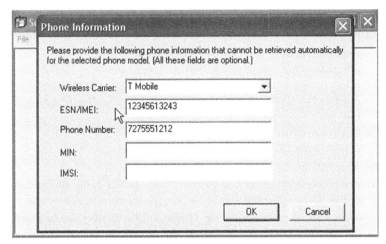

■ **FIGURE 5.101** Cell Phone information.

are no longer trapped in a single application. To add multivendor reports to the report, simply click the import data at the top of the report screen. A dialog box will ask you which type of report to include. You will then need to point to the folder that contains the data you wish to import. The report will then be dispalyed including the existing report.

To this point, most vendors have prevented or isolated their applications to a point where no one else can use the report in another report. With the inclusion of this added feature, the SVP stands alone (see Figure 5.102).

The SVP application comes with a new application called svProbe. We are going to look at the features of this application as this is how you will get to actionable intelligence with SVP (see Figure 5.103).

Capturing data from a SIM card using SVP

To acquire a SIM card, you will follow all of the instructions for gathering the cell phone except that instead of pressing the phone button, you will press the SIM card button. The application will load and run as it did in the cell phone mode.

Once you have collected all of the data from the SIM card, a report will be generated automatically. After you have reviewed the report, the SIM card can be analyzed using the svProbe tools.

Conducting digital triage analysis with svProbe

For the analysis of the data, we would like to pose a scenario to you. You are an investigator at an objective, you have four people in detention, and each of them has a cell phone. You exploit the cell phones at the objective

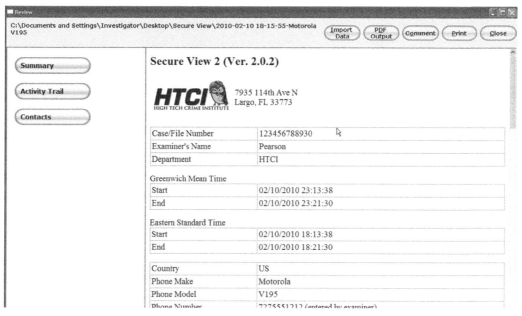

■ **FIGURE 5.102** Report.

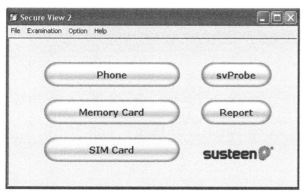

■ **FIGURE 5.103** Main Menu.

from the four people. Once you've exploited the cell phones, you have data that needs to be analyzed quickly so that you might be able to identify the four people who may have been involved in an earlier incident such as an IED attack. With the tools provided in the SVP application, you will be able to do this. SVP will provide the tools necessary to exploit at the objective the data gathered providing actionable intelligence.

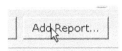

■ **FIGURE 5.104** Add report.

1. To begin using svProbe, simply select svProbe from the main menu (see Figure 5.104).
2. svProbe will load to the main application screen.
3. From the main application screen, you will have the option to add reports that you wish to analyze (remember that each report will be a separate device such as a cell phone or SIM card).
4. Select the option to add reports into the analysis function. (These do not have to be just SVP reports; these can be any reports in XML format produced by any cell phone forensic application.)
5. To add a report, simply click the "Add Report" button in the bottom right-hand corner of the screen (see Figure 5.104). There is currently no limit on the number of reports that can be added for analysis; this gives you great flexibility at the objective.
6. Once the report has been added, you'll see it appear in the "Select Report" screen. For this example, you have chosen four reports to conduct analysis on (see Figure 5.105).

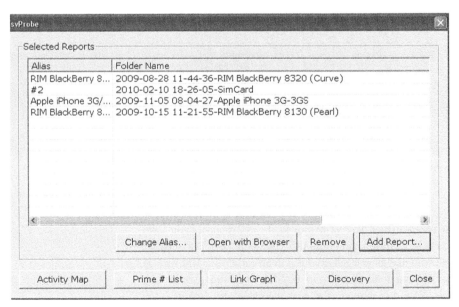

■ **FIGURE 5.105** Selected reports menu.

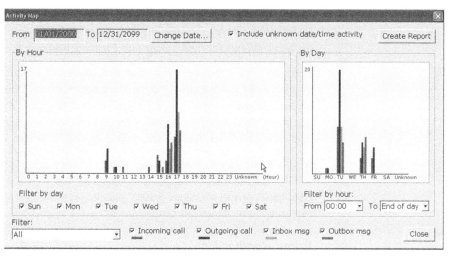

■ **FIGURE 5.106** Activity map display.

7. You now can choose from the four different analytics tasks at the bottom of the screen (see Figure 5.105):
   a. Activity map (see Figure 5.106)
   b. Prime number list
   c. Link graph
   d. Discovery

Activity map

Click on the activity map at the bottom left corner of the screen (see Figure 5.105). When the activity map loads, you'll be presented with a graph showing all the cell phones reports collectively.

This will show you the complete activity of all of the cell phone reports. If you wish to find an answer to a question such as, "did any of the devices being analyzed make a phone call at 1600 hours" quickly, you can see by looking at the map if any of the cell phones were involved in making a phone call at 1600 hours.

The activity map tool is a very powerful visual tool, providing the investigator the ability to quickly identify the devices by timeframe. If the investigator needs to filter the devices being analyzed, he simply needs to use the dropdown box at the top left of the screen (see Figure 5.106). This can isolate a single cell phone to do analysis on instead of the entire group.

The investigator can also filter the actual time and date parameters by filtering the data by date. To do this, the investigator simply checks or unchecks options for time groups (see Figure 5.106).

Currently, SVP is the only application that allows you to perform this type of analysis at the objective without a secondary device. There are other applications out there that will let you conduct this type of analysis but you would need to have a secondary application. Migrate the data into that application, and then preview that data using the secondary application.

If you would like to maintain the results of the activity map, you can simply create a report by clicking on the create report button in the upper right-hand corner (see Figure 5.106). This will create an HTML document capturing all of the results or the filtered results as you desire.

Prime Number List

Once you have completed your review of the activity map, press the "Close" button in the bottom right corner of the screen. This will return you to the "Select Reports" menu (see Figure 5.105).

The next analysis task to run is to view the Prime Number List. As with the activity map, the prime number list is going to review all of the cases in the selected reports and provide analysis (see Figure 5.107).

Once selected, the prime number list will appear (see Figure 5.107). The prime number list is designed to show all of the cell phone activities by phone number. The phone number with the most activity will appear at the top of the list. As you can see in the prime number list screen, the

Name	Phone #	Total	Call	Recieved	Dialed	TextMsg	Inbox
Steven, Suspect , Steve...	19497898213	17	17	2	15	0	0
James Smith	19492936880	15	5	2	3	10	4
Suspect 2 , Ted Richards	19498928231	10	10	5	5	0	0
	1121611611	8	0	0	0	8	8
	19493944945	7	0	0	0	7	1
Jim, Jim Jones , Jim o...	9494393370	6	6	4	2	0	0
Atsushi Fujimatsu	9493387861	3	1	0	1	2	1
	9497898251	2	2	1	1	0	0
	2024957148	1	1	1	0	0	0
Michael	8181112222	1	1	0	1	0	0
Darre l Jones	9195556666	1	1	0	1	0	0
	9492312876	1	1	1	0	0	0
	9492859721	1	1	0	1	0	0
Atsushi	9493410007	1	1	0	1	0	0
Ashley	9494447777	1	1	0	1	0	0

■ **FIGURE 5.107** Prime numbers.

"Stephen Suspect" cell phone had the most activity with a total of 17 different items. You can see that Stephen Suspect contains 17 phone calls, 15 of which he made and 2 of which he received. He had no text messages. This can tell us a lot about Stephen Suspect and the way that he uses his cell phone. From this analysis, we can assume that this user is not comfortable with text messaging and therefore makes more phone calls.

The next most active user is James Smith, who is much more proficient with text messaging. He is making far fewer phone calls but has sent 10 text messages. The prime number list can tell the investigator quickly who has been using the cell phone and who has not.

The detail of each one of the records can also be queried to provide a detail record.

To show the detail record, you can double click on any of the records in the prime number list screen. The detail record will be displayed showing all of the records that are associated with that record such as phone calls and text messages. The detail record will also show you the actual message from each text message. In other words, you can read the text messages and inbox messages immediately. You can see the phone calls that were made and received (see Figure 5.108).

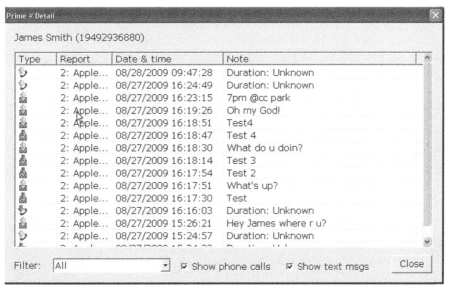

■ **FIGURE 5.108** Prime number detail list.

In our example screen (see Figure 5.108), you can see that James Smith made several phone calls and numerous text messages, as we identified from the prime number list. You can then read that record number 4 is a text message saying "Oh my God!" (If these messages were in Arabic, then the Arabic characters would be displayed).

This is an extremely useful screen as it allows you to read the messages immediately, identifing those individuals who may have been communicating with each other in the group of four detainees. This allows you to gather inculpatory and exculpatory evidence allowing you, as the investigator, to make much better decisions at the objective.

Remember, as with the other screens, you can filter the results to a single device or the group of devices.

If you would like to maintain the results of the prime number list, you can simply create a report by clicking on the "Create Report" button in the upper right-hand corner (see Figure 5.107). This will create an HTML document capturing all of the results or the filtered results as you desire.

Once you have completed your review of the activity map, press the "Close" button in the bottom right corner of the screen. This will return you to the "Select Reports" menu (see Figure 5.109).

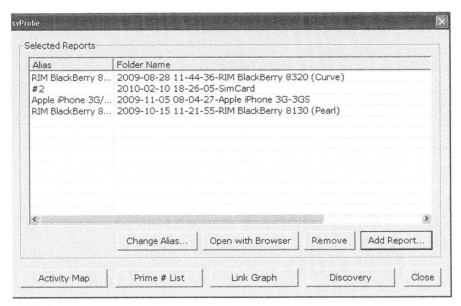

■ **FIGURE 5.109** Selected reports screen.

The next analysis task to run is to view the Link Graph. As with the Activity Map, the link graph is going to review all of the cases in the selected reports and provide analysis (see Figure 5.109).

Link Graph

Select the "Link Graph" button from the bottom of the selected reports screen, which will launch the Link Graph Analysis tool (see Figure 5.110).

The Link Graph screen opens, showing all of your reports that were selected.

The reports will be linked one to another in the Link Graph screen. The detail level can be adjusted with the sliding bar in the upper right-hand corner of the screen.

The Link Graph can show you immediately whether or not two phones have been actively communicating with each other.

In the example of four detainees that we are investigating, you may be able to tell that three of the individuals have been talking to each other. You may find that the fourth person may have just happened to be at the wrong place at the wrong time.

The Link Graph analysis tool puts powerful information in the hands of the investigator at the objective, as it allows the investigator to make much

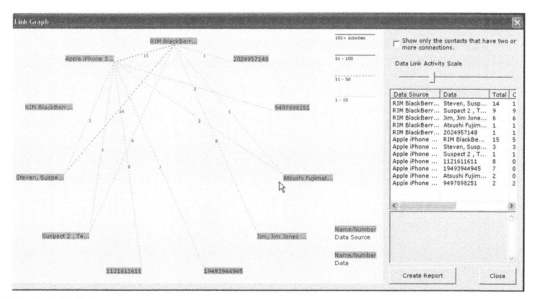

■ **FIGURE 5.110** Link Graph screen.

better decisions using the technology. The Link Graph can also identify whether a number was called that is not in any of the contact records on the included devices such as an IED phone number. Very quickly, the investigator is retrieving actionable intelligence (see Figure 5.110).

Once you have completed your review of the Link Graph, press the "Close" button in the bottom right corner of the screen. This will return you to the "Select Reports" menu (see Figure 5.110).

The next analysis task to run is to view the Discovery tool. As with the Activity Map, the Discovery tool is going to review all of the cases in the selected reports and provide analysis (see Figure 5.109).

Discovery tool

The Discovery tool is a basic search tool that will allow you to query the data pool of the selected reports looking for specific pieces of textual information such as a name, phone number, and text. To access the Discovery analysis tool, press the Discovery button in the bottom right of the selected reports screen (See Figure 5.111).

The Discovery analysis tool will be launched with all the select reports to be reviewed. You can filter to select certain phones by clicking on the filter in the top left of the screen.

To add a word to search for in the Discovery tool, simply type the word into the keyword block on the right-hand side of the screen. Select "Add

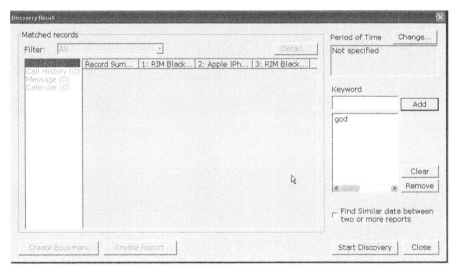

■ **FIGURE 5.111** Selected reports screen.

Word." The word will appear in the keyword list directly below the keyword add block.

Once you have entered in all the keywords that you would like to be searched, press the "Start Discovery" button in the bottom right-hand corner of the screen.

All the results that are found from your keyword search will be displayed in the far left column of the screen in one of the four categories. The four categories are the following:

■ Contact
■ Call history
■ Messages
■ Calendar

In the sample case that we have run the word "God," the keyword has been found in one text message. You can now review that message directly by selecting that category, which then displays the results in the center column (see Figure 5.112).

Double clicking on the record in the center detail screen will show the details of the text message. In the example, the test message is from James Smith who stated "Oh my God!"

This also tells you exactly which phone the message is located on; so, now you know which phone is a high priority phone (see Figure 5.113).

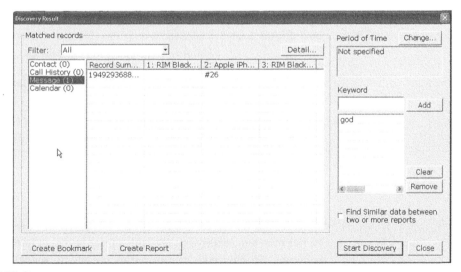

■ **FIGURE 5.112** Discovery screen.

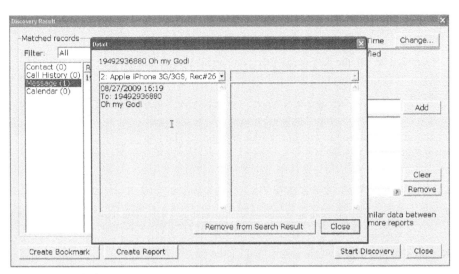

■ **FIGURE 5.113** Discovery screen detail.

Once you have completed your review of the Discovery Tool, press the "Close" button in the bottom right corner of the screen. This will return you to the select reports menu (see Figure 5.109).

Secure View 2 analytics

As you can see, by using the analytical tools in SVP, the investigator is given a wealth of power to be able to analyze the data that has been collected. This is one of the few tools available on the market today that provides the analytics package within the standard application without having to buy any additional or add-on software packages. Using SVP for triage analysis allows the discovery of actionable intelligence immediately. Since the application can be run on any Windows XP platform, there is no requirement for proprietary hardware. The SVP uses the standard cable sets and does not require proprietary cables. This reduces the amount of cabling required to be carried by the investigator. This application is also a part of a multidiscipline or cross-validation tool set allowing the use of multiple tools to evaluate a single day container.

HTCI SIM Analysis Tool

The HTCI SIM Analysis Tool is designed to provide a program that can be run from a thumbdrive or SD card without having to install any other software. With the application copied to any device, you will be able to launch the application. To process the SIM card, follow these steps:

1. Make sure you are wearing gloves to protect the SIM card from oils and dirt.
2. If you have not done so, remove the SIM card from the phone. Try not to touch the chip on the SIM Card if possible. To do this normally will require you to remove the battery from the back of the cell phone. Some newer cell phones have compartments that allow the extraction of the SIM card without removing the battery.
3. If you have not done so already, record the ICCID number located on the SIM card.
4. If you have not done so, record the IMEI number from the phone that the SIM card was removed from.
5. If the SIM card is an additional SIM card for the user, make sure to annotate in your notes the IMEI number of the cell phone that was seized with that SIM card.
6. It is common now to find dual SIM cards in the cell phone, allowing the use of two identities or accounts. (This is found most often in European markets where users have different rates from different providers.)
7. Depending on the SIM card reader that you are planning on using to perform the analysis, may require you to use a SIM card holder. (These SIM card readers and holders are available from www.forensicstore. com.)
8. Carefully place the SIM card to be analyzed into the card holder and place the holder with the SIM card to be analyzed into the SIM card reader.
9. Launch the HTCI SIM Analysis Tool from the shortcut icon (see Figure 5.114).
10. Once the application opens, press the "Gold" acquire button in the upper left corner of the program (see Figure 5.115).
11. A screen will appear to gather case and investigator information. Fill out the case information screen. The entries that you make here will be included on the report that you generate later.
12. Once you select the "OK" button, the SIM card is checked for a personal identification number (PIN). If the SIM card has a PIN assigned to it, a screen will appear that will allow you to enter the

■ **FIGURE 5.114** HTCI Sim Analysis Tool shortcut.

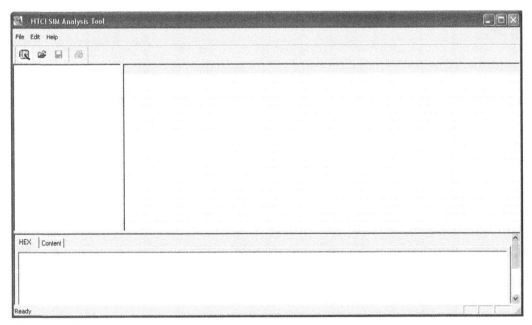

■ **FIGURE 5.115** HTCI Sim Analysis Tool desktop.

PIN number. Once the PIN number is entered, press the "Verify" button. The PIN number can be entered only three times incorrectly. If the PIN is entered three times incorrectly, then the card will lock itself until the correct "PIN Unlock Key" (PUK) is applied. The PIN and PUK (eight digit code) can be obtained from the service provider of the cell phone. Be very careful at this point if you need to use the PUK. If you enter the PUK incorrectly 10 times, the SIM card will be locked permanently and all data will be lost.

13. If the PIN is accepted, the box will say "Verified."
14. You can now launch the acquisition (see Figure 5.116).
15. After processing the SIM card, the analysis screen will be displayed.
16. At this point, make sure to remove the SIM card, as it is no longer needed; place it back into an appropriate evidence container for storage or use later in the cell phone body acquisition.
17. Elements that contain data will be shown and a green block will be displayed next to it telling you that data was recovered from that file element.
18. You can now move through the file elements looking for data for your case (see Figure 5.117).
19. If you wish to gather data from the SIM card, you have two options to choose from.

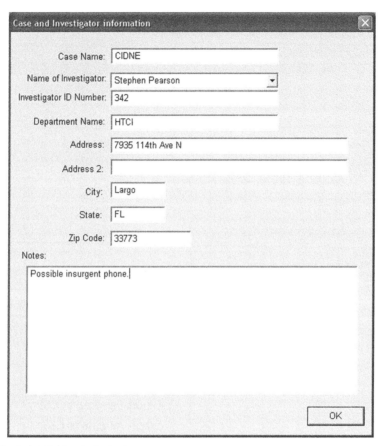

■ FIGURE 5.116 HTCI Sim Analysis Tool investigation input.

20. To select an entry, right click on the entry and select "Export Selected" to CSV. This will allow you to copy a single entry to a CSV file. You can then import the CSV file into a spreadsheet program for further analysis.

21. The second method to gather data is to use the "Export all items" to CSV. This option will allow you to gather the entire file element including all rows into a CSV file. You can now import the CSV file into your favorite spreadsheet program and perform analysis (see Figure 5.118).

■ The Toolbar offers several different options. Each one of the options is listed below:

  ❏ *File*

   ■ Open—This option allows you to open an existing file saved with the .hsa format.

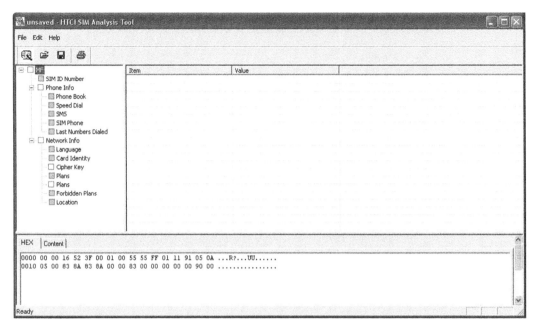

■ **FIGURE 5.117** HTCI Sim Analysis Tool review screen.

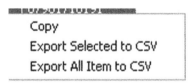

■ **FIGURE 5.118** CSV export.

- Save—The "Save" option allows you to save the data from the acquisition to a file. When you save the file, you will have a choice of what folder to save the file to. The saved file will have the extension .hsa.
- Save As—The "Save As" option allows you to resave the file under a different name.
- Print—This option allows you to print a report from the case including all elements.
- Print Preview—This option allows you to view the report prior to actually printing it.
- Print Setup—Allows you to choose the printer you want to print the report from.

❑ *Edit*
- Case Info—This option allows you to change the case information that you inputted earlier in the acquisition.
- Verify PIN—Brings up the PIN or PUK verification screen.

❑ *Help*
- Help Topics—Help menus for the application.
- About HTCI SIM Analysis Tool—Provides information about the HTCI SIM Analysis Tool.

HANDS ON
Add the HTCI SIM Reader to the Portable Applications Menu
In Chapter 4, we loaded a thumbdrive with portable applications so that we would have a device that we could carry around with us and use when needed. We are going to add the HTCI SIM Tool to the Portable Applications menu.

1. On the thumbdrive in the portable Applications folder, create another folder called HTCI SIM Tool.
2. Now copy the HTCI SIM Tool to this directory. (To get the HTCI SIM Tool, send an e-mail to info@gohtci.com requesting a copy.)
3. Once you have done this, the Portable applications will read that folder and add the program to the Portable Applications menu.
4. To run the program, simply click on it one time.

SUMMARY

In this chapter, we have covered the use of the digital triage analysis process using four separate tools, each being used to provide a specific result back to the investigator. The chapter also discussed the use of the Faraday container and the reason to ensure that the cellular devices are kept clean from the network. We have covered the need for nonproprietary applications in the world of DTF processing and why it is important not to get caught up in the marketing hype of the program.

Realistically, as the world progresses forward into the world of digital media, the cell phone is going to become more and more important. More uses are found daily for the cell phone. Who would have thought that you would be turning on your alarm system and monitoring the nanny cam from the cell phone, but there is an app for that. We are watching the growth of this industry explode, and we as investigators/operators, are holding on for dear life. The cell phone hackers grow in number every time a child is given a shiny new cell phone. Everyday the terrorist finds one more way to pervert the use of the cell phone to meet criminal means.

The next few years will be very interesting to watch and see how far the use of the cell phone will go and what devices will end up with the cellular capability. Throughout this chapter, we have reinforced the DTF process, as it will give the investigator/operator the chance to at least begin the process of identifying the threat and gathering the intelligence/evidence that will be needed to put offenders in jail. The second part is to make sure to use the DTF process to be able to gather the actionable intelligence needed by the battlefield commander.

The changing role of a digital forensic investigator

THE SOLUTION

Over the past 3 years, the High-Tech Crime Institute (HTCI) has been training weapons intelligence teams (WITs) in digital triage forensics (DTF). During this time, HTCI has seen a definite change in attitude toward the role of the digital forensic investigator. This attitude change can be attributed to several arguments.

Argument 1

An attitude exists that roughly says, "There are other people who can do digital forensics, so why not let them take care of it (in-country labs)." This argument, while partially true, is the worst argument to have. This attitude allows the small unit investigators to say they can pass it off to someone else and we don't have to worry about it. The problem should be clear with this argument. If you let it continue, you create a procedural model that is now bloated in the middle because of all the work being sent to them. It is an operational fact that there are more WITs than there are digital forensic labs in theatre. The WIT is poised perfectly to do the initial evaluation to determine whether an item has actionable intelligence or not. Unfortunately, we have learned from the mistakes made in civilian law enforcement that trying to use a single entity to do all digital forensics does not work.

Initially, your results are good, but soon a severe backlog is created. This was seen very clearly when the Federal Bureau of Investigation (FBI) began the use of the Regional Computer Forensic Labs (RCFLs). The RCFL was designed to take over all digital forensics in regions spread out across the country. The FBI then told Law Enforcement to send all digital media to the RCFLs, and they did. The RCFLs were overwhelmed with requests, and a huge backlog was created. The RCFLs had to begin

Digital Triage Forensics. Doi: 10.1016/B978-1-59749-596-7.00006-1

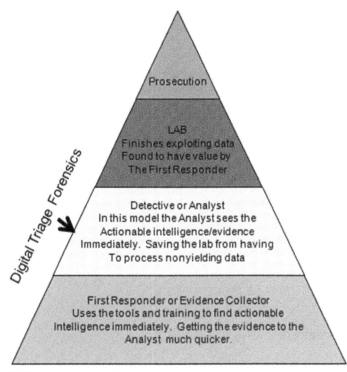

FIGURE 6.1 Processing pyramid.

placing prerequirements on the media being sent to them to try and reduce the backlog. This helped, but did not cure the problem. Even today, the RCFLs are still backlogged. Cases wait to be examined, sometimes for as long as a year.

Figure 6.1 illustrates what happens when one agency decides to try and handle all digital media exploitation as is currently being done in Iraq.

This attitude is the easiest of the issues to correct, as leadership can simply place the responsibility of DTF back on specialized teams like WITs. WITs should not be allowed to pass off media, but instead they should be required to use the tools and training that they have, and exploit the media that are either collected or brought to them. We are by no means incurring new costs; we are simply using the training and equipment already provided to accomplish the recognized mission at hand. Not to use the WIT in the role that they are designed for but to, instead, allow the passing off of work for no real reason is a misuse of the funding provided for these programs.

Argument 2

The second argument is that WITs do not have the tools necessary to conduct these investigations: that only these specialized labs with highly skilled and trained personnel are qualified to conduct the digital forensic missions. This is absolutely not true. In fact, the civilian world has a word for this argument. It is called "Job Security." The staff of the Weapons Intelligence Course (WIC) and HTCI conducts training at Ft. Huachuca, AZ, to provide the highest level of professional training in the field of battle field crime scene investigations and DTF. Both staff have dedicated their time to making sure that the teams in the battle space have the tools necessary to accomplish all of the WIT-assigned tasking, including digital media exploitation. After speaking with other contractors and organizations, we can, without any reservation, state that the staff at WIC Ft. Huachuca have compiled, with the help of HTCI, the best mobile forensic lab available to any team worldwide. As compared with the static labs found in Iraq and now popping up in Afghanistan, the WITs have identical if not better equipment in most cases. Unfortunately, in many circumstances, the tools sit idle, and the training expertise is lost over time.

Argument 3

It has been said that the WIT member is not trained for the task. We have heard this from WIT members both past and present, and from the leadership of the WIT members. This is a perpetuated lie that comes from teams currently deployed. The ones that pass on this information are the teams that are not conducting investigations or examinations. You will find that these are the teams that pass off the DTF mission to in-country labs, and, as already noted, afterward the team's skills wither and die. What skill doesn't if it is not exercised? WIT members are told by group leadership that they will not have to conduct these examinations or exploitations in the battle space, as there are other agencies that can do it for them. This leads to a training attitude of complacency and not caring. When the group leadership puts emphasis on the training, the results are amazingly different.

The bottom line is that the WIT member is more than capable of retaining the lessons learned in a digital forensics class. The amount of time that is currently dedicated to the training should be increased by 1 or 2 days to allow for more hands-on examinations, but the time allocated meets the minimal requirement to train someone to a skill level at which he/she is capable of conducting DTF examinations. To ensure that the team members are prepared, we can use the procedural model of DTF. We have referenced it as a model for collecting actionable intelligence for the field commander. As the name implies, it is a methodology for processing digital media from a given scene expeditiously, ensuring that the container and data are maintained in as pristine a form as possible. The DTF is best done by trained and equipped persons who have direct knowledge and input from the immediate battlefield crime scene. These trained and equipped personnel already exist in the form of WITs. WITs bring knowledge and expertise from the battlefield crime scene that an examiner who is afar may not recognize—for example, keywords or regional programs that are of importance to an intelligence entity.

To affect this new methodology, new rules or doctrinal policies must be used in the collection of these digital media, as the mainstream methods do not take into account the tactical and time nature of the battlefield crime scene.

For the purposes of this book, we isolated a specific media type and drew a comparison between the collection of it in a traditional crime scene and that in the battlefield crime scene.

We chose cell phones as the medium to compare, as this is the fastest growing medium in the battlespace. Even though we showed a specific media type for comparison, the principles applied in this model can apply to any digital medium found at the combat crime scene as well.

IMPLEMENTATION

DTF, in my opinion, will be the way digital evidence from a crime scene is processed in the future. The understanding that the tactical soldier can be competently trained to obtain actionable intelligence is a reality with schools like WIC at Ft. Huachuca. In this book, we have spoken of the methodology of applying the DTF procedure to a specific media type. The reality is this system or procedural model can be applied to all media items taken from the battlefield crime scene.

The procedures set forth here for DTF can be applied and instituted at any battlefield or tactical level. As was referenced in this book, WITs have both the equipment and training to accomplish the task of DTF. This training and procedural set should be continued and emulated in other environments. Currently, many other organizations are trying their own versions of the WIT. These other team types are being deployed around the world with the mission of providing the field commander actionable intelligence, which may or may not come from the battlefield crime scene.

This book covered the major components of the battlefield triage process. They are the following:

- The reality of triage forensics on the modern battlefield
- The employment of the triage forensics
- A comparison of the cell phone procedural model using the battlefield triage forensics
- The incorporation and uses of battle field triage forensics in today's modern battlespace

Glossary

9-Line Report Is a spot report used in tactical situations that request assistance such as Medical Evacuations or Explosives Ordinance Disposal support.

AFOSI Air Force Office of Special Investigations

AOR Area of Responsibility

ASI Additional Skill Identifier

ATF&E Alcohol, Tobacco, Firearms, and Explosives

BIP Blow-up in Place

BIT Smallest unit of recognizable storage

BYTE Single Keystroke or Character

CEXC Combined Explosives Exploitation Cell

CITP Counter Improvised Explosive Device Targeting Program

CLUSTER Combination of Sectors to form a single unit of storage

Computer Forensics Field Triage Process Model Those investigative processes that are conducted within the first few hours of an investigation and that provide information used during the suspect interview and search execution phase. Due to the need for information to be obtained in a relatively short time frame, the model usually involves an on-site/field analysis of the computer system(s) in question.

DIA Defense Intelligence Agency

Digital Triage Forensics The process of identifying electronic evidence containers that can yield Actionable Intelligence for the battlefield commander while maintaining the integrity and pristine nature of evidence. Actionable Intelligence is obviously the difference in the model. We defined Actionable Intelligence earlier as Intelligence that can be acted upon within a 12-72 h period of time.

EFP Explosively Formed Projectile

EOD Explosive Ordinance Disposal

FBI Federal Bureau of Investigations

FOB Forward Operating Base

HME Home Made Explosives

IED Improvised Explosive Device

INTEVIDENCE Battlefield material collected in a forensically sound manner to allow the use of the material as either Evidence or Intelligence

INSCOM United States Army Intelligence and Security Command

JEFF Joint Expeditionary Forensic Facility

JAG Judge Advocate General

MI Military Intelligence

MOS Military Occupation Specialty

NCOIC Noncommissioned Officer in Charge

NGIC National Ground Intelligence Center

ROE Rules of Engagement

RPG Rocket Propelled Grenade
SECTOR 512 Bytes
SOP Standard Operating Procedure
TECHINT Technical Intelligence
THT Tactical Human Intelligence Team
TEDAC Terrorist Explosive Device Analytical Center
TTP Tactics, Techniques, and Procedures
UXO Unexploded Ordnance
WIT Weapons Intelligence Team
WTI Weapons Technical Intelligence

Index

Note: Page numbers followed by *f* indicate figures and followed by *t* indicate tables.

Printed and bound by CPI Group (UK) Ltd, Croydon, CR0 4YY

03/10/2024

01040343-0007